PENGUIN BOOKS
WHERE THE STREETS LEAD

Sarayu Ahuja trained as an architect and town planner at Madras and Tokyo universities. The evolution and growth of cities, especially those in Asia, has been a focus of her research, and she has written extensively on this and other subjects for newspapers and magazines in India and abroad. She is the editor of *Indian Architect and Builder,* and recently scripted episodes for a Channel Four television series on major Indian cities. She lives in Mumbai.

Sarayu Ahuja

Where the Streets Lead

Design and Illustrations
by Sanat Surti

PENGUIN BOOKS

An imprint of Penguin Random House

PENGUIN BOOKS

USA | Canada | UK | Ireland | Australia
New Zealand | India | South Africa | China | Singapore

Penguin Books is part of the Penguin Random House group of companies
whose addresses can be found at global.penguinrandomhouse.com

Published by Penguin Random House India Pvt. Ltd
4th Floor, Capital Tower 1, MG Road,
Gurugram 122 002, Haryana, India

Penguin
Random House
India

First published by Penguin Books India 1997

10 9 8 7 6 5 4 3

ISBN 9780140259520

Typeset in Palatino by Digital Technologies and Printing Solutions, New Delhi

Printed at Repro India Limited

www.penguin.co.in

MIX
Paper from
responsible sources
FSC® C047271

For my mother,
Pradeep, Anshu and Ayush,
and Dom
without whom this book would not have been possible

Contents

Foreword

I first met Sarayu five years ago. She was introduced to me by a mutual friend. She seemed to me unusually intelligent and versatile: she was an architect; she edited an architectural magazine; she lectured; she also wrote somewhat minatory letters to the editors of various national newspapers, mainly on architectural matters.

Some time after we first met, she gave me a book of poems she had written. She knew, as she kept saying, nothing about technique, but these poems seemed to me remarkable. She had a natural ear for the rhythm and texture of language; she also appeared to possess an instinctive wisdom. I told her, not entirely in jest, that these poems were like good translations of the work of some fourth century Tamil poet, a female saint. I began to think of her as a writer.

She explained her interest in streets to me. She also told me of her experiences as she went around India collecting material for a book on its streets. She is a very good conversationalist, with a not always delicate sense of humour, and a great gift of timing. I thought any book she wrote on Indian streets would be very readable, possibly brilliant.

So I asked her to show me a couple of chapters of the book she was working on. She did, and I was amazed. I was amazed that so vital and alive a person could produce anything which was so abysmally dead. All the architects I have met, apart from Buckminster Fuller and Mies Van der Rohe, turned out to be bores when you looked into their minds. I did not think Sarayu was a bore. When she asked me what I thought of her chapters, I told her the truth and I also said, 'Why don't you write as you talk?'

To my amazement she took my advice, and rewrote the entire book. I was amazed all over again by what emerged. She is a natural writer; indeed I am surprised that she did not choose to become one, instead of embarking upon so dreary (and in India so wholly irrelevant) a profession as being an architect.

About the validity of what she says, in a technical way, I know nothing, expect that she is a woman full of common sense, perception, and idiosyncratic ideas, which come through in this book. In the end, it is her talking to the reader, with a clear and unfaltering voice. It is her being herself. To be able to make your own voice heard is one mark of a born writer. She has this rare gift.

I dislike much modern architecture and I do not know anything about it, nor do I want to. I have much more interest in ancient monuments, perhaps because I am rapidly turning into one. But if I cannot judge what Sarayu is saying architecturally, I can at least say this—*Where the Streets Lead* is the only book I have read on an architectural theme which has sustained my interest and made me feel that it is a worthwhile place to which the author is leading me.

Dom Moraes

Author's Note

This is my first book. There was another, a small book of poems, but that now seems to me a miscarriage. I don't really know why I am so obsessed with streets; it seems to me a fascination that has continued from my childhood days. 'A book about streets? What can you write about streets?' many friends and colleagues queried. They concealed their amusement or perhaps disquietude from me. My obsession continued.

I met Prakash Rao, a photographer and now a friend. He like all the others was wary about the subject of the book. It was probably because he possessed a singular brand of cynicism coupled with a wry sense of humour that he agreed to come with me. He became my travelling companion and sounding board as well as my photographer. He was someone with whom I shared my excitement about the streets, the buildings and people and activity in them, also my idiosyncrasies; he responded enthusiastically. If he wasn't really enthused, then he was a good pretender. I am grateful to him.

I am also indebted to S.K. Sharma who at that time was the Chairman and Managing Director of HUDCO, M.N. Joglekar, Director of Development and Planning of HUDCO, and the institution itself for giving me the financial support to travel to eight cities.

Many friends and relatives helped in their own ways. At the end of a year of travelling and a year of writing, the first manuscript was ready. Monisha Pinto edited it, smoothing all the rough edges. By then nagging doubts had begun to creep in, perhaps inevitable in anyone who is writing a 'first' book. I showed the manuscript to Dom Moraes. He said, 'It's too decorative.' Then he added more reflectively, 'It's too academic. Who is going to read it?' 'Architects and planners,' I replied with confidence. 'Do they habitually read boring books?' he remarked rather sardonically, as is characteristic of him.

It was rather out of being infuriated by someone who I surmised—wrongly, as it turned out—knew little of architecture that I succumbed enough to write two sample chapters for Dom in a way that he suggested. He liked the chapters written as an autobiographical account; he liked them very much, and fixed up a meeting with David Davidar of Penguin almost immediately. David, after reading the chapters advised me some more. 'Why don't you fictionalize a little?' he said. It is, I firmly believe, as a result of these two bits of pertinent advice that the book has taken an autobiographical, quasi-fictional shape. By quasi-fictional I mean that some people and events are made up of bits of other people and other events. In its new form it is not a book about architecture alone. It is also about people, how they live, their cities and their streets, the stories they recount. In a sense, therefore, it is essentially about the architecture of the city in every dimension: physically, sociologically, historically and culturally. I thank both Dom and David for moulding the book and me as a writer.

For their help I would like to thank, among many others, R. V. Pandit and Sushil Ansal for their continuous support, and my brother Murthy.

I am indebted to Pradeep, who with immense patience taught

me to use the computer and solved the bewildering problems I faced juggling with the electronic device. And who spent many hours of many Sundays formatting the manuscript on the computer. Also who understood, many times, and did not, sometimes, my preoccupation with the book. And to Anshu and Ayush, my children who laughed away my irritations which occurred with unshackled frequency. And to my mother in Bangalore whom I ran to in search of solitude, a prerequisite for any form of writing.

*

My mother, when she had read all the chapters asked, 'If I were to look for the book in a bookshop or a library, in which section would I find it?' Honestly, I had no answer.

Introduction

Some years ago, Sarayu told me about her interest in writing a book about streets. At that time I did not understand what she meant. For she wanted, though herself an architect, to write a book for people who were not. I did not believe this could be done. Then she began to travel through the streets of India and they carried her on her quest.

That quest, that journey, has been like a river for her, always carrying with it all that is around it and at a pace which understands the levels of the ground, the pressures of the wind and the supporting systems, the seasonal variations, velocities, depths, expanses. She comes closer to nature where she eventually finds her answers: in the nature of life, the cycle of growth and in the way people choose to live together. Unconfused by surfaces, she finds the invisible force, a law that brings order and the vulnerability inflicted by change; and in her book one sees the street through the eyes, heart and body as a whole: sociological, psychologically viable, cultural, ritualistic, climatic; even the economic situations, they are all there. Beside them are observations on symmetry, asymmetry, order, chaos, high and low scales, straight and undulating spaces with changing widths, thresholds and connections.

The street is a world where one waits, watches, contemplates, absorbs, transacts, cherishes through generations and history. It is not merely about architecture, engineering, economy; it is to be felt, breathed and absorbed. However, if you try to touch it, hold it, only a fragment will remain. To see the street as a whole one has to be totally sensitive: shed the external self and feel with the inner being so that one can conceive images of one's own choice.

Sarayu has innocence, curiosity and a capacity to absorb with wonder, and her belief in some kind of beauty that must exist and that people unconsciously aspire to impels her to interpret things beyond what they appear. She uses the objects around her, images from her memories and a whole constellation of events, however minute, and finds paths rich, good and wide. In her imagery the tangible becomes intangible, then once again she makes it simple and visible. This I consider a rare quality. In her streets there is nothing that does not seem to have been understood, held, lived, and known in memory's wavering echoes; no experience has been too unimportant, and the smallest events unfold like fate: a wide fabric in which every thread is guided by a weaving hand and placed alongside another thread, the warp and weft of which is supported by a hundred others. There is perhaps an analogy in this book with the growth of life: a tree rises, branches, becomes something which all those living around observe; in this sense the tree is like the street. A tree reaches up to the sky and has its roots in the earth. A tree rises and falls. So eventually does the street.

What Sarayu does in this book, page after page, is to create a picture of the streets of India such as has never been produced before, and, speaking only as an architect, I think of this as a great achievement. Because it is fluid and ambient and has roots, and her words reach towards the sky.

Balkrishna Doshi

. . . no human heart
changes half so fast
as a city's face

Baudelaire

Part I
Beginnings

Chapter 1

TANJORE: 'SHIVA, SHIVA, SHIVA,' ANDAMMA WOULD SAY, slapping her cheeks hard. 'I said to give a fistful of rice to the sadhu, not a vesselful of it.' He arrived each morning at nine as I sat in the square tinnai playing 'house-house' with small brass vessels. 'Chinna-amma,' he would call out to me, and I would run to the little room under the staircase where rice was stored in large gunny bags. I would gingerly untie one of them and fill a large gun-metal vessel; the white crisp grain smelled starchy, like unperfumed talcum, as it streamed into it. Then I would rush back to the gate to empty its contents into the sadhu's bag. He would say some words in Tamil which I did not understand, but whatever it was he said, his eyes would be kind, which made me happy. I had been giving him a bowlful of rice for a week, from the day I had come to my grandmother's house. I was six years old then.

Each summer and sometimes in the Deepawali holidays, I went

3

to my grandmother's house in the temple town of Tanjore. We travelled, my mother, my two brothers and I, from the railway station in a bullock-cart, as there was no other mode of transport. We would sit on the matted straw and listen to the sounds of the street under us: the wooden wheel on the rough, tarred road, the squelch of mud as it skirted the corners, the clop of the bullock hoofs. I couldn't see much as the carts had those vault-like bamboo roofs, but I recognised the streets through the sounds: the noisy commercial street which was a miscellany of sounds, the quiet inner lane with children playing and old people gossiping, and the temple street with its fragrance of flowers and camphor emanating from the small shops along the road, and the sounds of bells pealing and songs and prayers.

Every time we turned into another street, I would glimpse the corner. Street corners were always interesting and I remembered them clearly: the little corner restaurant with colourful pictures of gods, the tiny shrine against an old tree with oozy spots of saffron and strings of flowers, a pan shop, a cigarette shop, the peppermint vendor, the old paper-and-bottle vendor, the cycle hire shop, the broken culvert where people sat, and, always, the ebb and flow of familiar sounds. It seemed to me that I was coming back to where I belonged.

But the street I felt closest to was the street that led to my grandmother's house. It was called Selvanagar. It was a broad and straight street, unlike the narrow, winding lanes of the towns I had lived in. The street had dead ends, and all the houses had little gates except one, that of Nattar. He was a contractor and the only one to own a car, a strange looking black one.

My grandmother's house was in the middle of the street. She would stand at the gate, waiting for the bullock-cart to arrive. She was always there when we arrived; I don't know how she knew. Perhaps she heard the bells on the cart, which made considerable noise in the quiet street. She would stand there dressed, in spite of the heat, in nine yards of Kanjeevaram silk travelling between her legs. She always wore dark colours. She was thin as a stick, the buck teeth prominent in her long, bony face which was crinkled like rice husk. She did not change much year after year, only became more vulnerable and less distant. Her eyes would be moist as we got down from the cart. She would touch our faces, then crack her knuckles on her temples. She never let us in until she had exorcised the spirits clinging to us from the city. She would quickly fetch a bowl of water mixed with turmeric and draw large circles in the air with it, emptying it thereafter in the street. We were then hustled along to the well at the rear of the house and cleaned up. Once this was done, she would give us tumblers of boiled, frothy coffee in the dining room.

Everyone called her Patti but I called her 'Andamma', the other mother, because she was like a mother to me. She was kind and loving, and very traditional. She believed in every superstition, and lived in a continual ritual. This was her domain, a sticky womb in which she harboured herself. Unlike her, Tata, my grandfather, was strict and disciplined and he tried to be modern. He was fierce and short-tempered. Everyone was scared of him, even Andamma. I was not, and we had long discussions in his small study at one end of the house. He became violently angry if he was disturbed and no one dared to go there. As we were thirty-two cousins in all and at any given time there would be at least ten to fifteen of us in the house, someone or the other always gave him cause for anger.

'That is why I had to build such a big house, to accommodate all of you,' he would tell me in an exasperated tone. The house was indeed very large, I had never seen one so big before. It had a spacious hall on one side of which was Tata's study and on the other his bedroom. This had only one bed; Andamma slept in an adjoining room, on a pai on the floor which she rolled and put away in the morning. Upstairs, there was another large hall which is where we slept. It was empty except for a tall stack of mattresses in one corner. Outside the hall was a veranda. It was wide and long and redolent with the long afternoons we spent in it.

Tata was a civil engineer and had worked for the British. He was an executive engineer with the Public Works Department and the engineer in charge when Selvanagar was built. It was a suburb of Tanjore, some five kilometres from the old city, which had been developed by a cooperative society. He was therefore respected by his neighbours and friends. He was very tall—six feet three—and wore round glasses like Gandhiji and a white veshti which he would hold up in one hand as he walked. He walked swiftly, almost menacingly, and everyone in the house moved out of his way when he approached. He was very proud of the concrete and brick house that he had built because he believed it to be modern and unlike the houses that other people lived in. It was, however, modern only in material. In every other way, like the people who lived in it, it was traditional.

Before Selvanagar was built Tata and Andamma lived in the old city of Tanjore where I went before I was six years old. There was a palace in the middle of the city and around it were four streets called the four main streets. The palace belonged to Serfoji Maharaja, Tata had told me. He was a Maharashtrian and many Maharashtrian families lived in the old city. Tata's house was one in a row of contiguous houses on one of the main streets. I had then found this lack of space between the houses strange because my father had always lived in houses built within compounds. There were narrow lanes which wound their way from the main streets towards the palace. They were paved and some of them were full of shops. There were many small temples and shrines and Andamma would take me each evening to the ones that were close to the house. Beyond the four main streets was the fortress. Its rampart encircled the city. A gate in the rampart led to the Periya Kovil, the big temple.

The houses on the street where Tata lived, most of them Brahmin houses, were similar: they were long and narrow and I could see the entire length of the house from the main door, which was normally left open. Every house had a tinnai built over the open drains that ran along the street. The tinnai was built high above the drains, and all day long old Brahmin men sat there with

their friends, rolling betel leaves. There would be a brass bowl of water from which they would drink water from time to time, gargle and spit into the gutter. Then they would prepare another leaf. They spent the day watching people, gossiping and playing cards. Tata was busy and out of the house the whole day, so it was only in the evenings that he sat out for some time. I did not like to sit in the tinnai in that house because of the foul smell from the gutter. Behind the tinnai were a living room and a dining room and behind these the kitchen and storeroom. The rooms for sleeping were upstairs. There was a small backyard which contained the well and the bathroom. A long passage ran beside the house. It had a dry latrine with a door on the street side. The scavenger would come each morning with a long stick which had a hook fixed on it. She would pull out the bucket from under the latrine, throw ash into it and empty it into a large bin. I used to watch each morning though I hated the whole process, and I was glad when Tata began to build the large house in Selvanagar.

He used to take me to the site of the new house sometimes. An attraction for me was the circular trench that had been dug there. Two oxen moving in the centre drew a heavy beam of wood which in turn moved a stone wheel around the trench. The stone ground chunks of lime which was used to bind the bricks together into a sturdy wall. Tata told me it was called lime mortar. He also told me that over the years as the mortar dried it became strong and compact and did not let water seep in.

During my next visit to Tanjore, a few months later, I watched them make the roof. Tata told me it was a special construction and was called the Madras terrace. The masons laid teak beams between the two walls. On these they laid the bricks without anything below to support them, fixing them with lime mortar. When the mortar had dried they poured a thin layer of concrete mixed with fine sand and red oxide over it. They made deep grooves on it in a checkered pattern so that they looked like tiles. I used to ask Tata how the bricks stayed in place and he would tell me, 'When you grow up and become an engineer you will understand. You won't understand now.'

I was happy when they moved into the Selvanagar house; it was large and airy, with a large compound and a toilet that could

7

be flushed with a small bucket of water. There was a septic tank in the backyard in which the sewage was let and allowed to decompose. After watching the Selvanagar house being built, my concept of playing 'house' changed. I would dig small trenches in the mud. I would attach a stone to a stick and move it round the trench, pretending that my fingers were oxen. Then I would remove the mud from the trench and heap it and pour water over it. I used actual bricks and made rooms one brick high. There would be many rooms, a kitchen and a backyard in which I would plant branches of trees. Once, when I was being very imaginative, I emptied a new tin of talcum powder into the trench. Andamma, curious, poked into the heap and sniffed the paste sticking to her finger. Then, seeing the powder tin next to me, she let out a yell which brought Tata outside. He was quite amused and said, 'Very clever. I tell you when she grows up she will be an engineer. Just look at the house she has designed. It has all the rooms.'

Encouraged by him, my housebuilding games became more elaborate. I would build larger rooms and many of them, paint the bricks white and then colour them with extracts obtained from crushed flowers and leaves. My favourite was the bright magenta of Chinese roses. I was also interested in the tools the masons used. I made my own. A top with a string attached to it became a plumb line. I used a flat ladle and a wooden batten into which I hammered two nails for a handle. I mixed clay and smeared it on the walls of the house with the ladle and levelled it with the batten and checked its evenness with the plumb line. In the passageway beside the house I built many houses, all one brick high and with septic tanks which were nothing but small pits in the mud covered with cardboard. Tata had given strict instructions that they were not to be disturbed. He would proudly show them to his friends and say, 'My engineer granddaughter built them.' Since then I had begun to dream that when I grew up I would be like Tata.

Both Tata and Andamma were staunch Brahmin Iyers and they performed all the rites that went with being one. I found their conservatism perplexing, particularly Tata's because he was educated and also trained under the British. Sweepers were not allowed into the house because they were of lower caste. Also, whenever Andamma would give me a ball of tamarind to give to the washerwoman to clean the brass vessels with, she would scold me if I gave it in her hand. 'Leave it on the floor. You don't have to give it in her hand. Now go and scrub your hands with soap. Hard,' she would scream at me. There was another strange thing that she did. The dhobi, like the other servants, would come in from the back, and place the bundle of washed clothes near Andamma's feet as she stood outside the kitchen. As he left, she would pick up each piece of laundry and dip it in a bucket of water and ask the washerwoman to hang it to dry. 'The dhobi is of a very low caste,' she would say to me. 'We can't wear what he has touched.'

Andamma used to wake at four in the morning. She would then

9

bathe, dress and pray. Her next ritual was to mix cowdung in a bowl of water and sprinkle it outside the gate, on the street. She would sweep over the moist mud and then with rice flour draw a kolam. Women in almost every house would be doing the same. The milkman also came while it was still dark and he would milk the buffalo and hand over the fresh, warm and frothy liquid to Andamma. She would light the wood in the clay stove and boil the milk to make coffee for all of us.

The aroma would reach me as I slept and I would rush down to the kitchen. She made coffee in an unusual vessel, thick and heavy. 'It is aeroplane aluminium,' she told me once. 'It is good to boil milk in.' I would drink the milky coffee sitting in a corner and watch her churning curds with a mathu, using a cord to turn it until the butter separated from the whey. The morning light trickled in through the glass pane set into the roof and the gaps in the clay tiles; the kitchen would be dark otherwise. There was a bulb but Andamma rarely used it. If she did, it was only in the evening for a short while when she said her evening prayers. She cooked dinner in the light of the wood fire and dinner was over by seven-thirty. By nine she would wipe the clay stove with a

mixture of cowdung and water which she told me kept away the ants and flies and after that, that part of the house was in darkness.

There was only one bathroom and two toilets. The bathroom was just outside the kitchen and near the well. The toilets were further down in the backyard. In the morning Andamma would fetch water from the well and pour it into a concrete trough which emptied into a large masonry tub in the bathroom. It was used to store water for the day but at first I thought it was a bathtub and had a luxurious bath in it. That was the first time I saw how angry Andamma could be. Another time she was very angry was when I had a shower with grains. Above the staircase was a wooden loft. It had a little wooden shutter at the bottom which could be reached from the landing. It was normally locked, but one day I found it unlocked and since no one was around I tugged at it. Suddenly I was engulfed in a deluge of grain. The grain made an enormous hissing sound, like a hundred cycle tyres being punctured together. Andamma rushed in from the kitchen. 'Shiva, Shiva, Shiva,' she screamed, slapping her face. I was tied for the afternoon to the coconut tree which grew beside the house.

I passed the time talking to the girl next door through the barbed wire that separated our houses. All the houses had these wire fences, only the front had compound walls, and this made the houses close and intimate, just like the street was. The older people rarely visited each other, but they frequently talked across the fence and any kind of gossip travelled speedily down the street.

11

On festive occasions, like Haldi-Kumkum, Deepawali or Golu, the men stopped and talked on the street while the women visited one another. They returned with their foreheads smeared with chandan and kumkum and brought with them a coconut, a banana, some betel leaves and nuts and a blouse piece. Andamma quickly stitched her pieces on her ancient Singer and wore them with her nine-yard silk sarees. It did not matter that they did not match.

Each day Andamma would wash her long silk saree herself and rinse it in soap nut. 'It makes the silk shine,' she would tell me. Then she would wring it, fold it in little pleats and hoist it with a bamboo stick on the clothesline. Still using the bamboo she would spread the saree right across the line. I tried to do the same with wet towels but could never do it like she did.

The dining room had a long wooden table, old and blistered. There were no chairs, only benches, and we would eat in batches. Tata always was the first to be served. He always ate out of fresh banana leaves cut from the backyard each morning. He would pour a little water in his palm and clean the leaf with it after which Andamma would put a spoon of rice and a spoon of ghee over it. Tata would pour some water in his palm and move it around the leaf, letting the water spill. By doing this, Andamma explained to me, one offered food to God. After this offering, Andamma would serve him the rest of the meal. Adjoining the dining room was a small storeroom in which Andamma would keep sweets and savouries. She would pull me aside sometimes and tuck some sweets into my palm. 'Don't tell anyone,' she would whisper to me, because there wasn't enough for all the cousins.

Once in a while Tata would bring a large watermelon in the evening. Andamma would cut it into thin wedges and give it to all of us. We would bite into the pieces greedily, the juice running down our chins. Tata ate his wedges neatly, using a fork. On one such occasion he told me of his days when he worked at the PWD office: 'The executive engineers lived outside the city. There were only three bungalows. There were no fans, no lights. At six o'clock the peon would take out the petromax lamps and hang them in

all the rooms. In the living room there was a pai hung from the ceiling which became the fan. A cord was attached to it and it would be pulled by a peon who sat outside the room. His job was only to swing the fan throughout the day. He was paid eight rupees for the month. Women would come to sell vegetables. You could buy a whole basket of vegetables from them for one or two annas. The bungalows were all similar. They had three rooms in the front: the living room in the centre with two bedrooms on either side. A long passage connected the living room to the dining room, adjoining which were the kitchen and storeroom. When I built this house I built it like the British bungalow but without the corridor. It is a very large house,' Tata said.

The tinnai was the best part of the house. From it I could watch the street and the vendors who came in the morning one after another: the vegetable man, the woman who sold all kinds of spinach, the coconut vendor. Sometimes a snake-charmer or a man with performing monkeys would come and I would run out and watch the show. Or the knife-grinder, and it was always interesting to watch the sparks as the knife touched the wheel. But the most fascinating was the kalaiwala, as he pumped the charcoal fire with his bellows and dipped a piece of muslin into the molten lead and quickly rubbed it on the inside of the vessel to make it shine like a mirror.

The other thing I liked doing was to run to the panaham pandal. Here on a table rested two large earthen pots covered with damp cloth, one containing buttermilk, which was watery and spiced with green chillies and curry leaves, and the other jaggery water, (panaham) which was mixed with dry ginger. Both were very cooling. The vendor would serve the buttermilk in aluminium tumblers and the jaggery water in brass ones. But when people of lower caste came he would pour the liquid into their palms and they would rapidly drink from them.

*

Tata owned a large farm and once in a while he took me there. There were lush paddy fields and fruit and vegetable trees there. All through the year , fruit and vegetables used to come from the farm. Close by was a village where his farmhands lived. It was a small village and the villagers lived in clusters, different clusters for different castes. There was a single street which ended in the Brahmin agraharam. There was a fence around this and it was detached from the rest of the village. Tata would go and talk to the Brahmins in the village. At some distance from the village street were smaller groups of huts, all facing inwards. Tata never let me go there because that was where the untouchables lived.

Whenever he was talking with the Brahmins I used to wander around in the village. All along its single winding street were huts with drooping thatched roofs. One had to bend down under the thatch to enter the hut, and couldn't see inside from the street. Thinking about it now, I realise there were so many ways to be part of the street, connected to it, yet maintain privacy. So many ways by which the inside was separated from the outside: door, steps, platform, veranda, fence, wall or, as in this case, a low roof.

This became more evident to me when my father took me to some villages in the north, when we toured through the Gangetic plains. One village we went to was like a small fortress of clay walls. There was no street in this village (I could never imagine a village without a street), only many courtyards that connected and some of them had large wells. The courtyards became common spaces like the streets. Another village had narrow winding lanes along which were houses with high walls. Within each house there was a courtyard. 'The women here observe purdah; they cannot come into the street,' my father told me.

Once Tata took me to Kerala to meet his brother. He lived in an old, traditional house in a village. Tata was busy with him much of the day and I spent my time with my aunt. Patti was old and frail yet full of energy. She was busy cooking and cleaning all day. After she had finished her morning's work, she would sit with me in the tinnai and watch the people go by. The tinnai had a red oxide floor like Andamma's house and in the wall were two alcoves where in the evenings she would light oil lamps. On some days she would shout out to a man with an icebox on his cycle as he passed by and buy me an ice stick. It melted rapidly into sticky rivulets; I could never eat it fast enough.

Patti's house was large and rambling. It had many rooms, all with red oxide floors. When I was there, Patti was having fresh colour put on the floor. For days after the soles of our feet were smeared with red. I liked them that way, it made me feel like a dancer with henna on the soles of my feet. I used to follow Patti around the house as she went about cleaning it and came to know the house intimately. Behind the tinnai was a nezi, a small entrance hall; it was empty. It led into the tavaram, a large hall which also was empty except for a steel almirah in the corner with a mirror on its door. Next to it, on the window sill, was a silver plate with two small silver containers holding kumkum and chandan. Patti would open the containers and offer them to her friends when they were leaving and they would dip a finger into the boxes and apply kumkum and chandan over their bindis.

On one side of the tavaram was a storeroom, the machikkul, which was always kept locked. Beyond the tavaram was the kudom, an open courtyard with verandas all around it. This was where we used to eat. Then the kitchen, adukulai and after it another small hall, nadai. In the afternoons Patti would roll out silk mats here and we would sleep. I did not actually sleep, only closed my eyes and listened to Patti softly snoring. Next to the nadai was the pinnanadai which had the grinding stone where Patti would spend hours turning soaked rice and dal into paste for idlis and dosas. She would also mash leftover rice and mix it with chillies, salt and spices and squeeze it out into squiggly kuruvadams which we carried into the paved backyard, the kolai tavaram. We left the kuruvadams to dry on white bedsheets while crows watched from the pomegranate and guava trees in the back garden.

One trip I particularly remember was when Tata took me to Chettinadu. 'I am going to build a hospital for the Raja of Chettinadu,' he told me with pride. It turned out that he was to build a clinic in Rayavaram, a village in Pudukottai district, for a wealthy Chettiar. On the way he told me about Chettiars. 'You know the house opposite Nattar's house? He is a Chettiar. They are not Brahmins,' he said with disdain. 'They are merchants. In the old days they used to sell gems and so they became very rich.' There were many kinds of Chettiars he told me. 'It all depended on their trade and the temples they worshipped in. Each had their own village, the Chettinadu.'

The Chettiar we met at his enormous residence in Rayavaram was tall, dark and majestic. He had been educated in England and was decorous in his behaviour. I liked him a lot. He talked to Tata about the project as I looked at the number of sweets, savouries and fruits that his servant had brought. There were cakes and sherbet, both of which I rarely had the opportunity to consume. So when I did, it was with unconcealed greed. The Chettiar told me more about himself, telling his story like it was a fairy tale. 'My grandfather was a trader in salt and gems. He was not a farmer like the others and he used to travel abroad and he made a lot of money. Then with all the money he became a moneylender. When the British came to India they found it very difficult to talk to the natives, so they used the trading communities to act as agents. The Chettiars were famous in Calcutta and they also had trade contacts with South-East Asia, so the British asked them to finance rice-growing in Burma. They made money abroad and sent it to their villages and you will find many big houses here,' he said.

I was very eager to see his house. It was like a palace, and much larger than Tata's house. It was built on a base almost six feet high. 'It is because in their old village, Kaveripoompatnam, which later became the historic trading centre, the houses were built like this on account of floods,' Tata later told me. When we walked through the house, it was very confusing because there were so many halls, rooms and courtyards, and Tata kept telling me the names of the rooms in Tamil. But later I drew a pattern in my mind and it became simpler. There was an ornate door with a colonnade around it. All over the house there were splendid engraved brackets. There was a tinnai in the front next to the entrance which Tata told me was used by the men when visitors came to meet them. There were two small muttarams, or courtyards, immediately after the entrance and on either side of it. There was a large, main muttaram in the centre of the house, with the roofs sloping into it. The muttaram, Tata told me, was a common feature in all Chettinadu houses. 'It is used to dry the paddy and the aisles around it are used for sleeping and chatting.' The pattagasalai, which was like an inner tinnai facing the muttaram, was used by the men to sleep and discuss family matters. The aisles around the muttaram opened to a row of storerooms, and these opened into another row of storerooms behind them. Between the entrance and the muttaram was a large pillared hall. It was the main living space but was used as a wedding hall during marriages in the family. It had a high ceiling and polished granite columns. There was also a dining room, various other halls, kitchens, and food preparation areas for festivals and ceremonies. The upper floor had more halls and storerooms.

After the discussion with the Chettiar, Tata took me to the site for the clinic. As we walked along the street I saw that all the

houses were alike and were arranged in rows. Sometimes two houses were joined together. There was a grid of roads and there were four houses in each grid and roads between them. The backyards of the houses faced each other. The fronts of the houses were elaborately decorated. An interesting feature Tata pointed out to me were the tanks. These had steps on all sides and rainwater from each house was conveyed by underground pipes and collected in them. There were many tanks dedicated to different temples. When water in one tank flowed over, it was collected in the next.

When we returned to Tanjore, Tata's house no longer seemed so impressive. I only dreamed of the Chettiar's house and in all my games of 'house-house' it played a vital part: now there were marriage halls where dolls were married, large and numerous kitchens and preparation rooms, dining rooms to seat a large number of people and courtyards where paddy was dried in the sun. And storerooms and cellars where gold and jewels were hidden. It became my new dream house.

*

On Saturdays Andamma and Tata would take me to the big temple in the evening. There was a lot of preparation for the visit: in the afternoon Andamma would pluck the malipoo from a vine near the entrance and string it. She would then carefully plait my hair and tie the string to it. Then she would pat on large quantities of talcum powder on my face to make me look fairer and fill my large eyes with mai and put a dot of chandanam on my forehead. I was dressed in my silk pavadai. Tata would have arranged for a bullock-cart to take us to the temple. On the way he would talk to me about the gods and religion and serious things like that. My mind would be intent on what he was saying but my eyes and ears would be attuned to whatever was happening on the street.

At the Brihadeshvara temple we would leave our chappals in the cart and walk towards the large gopuram. The mud would stick to my feet and little pebbles and stones would prick them; later, at the temple, it was the feel of the granite, smooth and cool, that they reacted to. I would stand in front of the outer gopuram and look up. The gopuram was five storeys high, intricately carved and made of black granite, as was the rest of the temple, and looking at it I would feel awed and uplifted.

The vimana over the main shrine was much higher. It rose like a hollow pyramid and had sixteen storeys. On the first four storeys there were many miniature shrines and as I walked around the temple, I would look at each of them.

I also liked climbing up and down the steps, of which there were many in the temple. And I liked entering through the narrow doors and walking towards the dark interior. There was a large granite beam on the floor across the doorway with a lotus carved on it. Like the others, I would bend down to touch the lotus. As I proceeded inward, it would become warmer, because there were so many fervent people within. The sanctum smelled different: it smelt of people, perspiration, flowers, camphor, incense and perhaps God. There was always that peculiar smell associated with God—the smell of ghee, jaggery, rose petals, camphor. The bells would chime incessantly each time a devotee felt the uncontrollable urge to beckon God; the pundit would chant shlokas, his one hand ringing a bell and the other inscribing circles with a lamp. There was noise, yet it was peaceful. Going to the

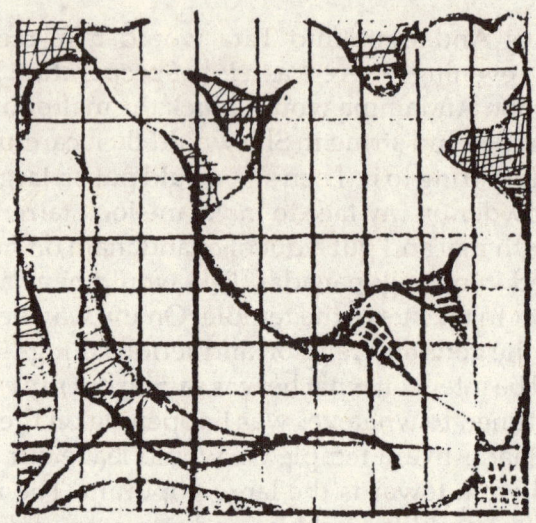

temple was always an exhilarating experience for me: there were so many contrasts—tall-small, warm-cold, rough-smooth, wet-dry, light-dark, peace-noise, plain-decorated, alone-crowded, God-people, spiritual-worldly and so forth. It exposed me to a variety of emotions and responses which then, given my young age, I couldn't translate into words but when I grew up, I could.

Tata told me that the temple was built by Rajaraja I. It had two enclosures and the outer one was surrounded by a dry moat. On top of the vimana was a circular cupola, the kalasam, which Tata told me was made of a single piece of rock. I always wondered how they had lifted the rock to the top of the vimana. Tata told me that they had to build an inclined plane with timber shuttering and planks, twelve miles long, and they rolled the cupola on it to the top of the temple.

Tata was religious but he also liked coming to the temple to understand its structure. He knew a lot about temples and their construction and he would talk to me about them, pointing out the various features: 'The temples are made to a simple plan, and they are built like mountains,' he told me on one such trip. 'There is a praggravira which is the vestibule. This leads to the mulaprasada which is the main hall. There is sometimes also a antrala, a hallway. Then there is the mandapa, a large hall where the devotees gather. The sanctum is the garbhagriha where the god is housed. The vimana represents Mount Kailasa or Mount Meru where the gods lived, and the horizontal tiers are the bhumi, the earth. The temple is the prasada, the palace of the gods. I too want to build a grand temple one day,' he told me.

He would buy packets of pattani (roasted chick peas) and chundal (boiled and flavoured gram) which were sold in front of the temple. While we ate these sitting on the temple steps Tata would tell me mysterious stories about building temples. He once told me about the Vastu Purusha who was, according to him, a powerful invisible man living in a sacred house which was the universe. From what he told me I quite liked the Vastu Purusha who was so powerful. 'There was a sacred mountain called Meru in the Himalayas,' he said. 'When the gods came they all lived there. Varuna was the main god and he looked after the whole universe and also Mount Meru. There were thirty-three gods who lived in Meru. They were all very powerful and they looked after the universe and the people. There was Indra the rain god, Surya the sun god, Agni, the fire god, Yama the god of death, Soma who was the source of nectar and others. Indra was so powerful that he became the main god instead of Varuna.

'The Hindus believed that there was a big universe and a powerful man. They believed that the universe had to be born again and again and for this to happen the man had to be sacrificed again and again so that a new universe and a new man were born. They called this man Purusha, the primeval man, he was the universal essence, energy from whom all other men would be born. He lived in a house called Vastu. Purusha had no substance, no form, so Vastu was his physical existence and because of this he had a form. So the whole world was made of Purusha, Vastu, prasada (palace), Ayodhya (the city) and Meru (home of the gods). But there was no symbol for worship. So the Hindus made a geometric diagram called the mandala. The mandala was a sign for the man and his home and was called the Vastu Purusha mandala and people used the mandala for their rituals, temples and cities.'

The mandala fascinated me. 'What does it look like?' I asked him and he explained: 'Like a square. The heaven touches the

21

earth at four corners, so for the Hindus the earth is not a circle but a square. The square is the basic form and all temples are built on a square. The square is achieved by the crossing of four circles; where they meet are the four corners. So the square was born out of a circle and also contained the circle. The square means order and the end of growing life, so the mandala is also a square. In the centre of the mandala is the navel of the Purusha which is the source of life. This is called Brahmasthana. Around this there are other smaller squares for the thirty-two gods. The squares also point to the eight sacred directions of space. Because the mandala contained the Purusha, the universe, the gods and the eight directions, it became a powerful symbol for worship and so people began to worship the Vastu Purusha mandala and it was also used for building temples and cities,' Tata told me.

Tata loved to talk about the construction of temples; it did not matter whether I understood what he explained. 'The horizontal and the vertical surfaces in any temple are spiritually connected,' Tata explained. 'You know, a plan and elevation. There was a sacred formula by which what was on the ground was related to how it rose up. There was a formula for proportions and also for plots and positions and the temple was always oriented according

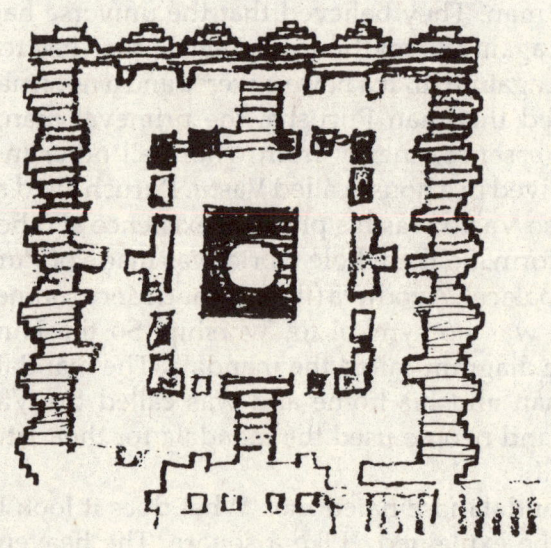

to the Vastu Shastras.' Many years later I learnt that the mandala denoted sacred space. Whatever was outside the periphery of the mandala was the zone of chaos and anti-life and whatever was inside had the unity of all existence. The idea of sacred space was derived from observing time and the idea of time came about because of the changes: morning to evening, day to day, month to month, because in a changeless universe, time would not exist. Therefore time brought about a pattern which was cyclic, and from this came the idea of rhythm, and from rhythm came the idea of numbers. I also learnt that the temple represented the mandala symbolically and not literally: the vimana reflected time through the idea of movement as it expanded from the apex into the four cardinal directions. This movement of time was visible in the evolving and dissolving structures of the temple complex, the smaller shrines and images.

What I found very interesting is what Tata told me about parts and the whole: 'The temple is not just one large thing. There is a step-by-step climax: there is a progressive way in which the parts come together and become the whole temple. That is why temples look so grand yet so intimate.' I was entranced by his stories about temples, their construction, the mandalas and the Vastu Purusha and fervently hoped that when I grew up and became an engineer I would also construct, besides houses like those of the Chettiars, large and mountain-like temples.

*

Deepawali in Tata's house was a week-long celebration. Andamma would recruit four cooks, two men and two old women, to make sweets and savouries which she would then pack in old biscuit tins and send to all her grandchildren. The cooks would sit outside the kitchen and fry the savouries in pure ghee. They would make a variety of laddoos and line them on a bench. Then count them and carefully place them in steel containers. Tata had many well-wishers and they would send him large boxes of sweets, baskets of fruits and fire crackers. We would carefully separate the bombs from the sparklers as we planned for Deepawali.

23

On that day Andamma would wake us up at two in the morning. She would rub large quantities of coconut oil on our bodies and hair, then bathe each one of us, rubbing our bodies with a mixture of gram flour and turmeric. She would rub fresh turmeric on the faces of the girls—'to remove facial hair'—after which she would rub a small piece of sandalwood on a stone and apply the paste on the forehead and neck. It had a pleasant and fragrant smell. Then she would dress us up in our silk clothes specially stitched for the occasion and by three we would be out in the street, all eager to light the first cracker. All along the street, children and adults from the other houses would venture out looking fresh and happy. That was one time in the year the entire street rejoiced together. In the evening little lamps would be lit and the street gleamed in their light.

The other festival which I liked and which was more privately celebrated was Vishu, the Tamil new year. Andamma would wake me up at dawn. Then, with my eyes closed, she would lead me from the hall upstairs, down the stairs to the puja room near the kitchen. She would make me sit and ask me to open my eyes. In front of me there would be a large mirror. I would look into it, staring the sleep out of my eyes. Around the mirror there would be large silver bowls of fruits, milk and butter and in front of it a large silver plate with silver coins of Laxmi and gold necklaces. The silver lamps would be polished and lit and the incense hung heavily in the small room. Tata would be sitting in his room in a new veshti with a new punal around his neck. He would read the Gayatri Mantra, the sound of which would diffuse softly like the tendrils of sweet smelling smoke. I would take one last look of my face in the mirror and run into another day in the rambling house that Tata had built and Andamma had filled with her mottoes and superstition, pursuing another dream that would possess me through the day.

*

One evening Tata brought home a British gentleman. He was tall and fair with blue eyes. I had never seen a foreigner before and gazed intently at him, unable to understand a word he was saying. I asked Tata, 'What language is he speaking?' 'English, stupid,' he replied. But it didn't sound like any English I could understand and he swallowed half the words. Tata told me that he was an architect. He was also a professor and he was writing a book on Hindu temples. I did not know who an architect was so I asked Tata. He told me that an architect was someone who designed buildings and engineers built them. I did not understand since I believed that the person who imagined buildings had to build them also. How could they be built by two different people?

Tata took the Englishman to see the houses I had built. 'They are very good,' he said. Then he turned to me, bent down so that he could look into my eyes and said, 'When you grow up you must become an architect.' He said it so gently I believed him.

Those were dreamy, inspired days. They taught me many things beyond the mundane, literal world which most people arrange in neat, dust-free shelves. It was perhaps because of those early days I spent in Tanjore that I became interested in architecture. I pursued it, when I grew up, for five years in the college of architecture in Madras. Tata was proud of me, but he did not live to see the few buildings I built. He died as soon as I

25

had finished my fifth year and obtained the degree, after which I went to Tokyo to learn about cities, because by then I had realised that architecture was created by a mere handful of architects; it was people and how they lived that made the city.

Chapter 2

TOKYO: JUST WANDERING THROUGH THE STREETS, TRYING TO grasp at facets I could not see, was a liberating experience for me. Perhaps it was a sense of primal freedom, walking the streets of a strange city, but it also had to do with the fact that I could observe the street and be part of it at the same time, be instinctive as well as evaluative, and this pushed me to explore.

The seeds of this obsession were firmly sown when I was a postgraduate student in city planning at the Tokyo University and enrolled in the studio of Professor Hiroshi Hara, an eminent architect who was researching settlement patterns. I lived very close to the vast university campus, in a private hostel with a variety of Asian girls, most of them from South-East Asia. I did not know the Japanese language beyond stuttering a laboured 'good morning' and 'thank you' in Japanese. My hostel mates spoke Chinese or something that sounded close to it. My Japanese professors, most of them PhDs from famous American universities, spoke English but relentlessly waited for me to learn Japanese before they spoke to me.

Off the main university road was a side street that wound its way to my hostel. It seemed long and endless at first, but later I came to know it quite intimately. Unlike what one imagines of Tokyo, this area, Hongo, did not have highrise buildings but single-storey houses and a few multi-storied apartments and offices.

On the ground floor were shops of all kinds: there was a bakery, a florist, a beauty parlour, a grocery store, a mini-supermarket, a vegetable vendor and several friendly restaurants interspersed with a few offices. One couldn't miss the parlours for playing pachinko, a very popular gambling sport, or the community bathhouses. I watched the street at different times of the day, through the seasons. It kept changing: at times formal, sometimes intimate. During festive celebrations and political processions it became vigorous with fervour and expectation.

It was at its best early in the morning or late in the evening. This was the time when it was like a stage before a show, a waiting ground for the unexpected. Some time during the day the street became accustomed to whatever was happening and so did the people; it settled into routine. Each morning as I walked to the university, I watched the street waking up: there were fewer people about, making it more personal and friendly, particularly as the shopkeepers opened their shutters, put out their placards and signs, and arranged their displays. Later in the day they had retreated behind their storefronts, become impersonal.

The evenings, however, were splendidly informal: after an early dinner, the local people poured into the street, casually dressed, some of them in their yukata, the casual version of the kimono. Everything was casual: their stride, their chatter, their attire, expression and gestures. They carried with them towels, magazines and toiletry as they made their way to the public bath. All along the street there were groups of people, and there were definite locations where they gathered for a chat. In front of the eating houses and bars, around the machines dispensing cigarettes or soft drinks, at the newspaper stands or in various niches and corners. The street was as intimate as a hostel corridor. As the evening drew on, the street seemed almost reluctant to retire, parts of it active till late into the night, like the jazzily illuminated pachinko parlours from where the incessant sounds of ringing drifted outside as people gambled away at the machines.

My guardian in Tokyo was Katayama Sensei, who was my father's professor when he studied at Tokyo University. Sensei was very old, almost eighty-five, and took it upon himself to acquaint me with the Japanese way of life. He took me one day to see a rerun of Kurosawa's *Dodeskaden.* It is about a very imaginative urchin who cries 'Dodeskaden! Dodeskaden!' pretending to be a train driver beckoning the passengers. This young tramp also fantasises about his ideal house: a bizarre blend of styles—baroque, rococo, Spanish—and colours. He eventually settles for a modern house of metal panels, flying terraces, roof gardens and large windows with dainty lace curtains. I saw the young boy's dream reflected in the modern Japanese houses: dream-like and ambiguous, moving from dream to reality, reality to fiction.

I talked about this fictional character of modern Japanese architecture to Katayama Sensei. In response, he immediately took me to his ancestral home. 'This is a Japanese house,' he said emphatically when we got there, after a long train journey. He wanted me to see Japan in a more traditional sense than through its modern idioms. It was summer then, and despite the

mosquitoes, we sat in the garden: a patch of grass, a few shrubs, one large and beautiful tree, a tiny pond with black and golden carp, a few rocks—all enclosed by a delicate bamboo fence. 'The house is primarily symbolic, ritualistic, and the spaces in it are important only because of the rituals of birth, puberty, engagement, marriage and, perhaps, ultimate death,' he said.

Sensei took me into the house. He was short and gaunt, and very alert, despite his age. 'A room, "ma",' he said, 'is a space without boundaries and so the rooms flow into each other, without a separate identity or function. You see, there are no bedrooms and dining rooms, there are only rooms, spaces. Do you know what a "furoshiki" is? It is a square cloth which is used to cover the head but which can be used for wrapping and carrying things as well. A traditional Japanese space is like that, like a furoshiki; it is all about wrapping. And the house is just like wrapping space. In the ground breaking ceremony, they insert four bamboo sticks into the ground and tie a rope around them. This is a simple way of defining inside space from the outside. You know "byobu"? That is the folding screen used in Buddhist temples to divide space. In Japan space must be flexible.'

He stroked the polished wood of a post and said, 'The post is very important, it is mysterious because God resides in it. That is what the Japanese believe. So space is seen in relation to the post,

it acts as the organiser of the plan and the distance between two posts, "ken", becomes the basic measurement of space. The Japanese believe in unity, unity with nature. That is why the traditional house is based on a horizontal unity between inside and outside, because the horizontal is unity. That is why, even though the pagoda is vertical, it is only the ground space that is used and people move in it horizontally.

'Do you know, Japanese space began with the idea of a parasol. In the old days when carpenters used to build houses, they used an umbrella to cast a shadow to locate the house properly. Because for them darkness and shadows were beautiful. Therefore the roof was important, like the posts.'

After I had been in Tokyo a few months, Katayama Sensei took me to attend a Japanese tea ceremony. 'You will understand so much more about the concept of space. You are only seeing space, you will learn to sense it,' he said. After the tedious ceremony through which I was forced to sit still, and after drinking the tea that was bitter and eating the rice cake which was too sweet, Sensei took me out into the manicured garden. 'The ceremony relaxes the mind, it helps to awaken all your senses,' he said. We sat down on a bench facing a small pond.

I looked at the tea house. It was set in a beautiful garden, and raised a foot or so above the ground. There were two flat boulders, one bigger than the other, placed before the entrance, so one could climb up. I asked Sensei about them and he told me about the idea of "mono-no-aware", the sadness of things. 'Because,' he said, 'the Japanese want to coexist with nature, to be born from nature and to return to it: it is all based on the idea of impermanence, "mujo". Tied to this is the idea of imperfection, because perfection is impossible to achieve so it is humble and beautiful to resort to imperfect ways. Those stones are just that, an imperfect connection to the tea house.'

'But,' he cautioned, 'imperfection is not a lack of sensitivity, it is a calculated imperfection, a perfection of imperfection—"miyabi". That is what we call it in Japanese. It means refinement; it gives an uplifting feeling. Like when you see something

31

beautiful, when you smell a flower, when you read something touching. It is something that is worked over without showing it.'

He patted my hand gently. 'Japanese thought is not simple, it is very complex and indirect. There is a duality in everything. We believe that the way to acquire the positive is to contain the negative. You will see this aspect in traditional buildings. It is because the Buddhist idea of space and time is very different. It believes that experience is pluralistic and all existence is divided into noumenal and phenomenal worlds. Our ordinary knowledge is of the phenomenal world and so only partially true. It is only when one is enlightened that one becomes aware of the noumenal world; this is higher knowledge.'

*

It was mid-term; I attended a lecture by Kisho Kurokawa, a famous architect who was to talk to us about 'the culture of greys'. '"En" is a bond,' he said at the beginning of his lecture, 'it is a relationship, an affinity. In a Japanese house there is an "engawa", a veranda built around the house, running under the extended eaves. It is different from the Western porch or the terrace. The engawa is a multi-purpose space: it is a corridor connecting the rooms, a shelter against rain, wind and the heat of summer, a space for entertaining friends, and a link to the garden. But most importantly it is an intervening space between the inside and outside. The "engawa",' Kurokawa said with emphasis, 'is the "grey" space—neither in nor out but a world in itself; yet not independent but an area where two spaces merge. That is the culture of grey.'

Then he began to talk about towns and the idea of 'grey' related to them: 'Traditionally,' he said, 'there were no public squares or plazas in our towns. The residential street, "roji", served their purpose as a gathering place. Hideyoshi, the sixteenth-century ruler, organised the city of Kyoto into units consisting of houses facing a street. This was also the period of urban culture, when city populations began to increase and the streets filled with homes, shops and craftsmen's workshops. The street became an engawa—a multipurpose semi-public space. The windows with parallel batons (renji), built-in bench-like porches (agedana) and the cloth curtains (noren)— all formed the standard design for a new urban architecture, and the facades grew out of a lifestyle whose focus was on the street itself. What the elements of the facade did was to blur the edge between the interior and exterior and present a transparent barrier between the private and the public realms. The street played a dual role. At times, it became an extension of private living and at other times a forum for public activities.'

I had to understand space in the Japanese sense; to do this I had to understand how the Japanese perceived the world: they believed in the elusive, the intangible, the greys; they believed in the dimness of the dark, in the essence of form that was impermanent, imperfect and incomplete. My Western education had taught me all that was tangible. My exposure to all that was Japanese, taught me the intangible, and what I made of it was intensely Indian. So to see 'space' in the Japanese sense, I travelled to Kyoto, Osaka, Nara, Sapporo, Nikko. I visited the temples and shrines, old Japanese inns and traditional houses. But most of the time I roamed the narrow streets, talking to people, experiencing the cultural hues. The people lived in a humid and relatively mild climate and surrounded themselves with gardens. Around them, at least in the smaller towns, were rolling landscapes since they naturally felt a oneness with nature. Even in large towns, where the houses were tiny, there was always a garden. However small, it had everything that a large garden had, almost like a bonsai, a microcosm.

Kurokawa Sensei had said that in the grey of the descending twilight, the spatial quality of Kyoto appeared at its best and I experienced all that he had said when I was in Kyoto: the roof tiles and plaster walls dissolved into shades of grey, they seemed to lose all perspective and three-dimensionality. He had strongly contested that the idea of grey deliberately attempted to create a world in a two-dimensional plane, temporarily frozen in time and space. And this grey was a condition of confrontation or collision

33

where the elements cancelled each other, so achieving coexistence and continuity.

I sat in an inn in Kyoto, in a narrow lane winding its way off the main street. The eaves of the houses leaned over verandas screened by reed and bamboo blinds. The intermittent "shoji" or rice-paper doors and latticework panels ceaselessly expressed glimpses of the inside, even the slightest movement within. As I looked on, the 'layers' of space and elements, from the street to the interior, kept changing in untold permutations, like the glass beads in a kaleidoscope.

In fact if there is one word that describes the esoteric quality of Japanese tradition, I think it is 'semi'. In architecture it denotes semi-permanent, semi-complete, semi-enclosed, semi-public, semi-visible, semi-tone, semi-dark, semi-manifestation. This 'semi' essence, to the Japanese, allowed coexistence and continuity without resistance or antagonism.

There was something else that I noticed in the temples and shrines in Kyoto and Nara: they were rigidly geometric in form, yet there was an unmistakable fluidity about them, a strange floating quality. Perhaps it was the curved edges of the roof that made them look so organic, and therefore one with nature. From a distance the roofs looked like birds, flying, their wings spreading

upward. There was this sense of tension—a pulling of things: the walls, roof, the stepping stones, boulders, pebbles, they seemed to be apart yet invisibly bonded together. It was like being alone, in darkness or in silence, in mounting strangeness, experiencing a compelling connection to a flicker of light or sound.

*

Many months later, I drove to Choshi, the easternmost point in Japan, to watch the rising sun. We booked in at a quaint little inn. We entered through a latticed door and walked through the front room into another, much cosier room matted with tatami. In the centre was a firepit over which was placed a quilt-covered table. This space I presumed was used to receive guests. I could see through a floor-level window a tiny garden, immaculately maintained. I couldn't see the whole garden when I was standing but as I sat down at the table, the garden lifted its flowers to my eyes. Light entered this space from the garden on one side and the street on the other. Beyond this room was a corridor running deep inside, reaching one room, then another.

I was amazed at the complexity of orientation and the density of space, more so because it was indeed such a small inn. Ever since, the phenomenon of "oku"—the inner labyrinth—continues

to fascinate me. Katayama Sensei had told me about it when he took me to the tea ceremony. 'It is progressive, heightened experience starting from the interior of the tea house to the interior of the inner self. Oku has the idea of the secret. It is incomprehensible and unattainable, and is essential to the Japanese sense of aesthetics and sense of place. In a traditional house, "omote" was a room facing the street and oku was the

innermost room. So oku also meant a direction facing inwards from the entrance and progressively reaching to the inner space. Also the degree of depth of space influenced the behaviour or sensitivity of a person. If the space was intimate, the behavior was intimate too. Personalising and interiorising space is very important to us.' In this remote inn, Oku revealed itself to me like the layers of an onion. There was a core contained within, it was dense and preserved by layers. Oku, the 'inner space', added depth to a restricted space, it generated a sense of distance within it.

There was such a contrast between the West and the East, and the idea of the centripetal and centrifugal. Whereas the Western concepts of house, architecture, city were centrifugal—an outwardness—in Japan, they were centripetal (okusei)—the idea of inwardness. Also 'ku', the concept of centre, did not exist in their realm of aesthetics. A Hindu concept, it was introduced through Buddhism. The sanctification of a place, the determination of a centre as a cosmic pivot, and the establishment of a microcosm was all a central part of Hindu philosophy. The philosophy of ku makes no distinction between existence and

non-existence—it embraces all contradictions. To make a city a microcosm, it was necessary to determine its centre and also demarcate clearly the surrounding territory so it became a finite entity. Centre was, therefore, necessary.

Centre played a major emphasis in European architecture and city planning. To the Japanese, however, the centre was open and visible, hence predictable. The centre required a uniformity of space around it. The idea of centrality, and demarcation within and without, be it in architecture or town planning, was an 'active' process. The Japanese tradition was about a passive act of 'envelopment', the 'wrapping' technique. Here space was used for 'wrapping', allowing flexibility, adaptation and spontaneous transformation. It was the inherent difference between the organic and the ordered. This was their concept of territorial completeness.

The determinants of a place in the Japanese sense therefore were layered space, inner depth and passive enclosure as different from the Western idea of defined space, pivot centre and demarcation. Centre theorists believed that only the manifested could exist absolutely, whereas the Japanese believed that space itself became formless and infinite. Architecture without space was naked.

*

A few days later, a friend asked me to see an artist and potter's studio in Kamakura. 'He is famous and eccentric, very moody and very angry, but you will like him. He knows a lot about Japanese art, craft and culture,' she said. 'And he speaks good English.' I went with her. He was in his studio, in a brown-black yukata, sitting at the wheel, totally absorbed, giving form to a lump of clay. The studio consisted of a long shed. The side we entered from was in darknes. At the other end, where he sat, the studio opened

on a neat garden and the light and the green flooded into the interior. In the centre was a long stone slab running the entire length of the room, supported on brick piers. On it were placed the most exquisite works of clay art. More than the shapes of the cups, bowls and other containers, what was so beautiful was the muted colours, the subtle textures, the patterns and motifs on them, all meticulous overtones.

He was silent. 'Why are your forms so simple and repetitive?' I asked. 'Do you know the meaning of "yugen"?' he asked in turn. I shook my head. 'Yugen is an idea of aesthetics that is intuitive, it can only be appreciated by the mind. It cannot be verbalised. It has a mysterious quality.' I prompted him, 'Like mono-no-aware?' 'No' he replied impatiently. '"Aware" has a more direct expression even though it may seem ambiguous, it is the inevitability of a natural phenomenon. But yugen is all about an innermost depth of feeling and consciousness. You like these cups?' he asked and I said, 'Yes, very much.' 'But you don't know why. You try to explain, to appreciate, but there are no words to define why you like them. That is yugen. Something that is intuitive. It requires no form. It is quite formless in that sense. The craftsman must possess the sense of yugen and so also the beholder,' he explained.

'Have you seen Noh?' I shook my head. 'Noh was considered to be the medium which best conveyed the idea of yugen,' he said. 'The bare simplicity of the Noh stage and scenery is the reflection of the aesthetic principle of Zen. The movement of the actors is based on the art of swordmanship which reflects loyalty, self-sacrifice, reverence and other such high feelings. The most enjoyable part of the play is the stop-action. When there is a stop-action then you get the clear idea of space and time. This was the aesthetic expression of yugen. It also captured the emptiness of Taoism. The idea of the void. This mere gesture suggested the eternity beyond. The expression in Noh is something beyond its representation. The same idea of formlessness. It was used in Japanese art also. There are some spaces in an otherwise detailed painting that are not defined. This is the essence of yugen.'

'Do you know about "sabi" and "wabi"?' he asked. I told him I didn't. 'Some time in the medieval period, there emerged the

aesthetics of poverty. Sabi and wabi were called the moods of poverty. Sabi was more specific and related to objects and the environment. Wabi was more general. It referred to the living of life. Associated with poverty, it meant insufficiency and imperfection. It is a feeling of loneliness. In a way it denotes nothingness. The sabi in a tea ceremony implies poverty, simplicity and aloneness in a metaphysical sense. The Japanese garden is also like that. It contains a sense of loneliness. Have you not seen a rock surrounded by circles of combed sand?' he questioned.

Before I could answer, he asked. 'What colours do you like?' 'The red of saffron, the lush green of paddy fields and the deep yellow of turmeric,' I replied spontaneously. 'Indian colours,' he said, 'We like browns and greys. We prefer monochromes to bright colours. It is again a sense of sabi, of poverty.' As he said this, I realised I could hardly see him. The browns of his yukata had slipped into the dimness of evening. The stars had appeared; they twinkled meaningfully like all the words in my mind, twirling in infinite space.

All through my journey back to Tokyo, I tried to sort out my thoughts. The last few months had been an experience of great intensity—almost like eating away a bit of a great culture. I could see now how in traditional Japanese aesthetics the 'perceived' was more potent than the 'felt'. How nature, the omnipresent, was glorified. And that it was much later, through the influence of Buddhism, that aesthetics became 'spiritual' and the 'invisible' became beautiful; the immeasurable, unperceivable, inexplicable became meaningful. Feeling, atmosphere, ambience, condition, which could be collectively felt but not explained, ruled aesthetics. Heterogeneity—inexpressible sensations with multiple meaning—was encouraged.

I understood why Japanese architecture was underscored by the absence of colour, its emphasis on the simple and frugal to produce a refined, subdued beauty. Their love for colours of clay, trees, straw and grass. Why the sombre colours like beige and grey were pulsating; and severe colours were avoided. Not surprisingly, there was a school of colourless aesthetics. Devoid of architectural colours, I experienced the colours of worship and festivity which were vivid and electrifying.

I looked at the notions of light and dark differently now. I sensed the 'darkness' that prevailed in traditional Japanese architecture. I remembered the shrine in Nara. As we had sat in the shade of its copious eave, Katayama Sensei had explained: 'Look how dark it is within. And how bright it is outside. We are sitting somewhere in between. This is the area of grey. Darkness is emptiness. It is a void. To our minds voids are more fulfilling than solids. In a shrine one's mind is processed from light to darkness. It is from this darkness that a new person grows, a new space grows out of shadows. Light is filtered by the darkness, shadows are formed. You don't see the geometry of the room but the depths of the dark, shadows and minimal light playing in the void.' I gathered the depth of his words. Space was essentially an object until you personalised it. Then it became an experience. Once I had figured this out I could perceive the idea of darkness carried forward in the modern works of architecture where simplicity was accentuated by a world of shadows. Through all this I realised that life to the Japanese was one of momentary contrasts in an otherwise harmonious environment. In the balance of contrasts, each object was respected, so each space. The transition from object to space in the past or present was a studied sequence of refinement.

*

41

And then, all too suddenly, the day of my departure arrived. I left Tokyo; the journey had ended. But in a way, of course, it had not, because my stay in Tokyo had broken the shackles of conditioning; my mind was moving on.

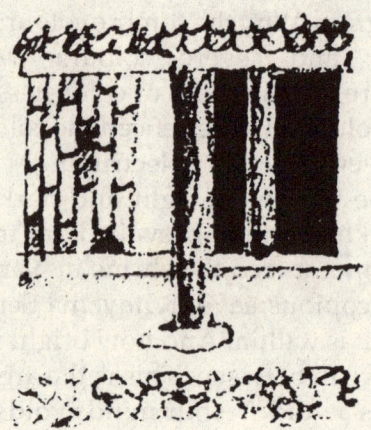

Chapter 3

MUMBAI: I RETURNED TO MUMBAI, OR BOMBAY AS I KNEW IT then, in the summer of 1972. My parents lived in a large flat on Malabar Hill and I lived with them for a while. Although I had visited Mumbai a few times before, it was the first time that I was living in the city. I set out once again, as in Tokyo, to know and adapt to a new place. I spent my time wandering through the lanes close to where I lived. There were tall buildings surrounded by compound walls and the streets were wedged between them. I didn't like the buildings or the streets but I liked the trees. They added history and age to the hill since the buildings were all new, usurpers of space once occupied by old rambling bungalows.

The two parks on the hill were the pulse centres of the locality. People came to them with religious fervour throughout the week. In the mornings I saw the same people each day. I did not know them, nor they me. But the fact that we met each morning created a certain familiarity. The half smile and nod silently endorsed this. And when I was away for a few weeks and revisited the park, the smiles grew wider. Their eyes questioned my short absence, and there was a greater sense of companionship. Small gestures really, but they went a long way in creating a sense of belonging. On Saturday and Sunday evenings, however, the parks changed. People arrived in large numbers, like waves which could only be calmed by subsidence into the sea. They left as suddenly as they came, strewing behind them the signs of their activity.

Perpendicular to the main street that led to the parks and dipped into Kemps Corner, was a little street. It was called Little Gibbs Road, till some politician changed it to a long Parsee name which I cannot remember. This road was narrow and intimate though it did not have any wayside shops or cafes. Instead it was bordered by the compound walls of those tall buildings I did not like. There were one or two regular rehriwallahs who turned up in the evenings selling bhelpuri and hot dosas and wadas. There was also a quaint cigarette shop put together from packing cases. This lane led to my house which was almost at the end. That I was familiar with it was not the only reason why the street felt so intimate.

It was intimate because the main street was different from Little Gibbs Road: the main street was wider, with more traffic and activity, and a sense of purpose, as it linked two major points. The little lane was narrow, softer in its movement and activity, and reached a dead end. This strengthened its sense of destination, of having reached somewhere. And it was also more personal. This was in fact what streets were like in small towns and villages, an inner space different from the large squares or chowks in a city.

In the evenings the rehriwallahs would park themselves at strategic points on the street. What was surprising is that they were never parked at the beginning or end of the street but somewhere between, particularly at the corners where a lane met the street. The most popular cart was the one selling dosas and idlis. It belonged to two young men from Kerala. They were dark, with curly hair, and wore colourful polyester lungis that were

44

brilliantly bright and tucked up at the knees. There wore gold
chains on their necks and flashy Citizen watches on their wrists.
One evening, munching a crisp dosa, I talked to them. They were
brothers and belonged to a village called Kullathoor in the
Attipara panchayat . It lay fifteen or twenty kilometres west of
Trivandrum, they told me. 'Our village is very different from
other villages,' the older one said, spreading oil on the hot plate.
'There is no clear pattern, no streets, no rows of houses or
buildings like this. You can see clusters of houses, open spaces,
coconut trees. This keeps repeating on and on. One village grows
into another without any boundary. There is some kind of political
boundary. We only know that we belong to this village. Because
of this the whole village feels like a family.

'There is a kutcha road at the entrance of the village,' he
continued. 'There are no streets?' I asked. 'No streets,' he said,
'there are houses here and there with spaces between them. The
richer ones have walls on the boundary. There are many coconut
trees.' He found it increasingly difficult to explain. He kept
turning to his brother and debated in Malayalam, which
fortunately I could follow. I asked him if there were street names.
Whether some common spaces or buildings like the temple or
school stood along the street. Or if there were small tea shops or
cigarette shops or even a tiny market. He was confused. 'No, there
are no streets, but the temple, market, shops and a small school
are all there in the village.'

I asked him about his house. 'We have a small house. My eldest
brother and his family and two of my younger brothers live there.
We also have land around it. We have our own well and a bathing
space. The walls are made of bricks. We made the bricks at home
ourselves and fixed them together with mud mortar. This time
there was heavy rain and the mud on the walls washed away. So
my brother remade some of the walls using cement mortar. Before
we had a roof made of coconut leaves. Now my brother has made
it with mangalore tiles. It looks very new.'

Housebuilding to them was so much like cooking or gardening.
It was an activity related to home: home-grown. They were totally

involved in it. It was quite different from the architecture in cities where the building was impersonal. The individuals were standardised, physically and emotionally, in terms of their needs and aspirations; they were all considered the same. Passing the brothers a few days later I saw another man with them. Seeing me they rushed forward, the other man behind them. 'This is my uncle,' one of them told me. 'He is principal of a school in Trivandrum. He knows a lot about building Kerala houses. Even the good omens and the bad ones. Ask him.'

We walked to the nearest park. The uncle was a tall thin man with a beard. Perhaps this was what made him look so learned. Even before I had phrased a question, he started talking deliberately and slowly. 'A traditional house in Kerala is built according to the set procedures. The moothasari or the perumthachan is the chief carpenter. He is like the architect. He is also a very good astrologer.

'The head of the family selects a number over twenty. This number becomes the number of "kol".' He clarified the term. ' A kol is a unit of measurement: one kol is about ten feet. The kol is then multiplied by the number designated to the caste of the head of the house. And another number is added to it based on the direction the house is to face. This total is divided by three. This gives the dimension of the perimeter of the house.' It was too confusing for me. I asked him to explain the numbers of the caste and the numbers of the direction. 'No,' he said, 'that is too difficult for you to understand.'

He continued talking. 'Afterwards, the final number is checked with the rules of astrology. If the number is a good one for the owner, then it is okay. Otherwise the whole process is repeated selecting another number above twenty. When the number is suitable, the perimeter is divided into a length and breadth considering the dimension of the plot. So the plinth is made. The roof projects out on all sides. Within the plinth the divisions for rooms are made according to the needs of the family. Almost everything—the doors, windows—are decided according to astrology.' I asked him about the streets since I couldn't imagine a village without streets.

'Streets?' He looked at me questioningly. 'I don't know anything about streets!'

The only other place I remember in Malabar Hill and where people gathered was a small Jain temple tucked away at one end of the main road. There were no other streets or spaces that expressed more than their physical attributes and utility. If I remembered any of them it was only because of their steep slopes and the fact that I had to exert myself as I climbed them. This aspect hardly seemed important to me then, but later I did realise that it gave a dimension to the form of the street. All the other streets tumbled down the hill in a rush, in different directions, like rivulets on a hillside after a storm.

By this time I had started teaching at the Sir J.J. College of Architecture. This took me twice a week to the college campus. At first I travelled by bus; it was invariably a double-decker and I liked to sit on the upper deck, close to the front, as it provided me an aerial view of sorts. During long hours of forced sitting, isolated in the half-light of the bus interior and the slow columns of traffic outside, I looked down at the patterns formed by the cars, the people, the signs, crossings, buildings and lights. Here lay the boundless conurbation of streets operating in perfectly controlled chaos. This was the Indian street for me.

Perhaps it was because I was in a bus that I learnt to watch more than listen. Initially my recollections of the street were more like silent movies with breaks in between when my mind took off to probe into some observation or the other. It was not that I did not hear the sounds in the street; I did. But I looked at people and their expressions from a distance; I could never really hear them or absorb the details. As the bus approached a junction, there was an increased momentum in the patterns made by people and cars. Later when I did see the details and hear the sounds, I experienced more closely the texture of the street.

After my lecture at the college I often walked along the length of Dadabhai Naoroji road looking at the buildings. I would walk from Crawford Market on one end to Flora Fountain on the other.

Both of them formed important nodes and the street bulged into wells of space at the two ends marked by buildings or elements one remembered: Crawford Market with its tower, and the graceful fountain. Between the two was the Victoria Terminus in all its Gothic glory and facing it, the municipal corporation building, a remarkable fusion of Gothic and Oriental styles of architecture.

Looking at the terminus, I experienced not just the building but its ambience. First I absorbed it piece by piece and then in its entirety. Designed in 1878 by Frederick William Stevens, it was built to be the terminus and the headquarters of the Great Indian Peninsular Railway. Its most notable feature was its dome which was considered to be the first masonry dome adapted to a Gothic building. This was a building I could look at for hours, taking in all its ornate embellishment. There was always some detail that I had not noticed before. The ornamentation seemed to stand out and at the same time fuse with the total form, enriching it. But above everything else was the total effect of the building: it conveyed a sense of arrival and destination. Hundreds and thousands of people poured out through its arcaded portico.

Complementing it was the chamfered facade of the municipal building that addressed the street in an extroverted way, unlike the buildings on Malabar Hill which were within high compound walls. Being a civic building this quality was much needed and the architect had provided it. It was designed in 1888 or so, also

by Stevens, in the hybrid style which came to be known as Indo-Saracenic, combining Western building forms and Indian decorative elements. This eclecticism could be seen in its essentially Gothic style used in combination with bulbous domes and cusped arches.

Going towards the fountain there were rows of tall buildings of hybrid classical and Italian styles. The repetition of style brought about a continuity to the street, and style in this sense became important since isolated styles did not matter on a street. My conviction about this matter was endorsed by the Asiatic Society building. It greeted the street in its classical glory in a sweep of wide steps. The building by itself was the focus of attention and demonstrated the visual dialogue with the street that was needed, but did nothing more to the length of the street since there was no other building around it that echoed its style or even parts of it.

Occasionally, I would also cross over from the terminus to the other side where there were many food stalls. Numerous people on their way to work would breakfast at these stalls. In the evenings it was the same; the corner was crowded with people. The food carts and people around them and the simple act of eating made the place appear intimate, particularly in the presence of the overpowering facades of the terminus and the municipal building. The street instinctively served the needs of the people: street stalls, hawkers, slums, they were all tied firmly to need and their undaunted presence indicated this. These were the adjustments that people made within fixed patterns which when established became a part of the street.

There was another kind of intimacy: this was in the stretch of the street between Victoria Terminus and Flora Fountain. There was a continuous arcade that connected all the buildings. It was crowded with hawkers of all sorts, and indicated a characteristic inherent in the culture of the Orient, to personalise a public domain, so that the demarcation between the private and the public was loose and nebulous, unlike in the West. Shops along the arcade opened into it through steps that marked yet another transition from one space to another. The arches of the arcade and its raised walkway and the steps into the shops all became thresholds marking and segregating one space from another. This kind of linking and delinking gave texture to the streets and spaces in the city as did the incessant change and chaos: the rush of pedestrians, the hawkers displaying their goods, the shopkeepers and their glass boxes and all kinds of signboards of all sizes and shapes hanging from every bit of space available, all this formed the mood of the arcade. An empty arcade would have been architecturally beautiful but lifeless.

The mood of the street was not made of just its tangible

elements—the width of the street, the buildings, their architecture, the spaces around, the street monuments—there was also something intangible, as though the street was made of several layers, one upon another, so that many elements and activities coexisted. This aspect was absent in streets which had only tangible, measurable elements and when they performed a premeditated number of functions. Streets that had grown organically, unplanned, in direct response to a collective need, were comfortable and intimate, full of layers. The layering of the street didn't happen all at once; it grew over the years through

continuous and intricate processes of superimposition of need and response that arose because of the subcultures that made the city.

This was confirmed when, in search of a particular address, I walked one day into Kalbadevi. It had rows and rows of narrow, crowded streets. There were streets selling only copper wire, streets selling lace, buttons and such gewgaws. There were streets selling only beads of all sizes, materials and colours. There were streets with temples. In this area, mainly inhabited by Gujaratis, I witnessed an entire subculture. In this maze of streets I could experience their culture: the people, their language, their clothes, their shops, the food sold in the stalls—each one of them indicated the cultural inheritance.

I came across many streets and localities which were culturally very distinct, streets where Muslims, Parsees, Hindus lived, or people from a particular region; they were all very typical and the difference could be seen in the streets, particularly during festivals. Such areas formed closed groups with an inner order. Like the slums in a city, they had the order of a village and clung together and formed a closed community. The streets in such localities were different from the new, planned streets whose homogeneous and undifferentated character killed all variety. Although the people were diverse, in conforming to a universal pattern of the urban image they slowly lost their intrinsic variety. Therefore the subcultures became the object of my intense curiosity, and I roamed the Mumbai streets and localities looking for all their peculiarities.

Much about society and culture was explained to me by a friend of my father's who had come to stay with us in Mumbai for a few days. Uncle Shivraman was around sixty, a professor of history and my father's bridge partner in Madras. One evening as they played a game of cards and sipped their whisky and soda, I asked him about culture. After much debate between my father and him on the subject, he tried to sum it up for me. 'Culture is the pattern of thought and behaviour. We share it, we inherit it by living together. It is something that is passed down to us symbolically, not by genetic inheritance. The birds build their nests, that is hereditary. But when we build our cities, without doubt it is because of culture.'

This explained all the subcultures, and why culture was not uniform for all groups of people but varied from one group to another. I understood easily the culture of streets and how they extended this idea to the level of the city. How one street looked different from the other. This then was the intangible factor in the street which gave it life. And, more important, the reason why modern streets, which were an assembly of technology and efficiency, lacked spirit. They personified the universal, robbing all the nuances of the way of life in the streets.

'There is also a double reality in people,' Uncle Shivraman said. 'There are two things in society. One, the collective order which tells us what to do. And the other is the factual pattern of what really happens. The city is made of both,' he said. 'It has a collective order which we must obey and a factual pattern. The difference between order and pattern is in the degree of flexibility,' Uncle said. 'Order is conclusive but pattern is inconclusive.

'In many ways the collective order influences the factual pattern; we can see this in the shared beliefs and behaviour. On the other hand, the factual pattern influences the control system because the rules arise out of the events in the real world. The crowding and chaos in the street are a part of this factual situation. It is a form of adjustment people make to change. But the problem with the city builders is that they look at only the collective order, of what ought to be, and ignore the factual order of what is. The collective order always control people's actions and it also often conflicts with their needs. What is good for a lot of people may not be good for you. It is the difference between Utopia and reality.'

*

Soon I had my office at Horniman Circle. Earlier called Elphinstone Circle, the idea for creating it came from the police commissioner, Charles Forjett, and the facades were designed by James Scott, the chief engineer of the Elphinstone Land Company.

He introduced an urban design style which, although popular in eighteenth century Britain, had not been used by colonial architects in India. The buildings were not in the Gothic style but in the Italianate mode. The complex had a covered arcade at the ground level which was useful during the summer and the lashing monsoon. What interested me was the fact that here at last was a space in the city where the street and its architecture responded to each other. The buildings curved and their arcades lined the periphery of the circle. Although the details of the buildings, their style, material and decoration, and how they appeared on the street, were important, what was more important were the links between the buildings and the street.

My work took me many times to Ballard Estate as well as Nariman Point, both reclaimed areas. Ballard Estate was like a part of a European city with its handsome office buildings and wide, shaded streets; it was a commercial development planned by the Port Trust in 1908 and designed by George Wittet, a consulting architect to the Port Trust. He evolved the control guidelines for its forty-three blocks of office buildings which were essentially built in a style close to the European Renaissance. Important to the design scheme was the street system which had carefully planned vistas and defined edges, with a subtle transition between the office block and the street.

Nariman Point, on the other hand, was congested with tall buildings in their separate plots. I couldn't fail to notice the difference between the two. At first I thought it was the difference between an older area and a newer one. I thought it was because of the material and the style of architecture. Or perhaps it was due to the height of the buildings. The streets were laid out in a gridiron pattern in both the places. The difference was in the manner in which the buildings connected to the street. At Ballard Estate, a commercial and urban architecture, the streets were part of it, unlike the buildings in Nariman Point which were like islands, encased within walls, reducing the streets to mere parking spaces.

Each morning as I drove to my office I passed through Marine Drive. It was a shoreline boulevard conceived as a part of the ambitious Backbay reclamation project. It was first conceived as a fusion of classical formality and ornamental landscaping—the original Davidge plan reflected the tenets of beaux arts planning and the street plan was laid out in a grid incorporating several broad tree-lined avenues, including a landscaped boulevard along the seafront. Intersections were marked with ornamental squares or circuses. However, because of the trade depression of the 1930s, this scheme was set aside for a more utilitarian plan. The Government, for monetary reasons, altered the plan to obtain maximum density. So long and narrow blocks were built with narrow streets between them. Many of the buildings were for residential use and were like apartments built of reinforced cement concrete; the style was a combination of the international style and art deco from America. Art deco was a new language of applied decoration based on abstract organic forms and geometric patterns and symbols like the sun's rays, palm trees, the moon, the ocean and so forth. Though the architectural style in art deco and its decorative patterns unified the street, yet something was missing.

This puzzled me and I walked right down Marine Drive

55

looking at it analytically. One question that arose was: What and who made the street? Obviously one was people, the other was architecture and the third was the surroundings. Once I established the participants it was simpler for me to experience the street, to see how these three elements reacted with each other. In Marine Drive, the answer was: they did not, they remained separate entities. There was the sea and the beach and the road which followed the curve of the sea, as did the buildings. There the interaction stopped. There was nothing else, no activity, no people, no life in the street—only the vast volumes of traffic passing through and the huge hoardings with their commercial messages. It was like a thoroughfare.

My impression was further confirmed when I came across Paul Klee's *The Thinking Eye*, which enabled me to look at the street comprehensively. He wrote:

'A man of antiquity sailing a boat, quite content and enjoying the ingenious comfort of the contrivance. The ancients represent the scene accordingly. And now: What a modern man experiences as he walks across the deck of the steamer: his own movement, the movement of the ship, which may be in the opposite direction, the direction and velocity of the current, the rotation of the earth, its orbit, the orbits of the moon and planets around it.

'Result: an interplay of movements in the universe; at their centre, the "I" on the ship.'

I read this, I remembered it. I looked at buildings in relation to people and the surroundings. For the first time, then, I looked at the domes over mosques and old British buildings and gopurams over temples differently, and what I had learnt early in life came in useful: when I saw a mosque with a dome, I wondered how it felt to be within a spherical form. It was different from the gopuram because it contained space within whereas the gopuram, as did the spire of a church, penetrated the space above; and the tiered mandapa terraced the space around it. The dome, spire, mandapa—this was how the building related to the sky, just as it connected to the ground through steps, platforms, verandas; I realised how important these connections to the sky and ground were.

I understood the idea of part and whole; I realised the

relationship between elements, openings, enclosures, arches, columns, walls, planes. I began to understand how the surroundings influenced the building—the street, the access, the topography, history, rituals and the person's need for intimacy, comfort and convenience and his cultural choices, which was all reflected in the scale, proportion and aesthetics of architecture. If I grasped all this, it was because I tried to see the connections between the buildings, how people used them and the surroundings.

At college, most of the time, we had learnt how to build buildings—how to build a pitched roof, how to build the floor, doors, windows, how to build cantilevers, tall buildings, how to keep the rain out, the sun out. We learnt to build through problem-solving experiments in a mechanical way. This became accumulated knowledge or science. But architecture was more than that; it was also an art of building—a spontaneous response, an awareness, a subconscious sorting of elements; it was about 'feeling', not 'resolving'. It was also about a shared experience—a collaborative consciousness which became tradition, a craft. It was not merely functional. After all, function was a need, and the material and method of satisfying the need was no more than a problem-solving exercise. The art and craft in architecture was its aesthetics, the rest was need-fulfilling mechanics. Art was the philosophical whole, craft improved the material, and their ingenious blending gave poise and essence to the building and the buildings to the street.

*

Eighteen months after I returned to Mumbai, I went to live in Bandra, known then as the queen of the suburbs. Although I continued travelling by bus into town, sometimes I preferred to take a rickshaw to Bandra station and then take a train to Victoria Terminus to reach the college where I lectured. As the train devoured the miles between the nodes, I would gaze out of the window trying to put the various fragments together, building the city part by part, combining one circumstance with another. Travelling through the streets in buses and cars was one thing, but

travelling through the city in a train was quite something else. To me this journey by train seemed essentially like a street travelling between places; like a moving street. But there was a difference: the buildings turned their backs to the tracks. It was like watching a city which had been turned inside out.

Front of the city, back of the city—I presumed such thoughts came to me because I was so used to drawing plans of the city and the buildings in it and their elevations as though they were two separate sections. Front and back, right side and reverse side—I was trained to think and see in this fashion. Even our body was like that, or, for that matter, the anatomy of animals and flowers: there was a top and bottom. There were sides. And a front and back.

The matter of debate, if at all, was on the degree of emphasis given to all these surfaces. I imagined a world without demarcated planes. Where everything was equitable. Front, back, top and bottom, sides. The image seemed, to say the least, alarming. But then, I was looking at everything as an object. It was objects that had planes as dimensions, not processes, which were continuous: they had a past and present and could be divided into linear sections. The street had to be looked at both ways, as object and as process. Right across my house in Bandra was the Pali Mala road which climbed over Pali Hill and down towards the sea on the other side. On my walk each evening I passed three quaint houses with distinctive balconies and tiled roofs. One of them had a parrot which would say a chirpy 'Good evening' each time I passed. Adjacent to this house was a lane visible for no more than two yards and at the end of this lane, I could see part of a house. I couldn't see if the lane ended there or continued. Curious, I walked into it. It turned a quick left and then a right. There were numerous clusters of small houses and it was like suddenly walking into a village. People sat around and talked across their

59

porches. I walked up to a man reading a newspaper and asked him about the place. He told me that the village was called Sherly. 'In fact,' he said, 'there were three villages, Sherly, Mala and Rajan. Now the other two have been almost entirely wiped out by builders.'

I saw a similar settlement near Hill Road; a side street led to another village called Waroda. Along its endless rambling length were shorter streets which emptied into courtyards. There were crosses to mark each node and corner. It was a living community architecture.

The main street led to what was the bazaar road. Beyond this was the Muslim area. The buildings here were taller, two or more floors with shops below and residences above. There were no clusters as in the area I had walked through before. I tried to find out whether the inhabitants had come at a later date, when the village was already well established. This would explain why it was so crowded. But the people were not very sure.

I walked through this village many times, drawn by its beauty which I tried to understand. The village was beautiful because the materials it was built of, its form, were familiar, simple, real and unpretentious, yet innovative. In the concept of 'beautiful' there is a difference between the basic, the derived, and the applied. The basic is about space and time, the ultimate constitution of things. The derived is concerned with ordering the natural phenomena and is strongly related to the basic concepts, but the applied breaks the chain of growth. The basic and the derived are purer than the applied; and the true values are never found in the conscious, calculated pursuit of things—the mechanical is not creative, innovation is.

I tried to relate beauty and the basic concepts to the city, its streets and people. It was not in the nature of things for any part of the city to come up suddenly; it grew step by step. What happened today depended on what had come before. What people did today also depended on what they did before. The streets were not born out of a single idea but the collective actions of a large number of people, each doing his little bit to add to the eventual structure, good or bad. And at the heart of this mesh of interrelationships, there was always an incredible simplicity. And at the root of simplicity was beauty. These interrelationships could never be invented, they were born. And any attempt to invent them resulted in simplification, which, totally different from simplicity, was not beautiful.

*

Those initial years in Mumbai were spent in learning. They were entrances to many ideas and thoughts: belonging, alienation, patterns, connections, values, forms, style, beauty. I had not learnt about them when I studied architecture at college. But they occurred to me when I was confronted with the city, physically, socially and psychologically. Actually it was the Mumbai streets that made me realise that people's dependence on the city and streets was not because of the way in which they reacted to things that were mechanical but rather from their responses to what meant something in their lives.

*

On my return home from college one day there was a letter from Professor Hara. I had not heard from him for two years, ever since I had returned. 'I have an assignment which will delight you,' he wrote. 'After you left we completed village studies in Africa and South America. Now we plan to come back to India to study urban settlements. Someone suggested Ahmedabad. There are five of us. Besides me, there is Professor Irinouchi who is an anthropologist, Keiko, a history student, Morita, an architect and Norman, an American architect. You will be happy to meet Norman. He has travelled all over Europe and makes interesting observations. He will be very useful in the team.'

My excitement now bubbling over, I read on. 'You will have to take a month off from whatever you are doing. Please think of all the places and people we can see and meet in Ahmedabad. I leave all that to you. We will also require some student volunteers to assist us. You will be able to manage that, I am sure. We will be there soon after your Indian monsoon.' This was precisely what I needed: a month off and a renewal of old connections.

I waited for it to rain. This time around I didn't even notice how the rain lashed at the mildewed buildings. Or how the water rose along the soggy streets leaving new tidelines against the walls. I only waited for the rain to stop. After several weeks of wind, rain, heat and mounting human grime, it did, to make way for a muggy September. Before its end, I waved to some dimly visible figures from the visitors' gallery at the airport.

Hara and his team had arrived.

Chapter 4

AHMEDABAD: VANDANA WAS AT COLLEGE WITH me in Madras. She was short, plump and full of momentum, specially in the way she talked. I suppose this is because Tamil is spoken rapidly and Vandana had spent most of her life in Madras although she hailed from Gujarat. After we graduated and I went to Japan, Vandana shifted to Ahmedabad. She had many relatives there.

It was Vandana I thought of when I made up my mind to take Hara and his team to see the pols of Ahmedabad—the old urban settlements in the walled area. I asked her if she could arrange for us to stay in one of the pols. As it happened, she was able to.

She fetched us from the airport and drove us into the city. It was Hara's and the others' first trip to Ahmedabad, and all through the journey they peered out of the window expectantly, looking for the unusual and the exotic. At some point the shapeless street broadened into what looked like a major avenue. 'Where are we?'

Hara asked. 'This is C.G. Road,' I told him. 'This is becoming a new commercial street.' Most of the buildings on the street had been converted into shopping plazas containing an assortment of shops and restaurants. They looked modern and new and the local people were proud of them. 'Why are the buildings so far apart?' Hara remarked. I wondered what he meant and asked him.

'The street must have some denseness, some enclosure. There is no enclosure here. For this to happen, buildings must be close together, and there should be a visible relationship between the buildings and the street and between buildings. Such connections and relationships when they exist give character to the street. Otherwise the street is impersonal,' he said.

As we approached the walled city, the streets became noisier and dustier. The roads were dense with traffic and people, who moved across in a solid mass each time the traffic relented. The still point in this flux was a group of cows which sat presiding over their territory. Vandana brought the car to a halt and told us that we had arrived at Manek Chowk, and that Muhurat Pol

where her uncle lived was just a short distance away.

As we pushed our way through the crowds, Professor Irinouchi, the anthropologist, asked Vandana about Manek Chowk. 'This was the main bazaar in the old days. It has many jewellery shops and cloth stores. It has a large vegetable market and the stock exchange is also located here,' she told him. Then she entered a dilapidated gateway and signalled us to follow. It was a narrow gateway which opened into a wide space just beyond it. As Hara walked through the gate he started moving around the open area with his arms outstretched as though he was trying to feel the space. 'What is it, Sensei?' I asked him. 'I will tell you later,' was all he said as he walked on.

We followed Vandana through the lane as it twisted and curved, and after walking for almost fifteen minutes, she turned into a small court surrounded by houses. She pointed to a three-storeyed building across the court. 'That is my Uncle Joshi's house,' she said. The front door was wide open and she went in to fetch him. Mr Joshi was an elderly man. As we followed his invitation to come in, Morita, the architect, pointed to the door frame, which one had to step over, and asked me, 'Do you always have that?' I nodded, and before I could explain Hara said, 'It is a kind of threshold, you see. This is interesting, temples have it. See how it makes you conscious of entering a place, marks the opening.'

We took off our shoes in an inner veranda and followed Joshi into a room on the right which had a few chairs and a divan with bolsters on it. The room was long and narrow and had windows opening into the courtyard. There was a shelf on one side containing a Sony television, some books, vases and framed family photographs. There was a money-plant in a Vat 69 bottle.

In one corner was a steel cupboard with a mirror and on it three suitcases covered in khaki cloth.

Mr Joshi's family walked in. He introduced us. 'This is Uma, my wife, my son Babu and my two daughters. My mother also lives with us. She is quite old,' he said.

Keiko, with whom I was to share a room, was slender and short like many Japanese women. She must have been around twenty-five. She was shy and quiet and not very fluent in English. She told me that she was completing her Master's in history at Waseda University, and that she was specially interested in the history of urban settlements.

'This is so beautiful,' Keiko said as she entered the room and saw the carved wooden jali covering the window that looked into the court below. Keiko peeped out of the jali and seeing Norman in the court waved to him. 'He won't be able to see you,' Uma told her. 'The jali works like a curtain; you can see only one way.'

A few minutes later we joined Norman in the court and Keiko explained to him about the jali. Norman had to almost bend to hear what Keiko was telling him. He was over six feet and well built. He was always smiling and I often wondered what amused him so frequently.

I glanced at Morita who was sketching one of the columns in the veranda. Morita was of medium height and about forty years old. He was rather chubby and serious. Irinouchi was just the opposite: he was tall and wiry and possessed a remarkable sense of humour. In fact he and Norman got along well and laughed a great deal together.

Later in the day we escorted Vandana back to her car. Babu also came with us. Babu was an engineer and had graduated only five years ago; he worked as a consultant to other small engineering firms. He showed us his office which he shared with a stockbroker: it was a tiny space beneath the wooden staircase of an old building whose ground floor had been converted into numerous shops. However, Babu's room was done up pretty well: it had a small table with a red telephone, two swing chairs on either side of the table, and glass shelves which held books.

The walls were painted a bright blue and the old flooring had been replaced by red ceramic tiles. That was another thing—the association with things that were bright: what was new was bright, what was clean was bright. So when someone put new paint on the walls it was always bright, particularly in small towns and semi-urban areas. It was, I supposed, because this gave them the confidence of having moved up in life, of having changed from what they were.

As there was no window they had to keep the door slightly open for fresh air. Nevertheless, what he had done to the little space was remarkable. It didn't matter that the facade of the old building was now completely changed by the shops. I looked at

67

it as a part of a natural process of growth and so inevitable, though a pity nevertheless.

As we walked back into the pol gate Babu asked us to wait a minute and ran up a single flight of steps to a room above the gate. It seemed a small room, just a little more than the width of the opening supported on one side by the temple structure and on the other by a three-storeyed residence. A few minutes later he returned with a parcel rolled in newspaper. 'That is our tailor. I had to pick up some dresses for my sisters which he had stitched,' he said. 'Why does the tailor sit up there?' I asked. 'It was the chowkidar's room to start with. You know all pols have a guard's room above the gate. Since we haven't had a chowkidar for so many years, the tailor and his family live there,' he said.

Professor Hara was making some hurried sketches in his notebook. 'Tell me why you were so excited this morning,' I enquired as I peered down at the axonometric sketch he had drawn of the five buildings around the space.

'See how this entrance is formed,' he told me. 'There are two buildings on opposite sides and there is a room that stretches between the buildings leaving an opening below which becomes the entrance. And see how the space between the houses has widened. This breaks the feeling of entering into a lane. And since the entrance is narrow and it opens into a larger space between the buildings it feels as though one is entering a court. Close your eyes and imagine it—the difference between entering a lane and an open space. What did you feel?' he asked me.

'A lane is different. One feels one will keep moving onwards in it. I am not sure, but here in the open space one gets the feeling of having arrived,' I replied.

'Precisely,' Hara said. 'Imagine the feeling. You enter through the pol gate and you have arrived. It was this that excited me. See, I have drawn a sketch of this space. It will be very useful to me when I design residential complexes or even schools and colleges.'

'Did you notice, it was the same in Joshi's house,' Morita said. 'We walked through a narrow door and into a space which was open to the sky.'

'Yes. Space is sensual,' Hara replied. 'We often look at elements, don't we? We think of the door, the opening, the window, the lane. These are all important, but what is more important really is the process—the act of entering. This process I think is manifested in "space" more than "form". This process activates all the senses and becomes sensual.'

'Why not form?' I argued. 'The door has a certain form, so do the window and the lane. Why are they not a part of the process?'

'Because form is tangible, space is not. It is fluid and ambiguous. Sometimes space is given form; it is arrested within the form and then it is contained. It's like a threshold. It's not just an element. That is what I am trying to tell you. It is a feeling.'

'What feeling?' I asked him.

'Look, when we entered into the pol, we did so through this narrow opening. The opening is the element. The street outside was crowded and noisy. It was also a major public road. But as we entered, it became quiet and secluded. It felt personal and more intimate. That is the feeling. Elements by themselves cannot create a feeling. It is a subtle combination of these elements that arouses this feeling,' Hara explained.

'What is this space called?' he asked Babu.

'Chowk,' he replied.

There were two lanes forking from the chowk. 'What is a lane called in Hindi?' Hara asked.

'They call it gali,' I told him. 'It means a narrow lane. It may contain houses and or shops.'

We walked down one lane which twisted in and out of groups of buildings, narrow most of the way but swelling into a node in places and sometimes enlarging into a chowk. Frequently the chowk was surrounded by houses. It created a feeling of culmination.

'Can Babu tell us something about the history of the pol?' Keiko asked me. I asked Babu.

'The only person who can tell us is Rasikbhai. Let us go to his house. It is just beyond the Mahadev temple,' Babu said. At the beginning of the lane there were many shops, mainly old

69

residences converted into shops. But as we went further in most of the buildings were old residences. The facades of the buildings were intricately carved with floral and leaf-like patterns and the windows and doors were also carved. I stopped and looked at each flower and leaf painstakingly chiselled into the wood. 'Did you see the beautiful carving?' I asked Hara.

'Yes, the carving is all right,' he said indifferently. 'But look at the way the facades of the houses form the street. They become the two vertical elements that hold the street together. Did you see how each house has totally different ornamentation, yet there is such a continuity and such a coherence to a total scale.'

'Sometimes, Sensei, you really confuse me!' I told Hara. 'When we drove through C.G. Road, you said there was no density and space escaped between the buildings. Then you said if form captures space within it, the space becomes rigid, as though it was arrested. Now you tell me these continuous vertical facades hold space together!'

'Because all three are different, don't you see,' he said. 'Here space is not let loose or arrested, it is contained and channelised, you see the sky above. The difference is what one feels in a room and in a courtyard of the same size with a grille or a ceiling. Space must be articulated, not regimented, not controlled.'

*

Rasikbhai was about sixty years old. He wore round glasses just like Gandhiji, and was dressed in a long white shirt and white dhoti. He was sitting in an easy chair as Babu walked towards him.

Rasikbhai got up with the help of a stick and welcomed us in. Except for Norman who trotted inquisitively in, the rest instinctively bent down to remove their shoes. The door immediately opened into the living room, long and narrow, stretching across the facade. Two windows with grilles opened into the front veranda; two more windows opened into the court on the other side. The room was bare but for a few imported items placed here and there. 'Only my wife and I live here. My two sons are both settled abroad,' Rasikbhai explained.

He led us into the inner court. 'We can all sit here. There is more light here,' he said. This was another thing: older people depended on natural light more than electricity and did not switch on the lights until the last glow of day had disappeared.

'First I must tell you about the pura,' Rasikbhai said. 'There are so many puras here, I think more than three hundred. Dariapur, Shahpur, Usmanpura are all puras. They were named after the noble living in them. Each pura contained the houses and palaces of the rich and the quarters of the servants. It also contained the subordinate streets and the chakala, which was the central square. Each pura has a number of pols. Actually a pol means a gate but it represents several clusters of houses. Within the pol there are further divisions forming smaller and smaller clusters called khancha, khadki and dela.'

Hara and Morita had walked over to a column and were inspecting the joinery detail between the post and the beam. Keiko and Irinouchi were listening to the old man rapturously. They also attempted to memorise the vernacular terms. 'Chakara, chakara,' they said, nodding to each other, failing miserably to get the pronunciation right. And Norman was softly humming a popular American tune. It was all very amusing—how each one was interested in his own thing. Rasikbhai continued his narrative.

*

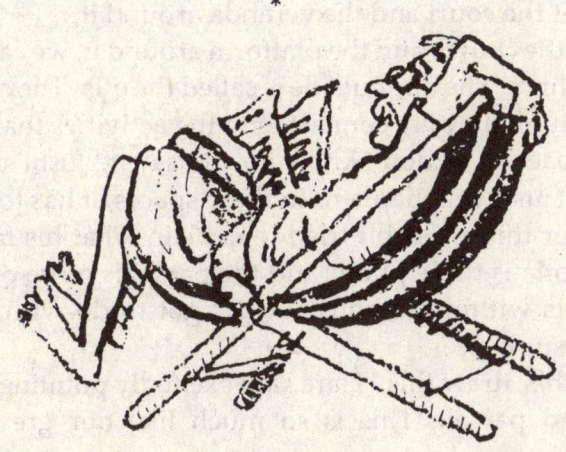

71

The first time I had met Hara Sensei, he was wearing faded denim shorts and a patterned shirt, two buttons of which were undone. His hair was long and poker straight and fell all over his face. He had questioned me for over half an hour, after which I had with curt impatience told him that I had an appointment with Professor Hiroshi Hara. Hearing this he had shyly introduced himself and the others in the studio. It was almost a year later that he disclosed to me that he was a bit nervous that day. It was the first time a foreign student was to join his research studio and the fact that I was an Indian had created a kind of myth in their minds. They had imagined me arriving from the land of snakes, elephants, maharajas and godmen. None of them in the studio had been to India. Hara had also been conscious of the fact that, India having been ruled by the British, my English would be pretty good, at least better than his; he had been wary of this.

I found Hara dressed in a similar way the next morning as Keiko and I joined the others in the chowk. Umaben was sitting on a swing in the veranda. She was combing and plaiting one of the girls' hair. The swing had caused quite a stir the previous evening as each member of the team took a ride on it. It seemed rather unusual to them to have a swing right in the middle of a house. I had convinced them that it was a familiar sight in almost every Gujarati's home, even in flats in Mumbai. Morita and Irinouchi clicked away some pictures of Umaben, her daughter and the swing. 'What is this place called?' Irinouchi asked Joshi, pointing at the court and the veranda around it.

'This is the chowk and the platform around it, we call it parsal,' Joshi told him. 'The one outside is called the otla. They are not just names; I think they are connected to the activities that take place in these spaces . . . I don't know how to say it,' Joshi said.

'It is not just what happens in these spaces, it has to do with so many other things.' Babu tried to explain what his father could not. 'The otla is more public and the parsal is more private. One feels one is within the house; it has got to do with degrees of privacy, I suppose.'

'Draw this, draw this,' Hara said excitedly pointing to the otla, chowk and parsal. 'This is so much like our grey spaces in

72

Japan—the in-between spaces. Imagine the hierarchy of spaces. First the pol is contained in the pura and then the pol contains the khancha, khadki and the dela (all this was of course brutally mispronounced). Then we come to the smallest house group. There is the otla which is semi-public and the chowk which is semi-private and then the ultimate spaces of privacy. Feel the degrees of privacy as one moves from the pura to the parsal. Feel the transition from one space to the other, from large to small. Feel the effect of layering. Feel the changes in activity, from a group to a family. Feel the changes in the sounds of the street. Feel it.'

We breakfasted in a room next to the kitchen. The children ate sitting on little wooden stools in the kitchen. Hara and Morita tried eating this way but found it difficult. Outside the kitchen was another small chowk. We had come down here in the morning to wash and bathe. The bathroom and toilet were to one side of this chowk. There was a washbasin against one of the pillars. There was also a locked room which Babu told us later was the ordo, a room for storing grains and other valuables.

Next to the kitchen was the prayer room. I instinctively knew this as I could smell the fragrance of incense sticks lit by Joshi's mother in the morning. I could also smell the oily aroma of the home-made ghee as it fuelled the wick in the diya. The floating odours in the house—from that of food being cooked to the fragrance of crisp sunlight and light breeze in the chowk, mingled with the exudations of plucked and strung flowers—made me think of how each odour in a house designated a room and the odours in the street, each place and activity. Subconsciously I was still trying to understand streets, although most of the time I seemed to be studying aspects that were indirectly related to them, like the form and space of the house.

Just outside the puja room was a beautiful painting of Balaji in a most brilliant blue. 'What is this?' Keiko asked. 'This is a painting of Lord Krishna. We call this form of Krishna Srinathji,' Umaben explained.

'The temple of Srinathji is in Nathdwara. Why don't you take them there?' Joshi told me. 'I go there every other month,' he said. 'They will like it. The ritual there is more elaborate than in other temples and follows a set daily pattern. This also changes with the festivals that take place throughout the year. The idol is dressed frequently. It is bathed, clothed and fed according to a strict routine. There are eight darshans during the day when people are allowed to see the dressed image. People gather in large numbers to see this. It is different from other temples where people can just walk in and offer their individual devotions.'

'We must go, we must go,' Hara repeated. He was always fascinated by rituals. He frequently told me how architecture was born out of rituals and so these should never be overlooked. 'The house, the streets, the village, the city—all reflect the rituals of life and society,' he used to tell me. I found it difficult to differentiate between ritual and behaviour, custom and usage.

Babu took us up to the terrace. We could see a large portion of the pol from there. I looked at the main lane as it broke down to different scales, subordinate and branching off, offering access ways to smaller clusters of houses and eventually serving only a few houses occupied by members of one joint family. At each level the transition was established sensitively to break down the order of scale. There were many transitional elements: the gateway, the level changes, the different paving, the inner chowks, the lanes, the outer chowks—all the elements that formed the structure of the pol which was dense yet porous because of the lanes that ran like rivulets between the houses; the chowks here and there appearing like pools of water. The dwellings were built against each other and their balconies projected over the street. People sat in the verandas and balconies, making the street a big community space.

Hara was taking hurried notes in his notebook. I peered into it and read the word 'contrast'. Below it he had written several pairs of opposite words—denseness-porosity, introverted-extroverted, ambiguity and hidden order, control and flexibility, connection-segregation, heterogeneity-homogeneity, unity-individuality. I asked him what they meant.

'I think these contradictory pairs are what energises the pattern of the pol. The pol is so formless, without pattern, yet it is this quality that allows flexibility. There is a hidden order that controls the pattern that is superficially heterogeneous,' he replied.

'Let's think of words to describe all this,' Hara told us all. 'Remember when we had done those village studies we had coined a few words—interface, threshold and domain. Let's see—threshold is the smallest contrivance of transition, like the space between the street and the house or the gateway to the pol. The interface is the transition at the level of the cluster or settlement. The domain is the limit of a group or territory. So there is an interface between two groups or domains and a threshold marks every domain. At the smallest level even a house is a domain that belongs to the family that occupies it.'

It was characteristic of Hara to think of final definitions. He loved terminology, especially when it sounded serious and theoretical. Nevertheless, to me the pol established an order that was complex, evolved and rich. In the pols I thought I could see a new concept of order: an order that was hidden and directional—an order derived from minor elements and not major ones, unlike the order prescribed by the modern planning concepts where everything was made to fit into a predetermined pattern. What I assumed to be disorder in the pol at first was perhaps only an excess of variety. But this kind of superficial disorder was different from the actual disorder which I had yet to come to terms with, and which I did that very afternoon.

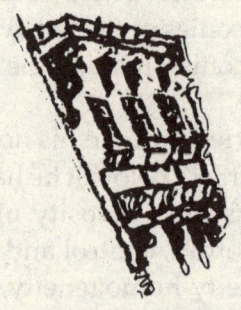

Chapter 5

AHMEDABAD: MUHAMMAD ALI WAS SITTING ON A WHITE mattress. He wore a white kurta and salwar and a white cap, and his beard was deeply hennaed. He sat behind a low counter with glass sides and within it were several small bottles with coloured liquids. It formed a barrier between him and me, and although I was standing and he was sitting, we were almost at eye level and could converse easily without having to look up or down. This was how the shop connected directly to the street and to the people on the street; I did not even have to enter the shop. The shutters of the shop were shelves in themselves and contained an assortment of bottles brightly packed and labelled.

Norman had been very keen to see the Jama Masjid and Babu had brought us here in a taxi as he had wanted us to meet Muhammad Ali. In fact, there were many shops that sold attar nearby, and the concentrated scents added another dimension to the medley of smells emanating from the diseased streets around.

Driving into this area, the first thing that struck me was the number of people—there were too many people in the streets, far too many cars and cyclists, also cows and dogs. The pollution stung my eyes and nostrils, and as I closed my eyes, I could even feel the congestion which swept through each lane and corner. At a distance I saw the mosque looming above the dust, noise and uncontained activity.

'This used to be the old city, these markets once traded with the cities of Europe,' Babu said, hopelessly attempting to put pride in his voice. But no one heard him as each of us, engrossed in thought, was looking at the Jama Masjid. It seemed a vestige of the structure of the city.

'What chaos!' Norman said, desperately trying to adjust his camera to get a clear view of the mosque. The word 'chaos' stuck in my mind; I had never looked at it that way. To me all this hurly-burly was something familiar, common in most Indian cities. But now I felt compelled to understand it. I did, to a certain extent, a few evenings later after a heated debate between Hara and Irinouchi about order and disorder. The discussion also answered some questions I had about familiarity, alienation and belonging.

At his shop, Muhammad Ali smeared various types of attar on every available surface of our wrists. The intensity of the scent disturbed my Japanese colleagues. I understood this, knowing their love for subtlety and understatement. In fact, I recollect how astonished Hara was the previous day when he saw the profusely carved columns and beams, doors and windows, the craftsmanship of which I had thought he would have been thrilled to see. Instead he had asked me, 'So much ornamentation? Why do people like so much decoration?' At first I had believed he had liked it. It was only later when he was looking at the wooden columns in Joshi's house that I realised that it was quite the opposite. 'Such a difference between those columns in the otla in the front and these. Those are intricately carved but in no way can they match the delicate texture of these plain columns. They are so beautiful,' he had said. I had understood then that ornamentation was not necessarily the epitome of beauty.

At the back of the shop, I could see a younger man sitting on a cushion on the floor. There was an assortment of bottles, small and big, on the table in front of him. 'That is my son, Yusuf,' Muhammad Ali told us, continuing to smear his various scents, this time on bits of cotton wrapped around a stick. Norman was thoroughly amused by it all and as usual seemed to be enjoying himself. He was a little like Moose in the Archie comics. Forever incredulous, and slow and lumbering in his speech. He was interested in everything Indian and his tireless questioning kept my mind rattling along, giving me an opportunity to test my own knowledge of things.

The others were curious too, but in a more methodical way and not as spontaneously as he was. By then I had gathered a striking difference between the others and him. While they were intent in observing and understanding what they saw, Norman participated in all that was happening. At that moment he had six cotton swabs dabbed with attar in his pocket as well as cotton buds stuck in his ears. Hara made enquiries with Babu's help about the kind of house Muhammad Ali lived in. Muhammad told him that he lived in an old mohalla just behind the mosque and had lived there since his birth. Hara asked him so many things about his house that Muhammad Ali finally invited us there. He put his son in charge of the shop and we started off in rickshaws.

We sped through the traffic and into a small lane. I did not know exactly where we were, and I regret now that I did not ask him.

The buildings were old and made of wood; some of them were intricately carved. The mohalla was a labyrinth of streets. It was denser than Muhurat Pol, and more dilapidated. Also, the houses seemed to look inwards and the doors were shut, although people peeped from windows and balconies. I noticed that the inner streets were like a connective tissue; once you had entered you became a part of the tissue. This was unlike Muhurat Pol which had an established hierarchy of streets and where there was a main street that moved purposefully inwards.

We reached Muhammad Ali's house: it was an old structure and quite large. It had been decorated profusely. 'My brother's daughter is to be married soon,' he said. It had been built by his great-grandfather. Now there were eight families sharing the place. There was a small ramp in the middle of the steps for taking scooters inside. We walked into a courtyard with a veranda running around it. The walls were painted in green and a metal grille formed the roof. Although the lanes were narrow and deep in shade, the house was open and full of light.

'See how the house has changed over the years, the little ramp, the grille,' Hara said to me. 'This is what I meant by flexibility. But because there is an inner order, neither adaptation nor change makes it disorderly. All these additions and changes may appear ambiguous, but ambiguity is not disorder. I mean it is not like the disorder we saw near Jama Masjid. That was something entirely different.'

There were a number of women and children in the veranda. The women covered their faces as we entered. I noticed that there were two groups: one of them was made up of small children and two women. The children were eating from a large plate, helped by the women. Their little hands would draw food from the centre of the plate toward themselves, mix it in a few rapid movements and pop the balls into their open mouths. The other group was of some women and girls decorating their palms with mehndi.

Muhammad Ali's wife Yasmin had placed a string cot in the courtyard and we settled down on it. 'These houses are so much like our old Japanese houses,' Morita said to Hara. 'They look very different, but spatially and in the manner in which the spaces are used, they are very much alike. All kinds of activities happen in a

80

particular space, the space is not defined by function. I think this makes the space fluid although physically it is compartmentalised into a number of rooms.'

Yasmin appeared with large steel tumblers on a tray. 'Sherbet,' Babu told Norman, who was unusually quiet. Hara took large gulps from his glass and pointed out to Morita the difference between the 'perceptional' and 'physical'. 'Here I can experience a perceptional degree of privacy, more than the physical,' he said. 'There is nothing physical to indicate this, no screens or partitions for privacy. Yet I feel the tension. Perhaps it is all in my mind. Perhaps it is the way they behave,' he pointed to the women and children. 'Perhaps it is because all the doors of the rooms are shut. I don't know what it is, but definitely I can feel several invisible thresholds within the house.'

Two thoughts excited me then. One was the similarity between the house-form and street-form. This pleased me because all I had to do was to understand the house-form and this would help me understand the street. Until then I had presumed architecture, that is to say the buildings, to be a part of the street. But now I realised that the entire street could be seen as architecture. And the parameters that defined architecture could be used to understand the street. The other thing was the idea of interface which Hara had talked about and which was the idea of the edge, seam or connective tissue which segregated and at the same time connected two parts together. It struck me then that the interface could be both a visual, physical as well as a social border as it was in Muhammad's Ali's house.

*

My appointment with Doshi was for late in the afternoon, and while Babu took the others around to see some more pols I headed for his office which he called Sangath. Doshi was short and thin and rather intense. He looked very much an architect. He wore his hair long but not as long as Hara's. He was dressed in a cotton shirt and brown cotton trousers. Doshi had worked closely with Le Corbusier, the French architect who had designed Chandigarh, and was a key figure in the development of an Indianised modern

81

architecture. I had known him since I was a little girl. He had a soft voice until something interested him. Then all of a sudden his voice would become louder and excited and his gestures would become restless and the words would tumble out rapidly. Whenever we met we often talked about architecture. Yet, somehow, through architecture he told me many things, about life, about intensity, about celebration. I always left feeling a lot wiser after these conversations.

We talked about many things that afternoon, but mostly about the character of the pol. Suddenly he smiled as though he had remembered something. 'There is a place I want you to see. I came across it rather accidentally when I was looking for a particular address. It is a single street. One street, that's all there is to it. Can you imagine?' he said. 'A small group of people who have migrated from Saurashtra have built their homes all along this single street.' He gave me vague directions to reach there. 'Oh yes, and Siddpur? Have you been there?' he asked me. I shook my head. 'You should go there also. These two places are exactly the opposite of each other.'

'What is so different?' I asked him.

'The plinth,' he said, 'you go to this street where the Saurashtrians live and also Siddpur; you will see what I mean. In one, the houses have no plinth and in the other they have high plinths.'

'So what about these plinths?' I asked.

'There is something psychic about plinths,' he said and smiled. 'Let me think of an example; it is not as ridiculous as it sounds.

'You have seen the plinths of temples, Humayun's tomb? You don't see any difference? But there is such a difference, can't you see? The tomb appears so monumental, and the temples look humble.'

'That's because the mausoleum is so huge. Surely it is also the size that makes a building monumental,' I argued.

'That's not so,' he said. 'Even though the temples are large they are not monumental and this gives them their own beauty. But the mausoleum is dominating and that is the difference.'

'Yes, I know what you're thinking,' he said laughing. 'I used to be confused too. It used to puzzle me so much and I kept thinking about this, about monumentality. I used to keep comparing the temples and the mausoleums. I think there is a certain sense of accessibility in the temples. Although the serration, mouldings and deep shadows make temples grand and monumental, there is still an intimacy about them.'

That was how the streets were. Some were monumental and some very humble and accessible. It had to do with size, but there was something else that made some streets so familiar, so easy to be in. I remembered the street in Tokyo. There was a familiarity about it although I was essentially in an alien place, without friends and ignorant of the language. The streets in the pol had the same quality. It was the difference between Joshi's house and Muhammad Ali's house. One was accessible, the other felt secluded.

'Have you not felt this in Fatehpur Sikri and in Jaipur?' Doshi broke into my thoughts. 'The difference between something that is awesome and something that is not. I felt it there. Both were monumental yet something about them made them personal; it was the shifting axis. Don't you understand? It has to do with space,' he said. 'Space is the most important thing and it has this dynamic quality, it flows, and in both these places space is fluid; it is not arrested by a predefined axis. Some buildings have a very defined axis and often this is what makes them so intimidating.'

'But Jaipur is like that,' I told Doshi. 'It has such a defined axis. What you say may be true of Fatehpur Sikri, but the first time I went to Jaipur I remember being surprised by the grid of streets. I hadn't really seen such streets before. I had lived in so many small towns and I only knew of meandering narrow streets. I always believed that streets twisted and turned and had many corners.'

'I know what you mean, but then you only saw the form of the street. The linear streets are imposing, but as you walk into them you lose this feeling and the street becomes personal. Do you know why? It is because of shifting views and the activity in the street. That is what brings life into a place—the variety of scenes and activity.

'Like in the pols, there is no axis; yet there is an instinctive sense of direction. You see some axis, a direction, only to lose it suddenly, and discover other areas and activities. The whole pattern is so ambiguous: the longer the route, the more the ambiguity, the richer is the experience.'

One word that had started bothering me was the word 'ambiguity'. Doshi seemed to be obsessed by it. What did he mean? Hara had also talked about it. I asked Doshi.

'Ambiguity makes a thing intangible. When it is too visible and too defined then it is tangible. When something is intangible it has more depth, it becomes more sensitive,' he said.

He asked the office boy to put some chairs in the lawn and bring us tea. As we walked out I noticed that the building looked different in the fading evening light. The rhythmic silhouettes of the vaulted roofs, their white china mosaic, had glistened in the afternoon sun when I arrived. Now, the form of the building merged into the darkness around it. What seemed tangible in the afternoon seemed intangible in the dimness. It wasn't exactly to do with the forms or spaces; they remained the same. It was the feeling or the perception of them that had changed.

Listening to Doshi's concepts, of self and architectural phenomena, I was able to sort out my own ideas. We talked about historic monuments, the terrain and the environment that formed the street's character, and how tradition and the community were responsible for the street-essence.

Doshi talked about the rapid expansion of cities which had brought about a new social order and how the form of the streets

had changed in response to this. 'This change is all about material benefits,' he remarked. I had seen this in the streets, the transition as they changed character, their adjustment to new functions. And I understood then that while society, as a whole, determined the development of the street, culture was responsible for the symbolic and ritualistic overtones. It was the latter that gave the street its essence which went far beyond its more obvious use.

The modern 'industrialised' street had been reduced to being a byproduct of an urban environment. It had become a conveyor belt for transporting traffic, people, sewage, electrical and telephone cables. The very purpose of the street as a public-private domain in the city was in danger of being totally destroyed when 'use' superseded 'custom'.

As I left Doshi's office that evening, I felt a bit more reassured. I had been able to work out some parameters with which to study the structure of the street; its physical, social and technical rudiments. I asked Doshi whether form, space, order and expression, which supposedly were the main physical attributes of architecture, could be used to define the street. 'Why not,' he said. 'Perhaps it will show some aspects of the street that we have failed to see.' Yes, I thought to myself, I would follow these parameters to find out where the streets led.

Chapter 6

SINGLE STREET: SHE WAS SITTING IN THE VERANDA. SHE MUST have been about forty and wore a bright nylon sari lavishly printed with flowers and leaves. The red of her bindi was deep and bright like the flame of the forest. The smile as she looked up was warm and spontaneous before she covered her head and bent down again to her work.

Her house was in the 'single street' Doshi had told me about. The first impression was of tall trees and a wide and open street. It was surprisingly broad, in fact broader than the street that led to it, and was lined with single-storey houses. Doshi was right, there was nothing to the colony but the street. And much more.

I had passed her house twice; it was almost at the end, the third house from the end to be precise. I liked it and this time I stood opposite it, encroaching on it with my eyes.

Then I went up to her. When I asked her name, she told me that she was called Lachmibai and continued to embroider a bedcover.

The veranda where she sat was more like a private pavement, lightly covered with a patina of dust from the street. Its flooring consisted of pieces of mosaic and cement tiles in a random pattern. Patternmaking is instinctive with village folk, and because it is so, it always appears natural and not contrived. A low compound wall ran around the house, except for the front, which was rather strange. Why have the wall in the first place? It puzzled me a bit but I could see why. The barrier that it provided was more psychological than physical, and perhaps that was what was intended. It made the entire street look spacious and more open, more friendly: the house connected easily with the street, and this aspect interested me, as always.

On one side of the veranda was an upright cot hung with several embroidered bedsheets. A girl sat below it hemming the sides of a sheet. Beyond this pavement, a single step reached up to an inner veranda, and just a few feet away was the main door which was open. I couldn't see anything within because compared to the glare outside it was dark inside.

I asked Lachmibai many questions: where she and her family had come from; whether the house belonged to her; who had helped her build it; who her neighbours were. She continued to stitch small round mirrors onto a bedcover. When at last she spoke, she sounded upset. 'Why have you come here?' she said.

She pretended to be busy, then asked, 'Are you from the government?' Norman had come in and was squatting on the floor, running his hand over the parrots and flowers on the bedcover. Seeing him she was reassured and said, 'So you are not from the municipality or something like that. You are only tourists.' She became friendly after that.

Norman draped a sheet around his shoulders, knotted it in front and strutted around like some berobed king. Lachmibai started to giggle. Her daughter started to laugh too in that marvellous way village girls have—dimpled, shy and yet free. Lachmibai asked us into the house. There was only one large room and behind it the kitchen. There was no furniture in the room except for a cot on which an old man slept.

'Father-in-law,' Lachmibai said, covering her face more fully. He stirred, hearing us, and Lachmibai told him we were visitors.

He sat up and indicated that we sit next to him on the cot. There was no mistaking his warmth, though he was very lean and very old. He was silent for several minutes and we waited—that is another thing about village people: they can handle silence with ease, unlike us, city-bred, to whom it is unnerving. Then he cleared his throat and spoke:

'We left our village in Saurashtra. First a few of us came here, then the others came. There was no water in the village. We were not poor. But you can't live without water. Don't think we came because we were poor,' he said shaking his finger. 'We had a lot of money; we were rich.' He spread his arms to indicate what 'a lot' was. 'But without water it had become impossible to continue. So we left and found this open area sheltered by these huge trees and built our homes here.

'We bought whatever second-hand building materials we could find, and we built our houses first in one row. When more people came they built opposite us. The men found jobs in factories and building sites and the women embroider and sell their goods to shops. Many people come here to buy. They make a lot of money.'

I looked around the room. There were two windows and the walls were bare. There was no calendar or pictures of gods. They were hung, perhaps, in the kitchen. There were no wall hangings or symbolic designs either. Somehow the room felt undefined, tentative, as though more was to happen. This lack of definition, strangely, felt more exciting than if it were well defined. I remembered the Japanese houses; they had a feeling of being transitory, of being 'in-between', though they were complete and not in any way tentative.

When we came out of Lachmibai's house, it occurred to me that the street also felt tentative and undefined, like something just begun and yet to take firm shape. Little children played in the street, and a large number of people sat outside their houses, working, talking, listening and looking. They looked towards us, acknowledging our presence.

Most of the houses had large paved areas in front of them. And almost all of them also had a low wall that demarcated the paved area of one house from the other. There was yet another aspect, the most fascinating of all in this street—the houses had no plinth. When Doshi had mentioned that there were no plinths, it was not something that I was greatly excited about. But now I saw what he meant. Despite the fact that it is rather undesirable not to build over a plinth and keep the rain, dust and insects out, it did incredible things to space. The spaces within the house and outside it seemed to mingle, making the street appear like a large community living room.

There was something very peculiar about this street. It was neither anonymous like a public street nor hostile and defensive as an intimate and private street would appear to a stranger. And it was such a short street. What was it that gave it this unusual quality? The only conclusion I could come to was that it was friendly: it was open and one did not feel like an intruder here. Was it because it was a new settlement that it was friendly? Or was it because it was not legal and therefore had this sense of impermanence? I didn't know.

These people were not poor. Their houses were large, sturdy and built in brick and concrete. There was another thing: I had always believed that when village people moved to bigger towns and built their homes, they always built in the way in which they had lived in their native place. This was not entirely true now, as in big towns you just moved into whatever was there. But in smaller towns, or even slums, this was what happened. Here, peculiarly, the buildings were rather contemporary, and with art deco motifs which were quite popular in Ahmedabad at one time.

Norman and I walked towards the others who were sitting in front of a house. Hara Sensei was sitting on a cot under a large rain tree and the others sat on the wall around the house. Hara looked as if he was in some sort of a frenzy. He was muttering to himself, his long hair was in a mess because he kept running his fingers through it, and his clothes were looking crushed. He looked, in short, as though he had just returned from a long and arduous journey.

He was talking, quite aptly, about chaos and order: 'It is only because of growth, more and more growth, that there is chaos. Growth is only about numbers, it is development that has quality. Even technology is used merely to cater to this growth; there is nothing creative about it. That is why there is so much chaos.'

Growth didn't seem wrong to me. I had thought that villages that grew naturally had a restful quality about them. 'Look at the smoke,' Hara said puffing at his cigarette when I told him that. 'See how it rises. It starts out in a straight line, only to diffuse swiftly into turbulence, disorder, chaos. That's what happens in natural growth. But chaos is not confusion. Remember, what often seems random is only a different set of rules in operation. We must find the rules. There is chaos because there is no order. Look at this street, for example. There is no chaos here. In fact, there is an order about it, and that is what keeps it intact.'

I looked down the street. The doors of the houses were open. Men and women sat around in the sitouts working, some cleaning

grain, others busy with embroidery. Even in the villages I had seen a certain amount of 'closedness', but here it was open, all joyous.

It was not so much the parts that mattered; one did not look at the style of the buildings as much or their material. All one experienced was space and a sense of totality of form. It was like a string of beads where each bead was important but the purpose and essence was in the formation of the string. I could see now why Doshi was so enthralled by this street. It was so simple and yet made such innovative use of space, unlike contemporary architecture, which was more often than not space-blind.

*

I tried to recapitulate the various observations Hara had made. He was more than a great architect. He was a great teacher. In Tanjore, I had felt interest stir in me when I looked at the streets. A history of itself existed in each. Hara's explanations of the morning had excited me. I wanted to hear more.

It was now evening, and we were sitting in the chowk of Joshi's house. I asked him to expand on what he had already said.

'Physical things are important,' he began, 'because we can see them. Like these pol houses, they are richly ornamented. You may like it, you may not, but they form an identity. They transmit the inner feelings of the people who originally made them, their myths and anxieties. These decorations become cultural history. We miss this point. As architects we fail to see this. We designate everything as good or bad. Too much decoration is not bad. I see this now because if people decorate, it shows their creativity.

'However, the facade and external form, no matter how beautiful they are, are only the container; the content is the space within it. Sometimes both complement each other and then the whole thing becomes beautiful. This physical aspect is not just of a "material" nature but is also cultural. But there is no culture in the cities today; I think the city has become anti-cultural.

'In the past, in the neolithic age, everything was about containers: pottery, jars, utensils, granaries; houses also were collective containers, just as villages were, and so also the street which is a container of space and activity. With storage came

continuity—storage of history. Without the containment, without the enclosure and order, the city, the street may never have appeared. What has happened now? The technical explosion has broken open the container and so the city has become largely demagnetised. That is why it is so random and unpredictable.

'You remember asking me what order was?' Hara Sensei cocked an eyebrow questioningly and said, 'Let me tell you—there are two kinds of order: one, the natural or organic order and the other, planned order. Both can be seen through physical and social patterns or sequence of events in a city. The natural order has an inner energy that drives these patterns. It is something like, shall we say, an organic force which creates a process and which stimulates these patterns.' He stopped and looked at me to see whether I understood him. 'Look at it this way,' he said. 'The natural order has patterns and processes; it is like a kaleidoscope. It forms colourful patterns, but it has to be turned to form these patterns. This turning force that causes the change in patterns is the organic force.

'This force is natural, therefore susceptible to changes. It is also structured to begin and end and this sequence continues in cycles. Continuity is important. I think it is a process of "unfolding"—you know, like organic evolution, where the whole precedes the part and gives birth by splitting—like it happens in the reproduction of seeds and cells. But I think the planned order is very different. There is already a preconceived idea and the elements are added in parts; this happens both consciously and subconsciously. When additions are made subconsciously it becomes a natural order. One sees many unforeseen events in an otherwise planned city or space, because of human ecology.

'It is not difficult to understand the organic system. Think of a tissue. It is like that. The main structure of the organic system is the individual cells that form the cellular tissue and the interrelation between these cells. This idea can be easily applied to cities and streets. The streets are like the individual cells and they form a network, a tissue of connections. Just as the quality of the organic system depends on the quality of the individual cells and the quality of their interrelation, the quality of the street depends on the quality of each of its individual parts and their interrelation, and also their relation with other streets in the network. The organic system is all about expression and interrelation. What they look like and how they relate. More often than not, both of these are missing in the streets or the city. Some streets are expressive, but the relationships are missing.

'One important difference between the natural and the planned is that the natural order is based on discipline while the other is dependent on control. Also, in nature there is order but not a modular system as in the planned systems. It has rhythm but it is not monotonous. This is because in the planned order there is a repetition of parts and not of their patterns and their interrelation. But in the natural system the patterns and their interrelation become important. There is also a rhythm of regularity and irregularity. This is how there is both order and variety.

'In the natural order, at first the patterns form simple sequences relating to each other. The sequences are linear and form a chain of events. Then they become complicated with multiple sequences like a web. In a growing village the natural order maintains the balance, but after a point this order is broken. As long as there is a natural order, streets appear natural, comfortable, timeless; they need no systems, they are spontaneous. But as the village grows into a town and later becomes urbanised, the balance is affected and it becomes complex.

'Have you ever wondered why you like old villages and medieval towns? It is not just because of nostalgia. It is because in those settlements there was a distinct order. Those towns were built, not planned; they were culturally constructive. Compare a village and a slum and you will understand what I am saying: one has evolved through time, the other is always "contemporary". Look at the layout of streets in the city, particularly the new streets—they have the right angular order, but they only are practical and technical. A medieval town is interesting because it reflects the tempo of growth and the changing conditions of life; it grows over a longer span of time, slowly, in a particular pattern.'

Patterns themselves are a result, not the cause of order. I had always believed order had a built-in permanence. But now I knew that it was vulnerable and susceptible.

'So you see,' Sensei said, 'both pattern and process make the street. In simple terms, pattern is more obvious because it is physical and visual. It relates directly to the street's form and space. The "process" is complex and is connected to the changing activities in the street.'

Hara flopped back in his chair, apparently exhausted by the deluge of words he had delivered. So, indeed, was I. Architects seem to speak in their own terminology, which is very far from

'the dialect of the tribe'. But like students who had sat at the feet of the Greek philosophers, I was not merely tired. Like all great teachers, the Sensei had left me with much to think about.

The next day was our last in Ahmedabad. We went to the single street which, like Doshi, Hara was excited about. I had a final look at the street. 'Single Street' is what we had started to call it. It was organic, as Hara had explained the previous night. It reminded me of *Dreams*, a film by Akira Kurosawa in which he dreamed of an idyllic village with thatched houses all along a stream. Each house had a watermill dipping wooden buckets into the water. There was no electricity. People worked only as long as natural light let them. There were flowers, birds, breeze and abundant sunshine. And people there lived to be very old.

Chapter 7

SIDDPUR: 'THE RIVER SARASWATI IS A VIRGIN RIVER,' RAM Shankar told me as he led me towards its banks. It was a beautiful sight, beautiful in a way that marks an absence of things. For my part I could only gaze unblinkingly at the river basin; it lay motionless and dry, unfulfilled. The sun poured mercilessly over the stretch of sand. I blinked as the glare singed my eyes. 'Saraswati after meeting with the Ganga disappears underground and never emerges; it is the only river that doesn't meet the sea,' he said. 'That is why she is called a virgin river.'

Ram Shankar was a pundit. It is a good thing to be named after two gods, I had told him, laughing, when he told me his name. We had met quite by accident. As we reached Siddpur and even before we came to a halt, several pundits ran to the car asking me whether I wanted to perform any puja. They gathered around me as I stepped out, refusing to let me go. They wore white muslin dhotis, their chests bare except for the sacred thread across them,

97

complemented by the tangled strands of long hair at the back of their shaven heads. They appeared to me like hawkers touting their wares, and I wondered what it was that they wanted to sell to me. I was standing there bewildered when Ram Shankar had confidently walked towards me and led me away from the throng. 'What is all this about?' I had asked him angrily. 'This is a special place for women,' he said. 'They come here to give their offerings to the river Saraswati and that is why those pundits were surrounding you. I,' he added, 'am also a pundit.'

I felt I had to explain to Ram Shankar exactly why we were here lest he also believe I had come here to barter with the river goddess for her favours. I told him we wanted to look at the houses and the streets and know more about the place. 'Then you must meet Abbubhai,' he said, happy to be of some help. 'Help' was always equated with 'tea-money', and being aware of this I agreed to use his help. 'He's one of the richest Vohras here. Come, I will take you to his house. Normally he doesn't like meeting strangers but if you are with me it is all right,' he said, and I understood that the 'tea-money' had also shot up because of this.

As he took us towards his house I began to notice the street and the houses on it. It was straight, part of a grid, and seemed ancient. The impression it gave was of careful planning. I began to think about hostility and friendliness again. There was definitely something hostile about this place—I didn't know why it felt that way. Despite the fact that the houses were built side by side they seemed isolated: isolated from the street and from the other houses. Perhaps it was because there was hardly anyone on the street, and the doors to all the houses had separate steps leading to them. I compared it to the pol which was alive and active; the houses participated in the life of the street. I couldn't help comparing it to the 'Single Street'; it had a spontaneity that was missing here. There was a rigid discipline here: the manner in which the houses connected to the street: the door, the plinth, the veranda, the gate, the balcony—there was something fixed about them all.

We entered a quiet lane with large houses on either side; they

were like town houses arranged in a row. 'Look,' Hara Sensei said, stopping to light his cigarette, 'this street is so urban; there is something powerful about it, dynamic, and all urban growth is dynamic because of a freedom of choice. You know, in the street day-to-day activities contrast, oppose, and the things that happen are both contradictory and complementary. And this is what stops a place from becoming too homogeneous, too boring. Don't be confused about this homogeneity bit,' he added. 'There is a lot of difference between homogeneity and harmony. We keep talking about harmony. In those newly developed areas of any city, large areas are homogeneous but that is not harmony. It is boring.

Uninspiring. This street for example,' he said pointing to the street we were in, 'there is the public part which is the street and the private part which is the house and both interface without losing their characteristics. This is what holds this street together, visually, physically and socially.

'See this,' he said, pointing to the steps and the closed doors of the houses, 'the stronger the contrast or conflict, the more defined the interface between the public and the private areas becomes; and the stronger this interface, the more "urban" the street—that is what urban dynamics is about.'

*

Abbubhai's house was on what looked like a main street; the street was broader and the houses were large. I was shocked to see such profuse decoration: every inch of the facade was ornamented and opulence oozed out of every pore of the structure. The houses stood on plinths almost three feet high and they seemed to me like some discarded colonial or Roman stage set; they smelt of a bygone era. And the colours—'Jesus! Look at these colours,' Norman exclaimed, pointing to the pista green, cobalt blue and baby pink-plastered decorations. 'They look like icing on a cake.'

We walked through the main door: there were two shutters but Abbubhai unbolted only one of them and we filed in sideways one by one; I couldn't help but notice this—the way in which we entered the house. It was almost pitch-dark inside, and I could smell old varnished furniture even before I could see it. In fact all I could see were dark blotches in the darkened space. It seemed mysterious, even in the manner in which each point of 'entering' was emphasised: the steps, the plinth, the ornate portico and the closed door. I remembered the various thresholds in Joshi's house in the pol and all that Hara had explained to me about 'the act of entering' as he had called it. Yet there was a difference between the two: Joshi's house so friendly, this one so uninviting and remote. I had experienced something similar about Muhammad Ali's house, but this one was more severe. I remembered Joshi's house: the front door was open and the house immediately within was bright and inviting. Abbubhai had opened only one shutter of the door and the house within was dark.

At first I thought we had entered a living room; it was a small room and had some furniture and screen that shielded whatever lay beyond it. There was a winding stairway on one side with a most intricate wrought-iron balustrade. All the windows in the house were shut tight; the only light coming in was from a small glass ventilator which I noticed as we reached the top of the staircase.

Abbubhai unlocked a panelled door painted in soft green pink and white, a very European colour, it seemed to me. He ushered us into a lavish room with a wave of his hand, bowing slightly. 'Ashraf,' he called out loudly, clapping his hands twice. Abbubhai was tall and thin with a slight paunch which showed through his fine white kurta. The kurta was embroidered around the neck and front and secured with gold buttons studded with glass diamonds. His loose salwar had the same embroidery at the ankle. He wore a large ring on his finger studded with nine big

diamonds, and a gold chain around his neck.

'Switch on the lights,' he told Ashraf, who must have been about fourteen. 'And bring us some tea quickly.'

Two huge chandeliers hung from the ceiling, salmon pink and white glass bits in circular tiers, the likes of which I had seen only in Hindi films and perhaps in Chor Bazaar in Mumbai, and the carpet was in almost the same colours as the pink and green of the ceiling. As we sat down on the plush sofas I noticed that some of the furniture was covered. 'We don't live here,' Abbubhai said, following my glance. 'My grandfather died many years ago, and after him my father. We shifted to Madras; my brothers live in Mumbai now. I come here once a year to check if everything is all right.'

I looked around the room. There were three doors, all with arched frames and a ventilator. But for the main door, the other two were polished the colour of rosewood. The window frames were similar, with stained glass in the ventilators, and I wondered why no light came in. Abbubhai later explained to me that there were shutters outside. 'It is common here to have two sets of shutters, many houses have them,' Abbubhai said, seeing my surprise. The shelves and cupboards were full of photographs and souvenirs. 'We Vohras have a habit of collecting expensive things during our travels and we like displaying them,' Abbubhai proudly explained.

I heard a melancholy old Hindi song coming from a radio. 'Tabassum, is that you?' Abbubhai called out and a young girl in her teens walked into the room. She was wearing a frock gathered at the waist and reaching her ankles. Her hair was long and plaited on either side of her head. 'Call your mother,' he said to her. 'She is my granddaughter. My daughter Naseem is also here,' he told us.

Naseem walked in with Ashraf who carried the tea tray. She acknowledged us with her eyes but did not say anything. She wore a long gown gathered at her waist just like her daughter. She was already fat; it made her look fatter. She had also wrapped a black georgette dupatta around her head. Her skin was white and pale, almost European, just like the house.

'Naseem, they have come from Japan and America to see Siddpur,' Abbubhai told her as she served the tea. 'There are two different stories about the Vohras,' Abbubhai told us as he poured his tea into his saucer and slurped at it. Norman was a bit startled at the noise, though the Japanese were hardly surprised as they were used to slurping their soup and tea with enormous slushy sounds. 'It helps to cool the tea if you roll it on your tongue and make a noise,' Hara Sensei had once told me.

'The eighteenth Imam sent Maulani Ahmed to India to spread their religion in the east,' Abbubhai said. 'He landed at Khambat, a prosperous port of Gujarat. He stayed for a long time and got to know the people, their language and religion. When he returned he took two Hindu boys with him and converted them to Islam in Egypt. They then returned to spread Islam in India.'

'That is one story.' He poured the remaining tea into the saucer and slurped again. I noticed that Norman was doing the same and thoroughly enjoying himself. Only that he made the noise much after he had sipped the tea. I had never realised it was so difficult. 'There is another story that missionaries were sent beyond the valleys of Sindhu and two of them were sent to India from Egypt. In fact their tombs at Khambat are visited by Dawoodis even today,' Abbubhai said. 'In those days,' he continued, 'the Hindu faith was very strong and opposing the Hindu saint was dangerous, so Abdullah who was one of the missionaries became the saint's disciple. Abdullah studied Hinduism and in the end converted the saint to Islam. Many of the saint's followers also became converts, even the kings. Do you know, on a single day in Patan, 260 pounds of sacred threads worn by Hindus were taken off!'

'Why are you called Vohras?' I asked him.

'Because it was the trader class who were converted,' he said. '"Vohruvu" means to trade and those people engaged in it and who were converted were called Vohras or Bohras.' From the corner of my eye I noticed that Norman was signalling to Naseem and she was ignoring him. 'I wanted to know what kind of tea this

is,' Norman said when I asked him about it. 'It is so sweet and
flavoured. It's very good, almost a meal,' he said. 'It's masala tea,'
I told him. 'It has cardamom and almonds and a number of other
spices. It is brewed with lots of milk and sugar.'

'It's too sugary, milky and tea-ey,' Hara commented. 'It's
terrible—it's like nursery pudding. You know Japanese
tea—ocha—it is so shibui, subtle. I like things that are enigmatic,
a little unfinished.' I could have expected him to say nothing else;
it was so like him. 'Tell me why you Indians like so much
exuberance, the decorations, so much furniture, colours, clothes,
this tea.'

I couldn't tell him why. 'Perhaps it is so because we are so many
cultures put together and unlike Japan which was isolated, we

weren't and so couldn't evolve in a singular sense,' I said.

'No, I don't think so,' he said. 'If cultures mixed then there should be hybridisation—it's even better. There is some problem here,' he said. And I wondered what the problem could be—just because the tea was so sweet we now had problems!

'Why did the Vohras settle in Siddpur?' I asked Abbubhai.

'It's not just Siddpur,' he said. 'They built their own settlements called vohravads where they lived together. And there are so many vohravads in Khambhat, Kapadvanj and other places in south Gujarat. At first they lived in Hindu houses, then they built new ones or adapted them to suit their Islamic lifestyle. Our houses are built for the privacy of our women,' he said, proudly explaining the purdah system that they strictly followed. 'But as the business with European countries flourished, their houses, particularly the reception areas, showed how rich they were. Perhaps they did this because they were a minority community and they had to show they were different from the Hindus.'

'By using European decorative elements?' I asked with surprise.

'Yes,' he said. 'Actually these traders frequently travelled abroad and they saw European and colonial architecture in those countries and when they came back home they copied them. When the British consolidated their power, the Vohras identified themselves with the British and broke with their Hindu roots and beliefs. You can see this in Siddpur,' he said. 'You must have noticed all the mixed up European styles here. It must seem different to you,' he said looking at Hara, Keiko and the others.

'When exactly was Siddpur built?' I asked him. 'I will tell you exactly,' he said. He went out and came back with an old book. 'It says here,' he said reading in Gujarati and then translating into English, 'Siddpur was built between 1890 and 1930. There are survey records particularly because they had started to build with brick masonry and stucco, unlike the earlier houses that were built with wood.'

He read through some more pages of what seemed to be an old book. Bits of paper crumbled and fell to the floor as he turned the pages. 'It says here that since the Vohras were basically Hindu converts,' Abbubhai said, 'their behaviour and houses and other objects of daily use were very much like those of the Hindus. They evolved very slowly in modifying them to suit their new social and religious beliefs. It seems this process was one of additions, particularly in the way in which the house was planned, its decoration, inner spaces and furniture. You can see the difference in the old and later Vohra houses, in the facade, furniture, openings, partitions—the later houses have a strong European influence.'

'You have seen the pol in Ahmedabad?' he asked. 'You must have seen the European decorations there also. The vohravads are built like the pol which is like the medieval row house,' he said. 'But this is so different from the pol,' I said. 'Siddpur is different,' he agreed. 'The older vohravads had long and winding streets but in the later vohravads there was a strong colonial influence and the streets became straight and intersecting. The vohravads are more like the Hindu neighbourhoods—very different from the British neighbourhoods in India. They are not one big bungalow in a large plot; they are close, all grouped together in rows. They are also looking inwards; and this gave them security socially and economically. Some of the row houses even had controlled street facades—they acted like models,' he said.

'So the Western influence is only superficial; the Vohra house is like a Hindu house,' I said. 'I think it is only in the Western houses that there are several rooms that can be used separately,' he said. 'It is not like that in the Hindu or the Vohra houses. Here all the rooms come one behind the other so it is not possible. Only the last room in fact is free from people moving in and out.'

'This maybe because they need more privacy,' I said. 'Yes,' Abbubhai agreed, 'it also shows that within the house not much privacy is required. The house is one large space. Did you see the screen downstairs?' he asked us. We nodded. 'That room where you entered is called a dehli—it is a small anteroom and beyond the screen is the inner house.'

'Why don't we go down, I will show you,' he said, summoning Naseem to precede us.

As we went down the stairs and walked behind the screen in the dehli I noticed that the house had become brighter. 'Visitors come into the dehli and are taken up to the living room,' Abbubhai explained. 'They don't come to this part of the house; we observe purdah, we are very strict about this.' I still wondered why the formal areas were dark and the more private areas bright. We moved across the court, paved in patterned tiles; the water place which Abbubhai called 'paniara' was to one side of the court. He told me that the paniara was very symbolic to the Vohras. The kitchen was a part of this court and it seemed as though all the activities happened here. Beyond it was the bahrni parsal, a small room; it was empty except for a large box-bed kind of arrangement, but much larger, which had shelves and drawers built into it. It had a mattress and large white bolsters on top. 'This is the baithak, this is where we sit together with the family. We don't use the living room upstairs—that is only for guests.' Two fading photographs hung on the wall—'My grandfather and grandmother,' Abbubhai told me.

'And this room we call the andarni parsal,' he said as we walked into the next room. 'This is just a room; we sit here, we eat here, when it is too hot in the bahrni parsal and also when it is raining.'

This room was also bare except for a large swing. 'Why is there always a swing in Gujarati homes?' I asked him.

'Oh! Because it feels good—and also it helps stay cool; it is because of the hot climate really,' he said amused at my question. 'Behind this is another room, the ordo. It is like a family room; my grandmother used to sleep there. Her cot is still there, see.'

There was a cot against one of the walls and the room was richly decorated with colourful mattresses and cushions on the floor. Against the rear wall was a cupboard which caught my attention; it was intricately carved. 'This is a traditional cupboard—it's nice isn't it?' Abbubhai asked. 'This is an Islamic design of nine squares called the navkhand and it is kept in most Vohra houses. This room is used to entertain close relatives and family friends and also for sleeping,' he said. 'Actually the older people in the family always use the ordo and the andarni parsal.' I looked around the ordo. Although brightly furnished, it was dark, not bright as the previous two rooms; there were two windows but they were shut. As I tried to open one Abbubhai opened the other and it was still dark and not much light came in. I peered at the high compound wall which cut away the light. 'What is beyond the wall?' I asked him. 'There is a small lane,' he said. 'The wall has an entry for the sweeper and the cleaning women.'

'The other sleeping rooms are all upstairs,' he said. 'They are used by the married couples of the family, and these sleeping rooms also have a bathroom next to them; the ordo doesn't. In our custom we must clean up in the night—after sex, you understand. This is very important to us Vohras,' he said but I wondered about it since the custom of an attached bathroom was not common in many Muslim houses. I thought it was the European influence and perhaps it was therefore also a status symbol. 'But most of the time in the hot months we use the terrace—the agasi,' he said. 'It is right on the top and is an important part of our living—it is the only open space we use. We don't use the otla—the veranda in the front of the house; the Hindu families use it—they sit outside most of the time but we live totally indoors. It is our custom; we are very

private people,' he repeated.

I understood this as he showed us the upper floors and the terrace which also had a patterned flooring. I was surprised as the terrace was not like an unused space; just the top of a house as it often was, but clean, decorative and well kept. I was also surprised at the staircase; one flight led to the landing that opened into the living room on the first floor. The flight leading to the second floor was along the walls of the court and looking into it. 'Because it is more private,' Abbubhai said when I asked him about the two separate stairs which was rather unusual, and I realised then how closely the spaces in the house responded to the lifestyle of the occupants; how it changed as they did. I thought of the streets and how they also changed gradually with the changes in people. Some streets preserved the geography of a place and not its history, as those on Malabar Hill, and others preserved history, like these streets in Siddpur.

Hara told me: 'The history of the street is tied to its geography. You must remember that architecture is a deliberate creation. It is an application of aesthetic and scientific principles, consciously or subconsciously done. But the city is not like that; it grows.'

And it is the architecture of the street that changes the city into art, beyond mere function; it reflects places and events, situations, social life terrain and also reflects the adjustments to change and need. There was another thought that came to my mind: the street's character is not always because of its regional base, its terrain or its local customs and beliefs. It could be totally different, alien and borrowed as it was in Siddpur because of various external influences and hybridisation.

'You are going to Madras? You must come and stay with us when you are in Madras,' Abbubhai said as we left.

'Why such a high plinth?' I asked him as I walked down the steps. 'My grandfather was a very wealthy man,' he said. 'He made a lot of money trading with the European countries. He often took my father and my uncles with him. In fact I and my brothers used to go with them when we were young. The women in the family were left alone in this big house when we were away.

The whole house is built with the idea of privacy and security. Perhaps the plinth is also because of this. It is also because we were rich. It is a symbol of prosperity—like living above the others.' He laughed. 'Surely you must bring them to Madras,' he said again. 'Stay with us, I am in George Town.'

'Yes,' I said. 'Yes, I would like to see George Town again.' It was such a long time ago that I was there.

Part II
Connections

Chapter 8

MADRAS: THE ROOM SMELT OF FRESHLY BURNT INCENSE. IT also smelt of whitewash. Two distinct smells and the white of the room enhanced the quiet within, but through the partially open window I could hear the soft noises which presaged what it would be like a few hours later. It was early yet, about six in the morning, but the day seemed to have begun hours ago, and it was already hot, sultry and bright.

Meenakshi walked into the room, freshly bathed, her dark skin lightly coated with talcum powder. Her long hair was wet and dripping, and she wore a starched white saree with small mango motifs—a favourite with south Indians, as much as talcum powder, which they use copiously. I remember my grandmother had given me a gold necklace strung with mango-shaped gold drops. She had told me it was traditional and was always given to a girl, particularly when she was to marry.

Meenakshi had not changed; she was just as I knew her in

college in Madras: small and thin, but wiry. She could then climb up trees very fast and with such expertise that I used to tease her that she was a monkey. She could ride a motorcycle without fear and I used to envy this; she was a tomboy, yet very shy when it came to talking to boys. Her face was all eyes and mouth, not surprising really as she was trained in Bharatanatyam, and these endowments were like a prerequisite. As she set down the steaming hot idlis and coconut chutney on the table along with plates and tumblers, she asked with pointed thumb and clenched fist (meaning 'why?'), 'So why are you here in George Town?'

I thought about Pierre. 'He is a French architect,' Hara had said. 'I think you had left Tokyo when he joined my office. He was there for a year and then returned to Paris. He wrote to me a few months ago from Auroville; he has been there for many years now. He wrote that he had designed his house with lightweight, fibre-reinforced concrete. It sounds interesting. Anyway I have wanted to see Auroville; so I wrote to him that I will come. Irinouchi wants to see it too. Why don't you come? You have not been to Auroville, have you?'

'I have,' I had replied, 'but that was a long time ago.' I had been to Auroville when I was studying architecture in Madras. And ever since Abbubhai had mentioned George Town I had wanted to go back to Madras and meet people I knew there and walk through its streets on which so many cultures had left their mark.

I had called Meenakshi from Mumbai and also Altaf and Arun who lived in George Town and were in college with me. Meenakshi had shifted to George Town after she had married. As soon as I had arrived at her house last evening she had introduced me to her husband and two daughters. The daughters were both state champions in swimming. Her father-in-law was unwell and resting and I didn't meet him, but I met her mother-in-law, a formidable woman who seemed to run the entire household, which included four sons and their families. I appreciated her dark blue saree with a turquoise border. 'This is Kanjeevaram silk; I only wear this,' she said. She wore huge diamond earrings, so large they popped out of her ear lobes, and on her nose were two large nose-studs that shone like beacons. When I complimented her on the diamonds she said, 'I am sure you have seen nothing like this before—this is the best blue jaguar ever.' I tried not to comment about her enormous gold bangles.

The house was more like an old apartment building; it had a stairway at one side which led to the various floors. Everyone lived here: each of the six floors was occupied by the brothers and their families. 'When my husband's parents lived here years ago, there was an old house, very traditional. They pulled it down and built this one as the family grew and we needed more space,' Meenakshi said.

Meenakshi's apartment seemed somewhat impersonal. As in many other homes, everything seemed to be pressing towards utility and convenience. There was the painted steel table with four steel chairs where we were sitting. In front of us was a yellowed Allwyn refrigerator. The refrigerator in the south, and elsewhere in India too, is often placed in the living room. It may be kept there for convenience or as a showpiece, as proof of progress, while the families themselves hold on strongly to the old ways.

Although traditionally the dining space was part of the kitchen it had also become a matter of prestige to have a living-cum-dining room, a fashionable fallout of American apartment culture. There was nothing much about this house and its whitewashed walls except for the brightly coloured kitchen and its bright and shiny oil paint that was a deep blue-green, and the pervading smell of ground coffee.

Meenakshi's mother's house had been very different. I remembered it well as I used to visit the house frequently when we teamed up on college projects. It was in a quiet lane in Saidapet, an area where there were many old houses, single-storey constructions with mangalore tiles on their roofs and wooden pillars in the verandas.

Meenakshi's maternal aunt would sit in the veranda in the evenings, stringing white jasmine flowers which she would promptly give to Meenakshi and me to wear in our hair when we returned from college. Within, the house opened into a courtyard. The courtyard was paved with rough granite slabs but the verandas around it and the rest of the house had the traditional red oxide floor which was redone every Diwali when the house was painted. I particularly remembered this as the soles of our feet would turn pink when we walked barefoot on the floor, which was all the time, since we couldn't wear any footwear indoors.

What I liked most were the large pillars. They were made of Burma teak and didn't warp in the rain; and though with time they appeared discoloured and badly in need of varnish, they remained smooth to the touch, like marble. Their beauty was in their simplicity and proportion; they were not delicate and carved but stark and bold. The entire house was like that; the entire lane was like that. There was a sense of belonging even as one entered the lane, which was a cul-de-sac, and the sense of privacy gradually increased as one walked into the house.

This apartment block in George Town was quite different; it was closed and the links to the street and between each floor could hardly be felt; the transition as one entered was not gradual but sudden.

*

'We have to go to Altaf's house for lunch. He called this morning. What would you like to do before that?' Meenakshi asked. 'Nothing in particular, let's walk around in the streets. Has the area changed a lot?' I asked.

'Do you want to buy jewellery?' Meenakshi said. 'My husband's family is in the jewellery business. I will show you our shop.' She led me in and around a number of streets: streets with shops that sold only utensils, others for hardware, building materials, electrical goods. Then there was a lane which was full of reed mats, 'pai', intricately woven, in various colours and designs. My grandmother used to spread a pai on the floor and lie down in the afternoons. They were much cooler in summer and very convenient: they could be rolled up and put away. For some

reason all the shops selling these pais invariably belonged to Muslims. I had noticed this when I used to come here with my mother who, like her mother, also slept on a pai in the afternoons. When I asked her about it she told me that originally pai-weaving was a traditional occupation and the weavers were Muslim converts who belonged to a lower caste. Next to this lane was Burma Bazaar which was full of smuggled goods. 'This used to be China Bazaar where one could buy the most beautiful yards of soft Chinese silk,' my mother had told me.

We came to Kasi Chetty street and to Meenakshi's shop. It had large show windows and many pieces of jewellery fashionably displayed within. The door, the show windows, the illumination, everything was very stylishly done, presumably it was done by a young interior designer with trendy ideas. The shops adjoining it were more flashy: black granite polished to a deep gleam, chrome and imported smoked glass. I preferred the old shopfronts: small, simple and not overwhelming. All this glitter and shine did not appeal to me.

Meenakshi's husband, Shetty, showed me the latest designs in gold and diamond jewellery. A peon fetched us cold buttermilk in silver glasses. I drank one glassful and asked for another; it was most refreshing in the Madras heat. Shetty told me about George Town, its past, how it was changing. 'It's not only that the streets have shops which sell particular goods,' he said when I pointed out the row of shops selling the same goods, 'there are separate streets for wholesalers and retailers and these shops are also monopolised by various ethnic groups.' This explained the cultural texture of the streets. It had not occurred to me before that texture and grain was so much more visible than the shape of a street.

I wondered how all this came about, whether there were rules permitting only particular kinds of shops, but I realised it was more of a natural process. George Town was a convenient centre. 'It is the centre of the city,' Shetty said. 'The raw materials suppliers and transport facilities are all here.

'All this was commercially attractive before, the amenities and the natural advantages,' he said after a little thought, 'but there is too much competition now and land prices have gone up. Only firms that could exploit the amenities have survived. The families who lived here had to move out. In fact the people moved out faster than the new residents moved in. Only some of the older houses have remained. The family who own the shop next to ours, for instance. They came from Gujarat and were traditional jewellers. They have lived here for years and years—several generations. They are just like south Indians; they speak and behave like them, you can't tell the difference. I think they are more traditional and more orthodox. I think people from different communities try so hard to conform to a new place that they remain strictly traditional for a long time even though the natives may have changed.'

The cultural aspect of the streets began to become clearer in my mind. When an entire street was made up of a single community who had migrated from their native place and settled there, the entire street wore the character of the particular community. But if only a few families were in a street occupied predominantly by the native families, they adapted and conformed to the native characteristics.

George Town began to grow on me once again; it was more than a place, it had become a way of life. In its streets, each so different, I saw the tempo of life and work, their constant transition and fluctuations; the habits, thought and behaviour of people and traditions that resisted change. But as we walked to Altaf's house which was in a more congested part of the commercial area, I felt as though it had grown all too suddenly. It seemed to be largely unprepared for whatever was happening to it. Caught up in a rapid process of urbanisation, it was breathlessly striving to stay abreast of all the changes. It was a melting pot of successive instances of history and industrial progress. Ruins of both were strewn all along the streets. Yet, remarkably, behind it all I sensed a staying power. And while residences had given way to commercial premises and small buildings had grown larger allowing greater concentrations of people, the streets had

119

remained the same, though cobbled and patched up in many places.

*

Altaf's apartment was in a corner house. It was in a building like Meenakshi's, three storeys with a staircase on one side. His apartment on the first floor had a panelled door, painted a mixed shade of green and decorated with green and blue glass beads hung in the shape of an arch. We rang the bell and Altaf opened the door; around him were five or six little children of varying heights. 'Those two are mine, the others are my sister's,' he said. He had become chubby and looked fatherly and responsible.

The last time I had been to his house was when we were in the final year of college. One of our friends was to be married and some of us girls had come here to have mehndi put on our palms. Altaf's two sisters were very good at it. The house hadn't changed; it was much the same. Even the upholstery was, if not the same, similar—bright with gold motifs and tassels. There was a lot of velvet used: curtains, chairs, all done in maroon velvet.

The chandelier lights were on despite the fact that it was a bright, hot afternoon. The room was dark and gloomy because the windows were lined with a green sun film. The windows had frames in the shape of pointed arches and they were laminated with Formica. I didn't like Formica. I didn't like the linoleum on the floor either, which felt like plastic under the feet.

'I am sorry,' Altaf said. 'My sister is here from Hyderabad; her friend is getting married and they are all over here to have mehndi put on their palms. It would be best if we went to a restaurant.'

'Sure,' I said. I walked into the next room to meet his sister who was busy squeezing the henna paste out of a plastic bag onto a friend's palm in exquisite fibre-thin motifs. Another friend rubbed the other palm with eucalyptus oil. Nearby sat four women around a large brass plate on which was piled a variety of food: rice, mutton, vegetables. Their mehndi-smeared hands rested on their laps, face up, while Altaf's younger sister fed them bits of

120

food from the brass plate. The room had a heady smell of mehndi, eucalyptus oil, sugar syrup and lemon. There was also the smell of the food.

Altaf came up behind me. 'What do you want to eat?' he asked. 'What else? Your Hyderabadi biryani, of course,' I said. He used to bring it for us in college: it used to be pungent, full of whole red chillies fried a deep brown and mutton pieces as tender and soft as the rice. 'Then let's go to Ahmedbhai,' he said. 'Do you remember him?' 'You mean the restaurant opposite the bus stop? Of course I remember,' I said.

Ahmedbhai's restaurant was just the same. It hadn't improved, neither had it deteriorated: it remained untouched by time and change. It was a small place with a counter on the street for fresh fruit juice. All around and above it were fruits that hung down from the roof: pineapples, oranges, grapes, even large watermelons. Whatever could not be hung was suspended in a net bag. Within, there were square tables with four chairs each and on one side curtained cubicles with 'Family Room' painted on the partition wall.

Ahmedbhai sat behind a table in one corner, stroking his hennaed beard. The waiters filled in the bills and poked them through the spike on his table. Ahmedbhai looked around frequently to ensure that the customers were being served. The decor was in green and pink. Even the lights were covered with coloured cellophane paper. On one of the walls, rather unusually, were faded photographs of George Town.

There were all kinds of people eating. People from the offices around, some even with a tie on; bus drivers, truck drivers and workmen in lungis, presumably loaders. Everyone came to eat what the place was famous for—Hyderabadi biryani.

Seeing Altaf, Ahmedbhai came over, calling out to the waiter to get freshly cut onions for our table. He then sat down and started talking to Altaf. I asked him about the photographs on the wall. 'That was what George Town looked like when I was young,' he said with pride. 'That one is taken from Wall Tax Road,' he said, pointing to a photograph. 'Why was it called that?' I asked him. 'Under the British a tax was collected to build a wall around the town. But all that is left of the wall is the road by its name,' he said laughing.

'Street names are very important,' he said, becoming serious. 'I don't know why these politicians want to change them—they have nothing better to do. Street names tell the history of the place.

You know, there is a Mint Road here where the rupee currency was first struck by Lingi Chetty. There is also a street named after him. He was very important and influential. There are also many streets named after other prominent businessmen of the age. There are so many stories behind the street names.'

Ahmedbhai came back after attending to a fussy customer. 'Some people,' he muttered and resumed where he had left off. 'There were many trading communities who came and settled here. This town was very important for trade. That is why you will also find streets named after these trading communities. Have you been to Sowcarpet, Armenian Street?' I said yes. 'These were named after the Sowcars and the Armenians and there are many such areas. But the most interesting is the Kotwal Chavdi market. Do you know why it is called that? There was a royal official who supervised the functioning of the market in those days. His name was Kotwal Chavdi.'

As we stepped out of his restaurant I noticed many people were gathered around the juice stand outside. I looked down the street; there were no other restaurants like this one. This one formed a knot of activity on the street, relieving the tediousness of a stretch of office buildings with closed fronts.

*

We walked to Kotwal Chavdi. It was like a palpitating organ of George Town; it was the city's principal market. I used to come here often with my mother, at least once a week. She argued that the vegetables were fresher and gave better value for money. She had particular stalls to go to for coconuts, green vegetables, potatoes and fruits. There was a middle-aged woman who used to sell all varieties of bananas, and that being my favourite fruit, I used to be particularly interested in going to her stall. She used to perch herself high up on her stall surrounded by bananas of all shapes and sizes. 'I am Muniamma,' she said pointing to her chest when I went to her the first time. 'Buy bananas only from me—okay?' When I said a few sentences in Tamil, not very

fluently as it was really my first year in Madras, she said with an
air of condolence, 'So, you are a papati.' I had wondered what that
meant and why it sounded so derogatory. My mother told me later
that Muniamma had wanted to know whether I was a Brahmin.

She used to swear and complain a lot; she also gossiped and
told far-fetched stories. They were observations really, but, she
wove them into stories as a grandmother would. 'Is Muniamma,
the banana woman, still there?' I asked Meenakshi. 'Yes,' she said.
'She's got two stalls now. She's grown old but is still full of guts.'

We found her, much thinner now but with a voice that was still
clear and razor sharp, much like her temper. She didn't remember
me but that didn't stop her from talking. 'This is my life; I will live

selling bananas and die selling them,' she told me with a bit of drama when I asked her about the market and how long she would be selling bananas. 'The trucks come here in the middle of the night carrying vegetables, fruits from the surrounding districts. One of them brings me my bananas. No, they are not all for me,' she said, shaking her finger. 'The truck driver doesn't sell it to me directly. But he sells it to the godown-walla. They keep fighting about the price each night. It is always the same. Then he buys the whole truckful. And he fights with me when he sells them to me. He is a bad man. He makes money from both of us.'

*

The first thing I saw the next morning, and the strongest picture of all I observed, was the rows of trucks unloading on the narrow street. It was four a.m. The floundering light of dawn ran in little rivulets, illuminating, now and then, the activity that unfolded in a great hurry at the Kotwal Chavdi Market.

We went in search of Muniamma and found her in the market cleaning up her stall. She walked with us to Godown Street where there was an endless row of lorries being unloaded in front of the godowns. Muniamma kept lifting the ends of the tarpaulins covering the trucks and peering into the stock, announcing loudly and emphatically, 'There are coconuts here. This one is full of potatoes. Look here, these are very sweet pumpkins.' She picked up a bundle of betel leaves from a truck overflowing with them, much to the annoyance of the truck driver and his helper. And she let out a squeal of delight as we passed a truck-load of bananas.

We stood on a shop step to watch the proceedings. Little boys with tea trays meandered through the crowds. Stalls started appearing all of a sudden, between the trucks, in the middle of the street, outside the shops. The sequence of events was rapid. Plates of breakfasts of all kinds appeared and the truck drivers ate off their truck bonnets. Hand-carts, rickshaws and coolies added to the confusion. Memory normally consists of pictures, but with Kotwal Chavdi, I felt I would always remember the sounds.

Among the hundred, perhaps hundred and fifty trucks that came here, thirty to forty trucks unloaded at the same time. The godown and goods owners transacted at wholesale rates to the retailers in the Kotwal Chavdi market, who then sold the goods from their stalls in the market place. The people started to arrive from 6 a.m. By 7.30 the market was in a frenzy of unloading, buying, selling, transporting, cleaning vegetables—all in an unhygienic environment of ever-increasing dirt and stagnant water. Kotwal with its intimate scale of space, people and traffic reached a crescendo which I had not seen elsewhere in George Town. Despite the filth and rotting vegetables underfoot, there was something about the place that was missing in the lethargic suburban markets. I realised that the conditions of the environment were really secondary at this point; they could be upgraded, regulated. But what was most important was the sequence of events and its organic, interrelated structure.

After Muniamma left us to attend to her duties, I walked up to a truck driver to talk to him. His name was Hira Singh, and he told me that he belonged to a village in Punjab. He was quite amused by all that I asked him. He said he came to Kotwal Chavdi with market goods, bags of onions or potatoes or heaps of bananas. 'I drive through the night to reach here early in the morning because all the transactions happen in the early hours. If I am late I will be stuck with my goods. It is very bad when I carry perishables. Also I can't go back empty. I have to load my truck with goods. There are so many trucks waiting and sometimes I have to wait several hours to procure the goods from the harbour or the railway station. There are agents for all this. Sometimes we have waited days to transact business,' he said, waving his hands around.

Surprisingly, Kotwal Chavdi market made me think of Crawford Market in Mumbai. That building with its trussed interior had a quality of its own, very much like what town architecture should be. I recollected every part in detail and also realised that unlike Kotwal Chavdi, this building was a historical landmark on the street. Yet Kotwal Chavdi with no building to boast of was no less of a landmark. I had until now thought of landmarks as physical entities: monuments, important buildings, gardens, mountains and so on. But I could see now how a hub of activity gave an identity to a place.

*

George Town was rather small and essentially suited to an older and slower mode of traffic which was the case in any city centre which had become urbanised. Its street pattern evolved at a time when most movement in the town was on foot or by carriage. Some streets were still cobbled. There was still a great deal of pedestrian movement, but the pattern had changed with the changes in land use. Though essentially a business area, people were seen all over the area throughout the day.

In the afternoon, food vendors and others started setting up their stalls along the pavements and by evening the activity was in full flow. There was an atmosphere of festivity as vendors cried out their wares, their voices rising over the hum of vehicles. A colourful melange of ribbons, bangles, plastics, leather goods and

127

toys appeared on the crowded pavement, backed by the brightly lit shops that presented their own range of goods.

But something wholly different I experienced in George Town was the manner in which the high density of activity was distributed over very nearly a twenty-four-hour period. While much of the city lay inert after dusk, George Town lived through the night and into the morning.

Chapter 9

PONDICHERRRY: I CAN BE FASTIDIOUS, SOMETIMES TAKING hours getting dressed. That morning, in under twenty minutes I had made up, dressed in a bottle-green cotton saree, patted on some of the attar that I had bought in Ahmedabad, breakfasted and spent an equal amount of time waiting for Arun to fetch me.

He had called the previous evening and told me about his aunt whom he intended to visit, and about his friends in Auroville and his uncle at the ashram in Pondicherry. He had told me that his uncle looked after the library and the bookstore at the Aurobindo ashram, that he was a learned man, a philosopher, and that he was certain I would like talking to him.

Arun arrived; he was tall and thin as always, with a stubble covering his face. At college he had a perennial stubble which never grew into a beard even after many days. As Arun walked into the room I saw that he was not alone; behind him was a short, fat, middle-aged gentleman.

He offered his hand and said with unusual confidence, 'Mother Victory Ramakrishna is my name.' Noticing my startled look, he chuckled, his cheeks dimpling, and held the tip of his nose with three fingers, which I later realised was a mannerism. And he explained proudly: 'Dr. M.V. Ramakrishna, I am Arun's maternal uncle.' Later, as we proceeded to Connemara Hotel where Hara and Irinouchi were to meet Pierre, he told me that he was an urban sociologist.

Pierre was not what I had expected him to be. His eyes were a brilliant blue, as I had anticipated, but the rest of him was unexpected: he was small built and bald except for a crop of red-brown hair at the sides. He had a nice brown tan and together with the very native mannerisms he seemed to have adopted, nodding his head frequently or speaking loudly, he hardly seemed a foreigner.

He had also acquired a new name: Satguru. He looked jolly, full of verve as he hopped around in a psychedelic T-shirt and white bermudas in sharp contrast to Dr. M.V. Ramakrishna who was standing beside him dressed in a dark suit. This brought a smile to my face, which was indeed a good way of starting a journey. After seeing Hara and Irinouchi drive off with Pierre, we started off too.

Dr. Ramakrishna sat in the front of the car with Arun. While Arun concentrated on driving, Dr. Ramakrishna turned around, fastened his prominent, bird-like eyes on me and asked me about George Town. Having started a topic which was of particular interest to me but of even greater curiosity to him, Dr. Ramakrishna engaged me for the next one hour in a detailed interpretation of urban processes.

'They happen in pairs,' he said, 'these urban processes— such as concentration-dispersion, centralisation-decentralisation, aggression-regression, obsolescence-rejuvenation. They oppose one another. It keeps happening in cities and that is how they grow and change. One process begins, then there is a feedback and the opposite process starts. They balance each other.' He gestured with his hands to indicate balance.

'First George Town attracted people to live and work there,' he went on. 'Then all activities began to be centralised, also the services, and the centre became commercially powerful. When it became too crowded people started moving out, dispersing. Some of the shops also moved to the suburbs as people began to live there in larger numbers and they did not journey to the centre except on special occasions. This started a natural process of decentralisation. So what was left in the centre was basically the wholesale activities and retailers who maintained their links to the centre. George Town is all this: concentration of people, centralisation of goods and services and also dispersion of people and commerce.

'Let's consider the other two processes—aggression and obsolescence.' I noticed his enthusiasm, as also Arun's frown. Obviously he wasn't enjoying all this. I was.

'Aggression had to do with land use. As it happens everywhere, new commercial uses displace old functions. So a new land use becomes important and the old one recedes into the background and sometimes fades away. This happens to particular groups of people also: a new community displaces the older community. I don't see the new user as an invader; I think the displacement establishes growth.

'You must have noticed how the traditional shopfronts have changed: they seem more prosperous and modern. In Rattan Bazaar also there are hardly any cane workers though at one time the entire street had shops selling cane furniture. There are all kinds of shops now. It is a pity, really. The older streets had some identity because they sold particular goods and because they had identifiable shopfronts. Now shops selling cane goods, or shoes, or ice-cream, all look the same. A pity.'

Though I was delighted with his observation about streets and shopfronts, I received his explanation about growth and change negatively. I preferred to believe in the permanence of things, that cities lived on and on. 'Why must places become obsolete?' I asked him rather sadly.

'There is a brevity in all natural things, and cities grow naturally. There is an inevitable phasing out of things, of use, and obsolescence is a necessary fallout of growth and change. Something interesting is the speed of obsolescence or change. Traditional elements don't get obsolete so fast; they become useless only after they have fully served their purpose. This is because they don't fit into narrowly defined purposes. They are not specialised like modern technology where things become useless faster and abruptly. It also depends on how easily they adapt. Those that do, continue. The organic process is like this, very adaptive, so it continues and evolves. This organic aspect in cities or even architecture is really important.'

*

We had been driving for over an hour in the scorching heat. The lumpy red soil stretched for miles along the road, dry and crumbly, and dotting the landscape were gigantic anthills. There were many of these, tall and abandoned. The landscape, the smell—the place smelt so different, perhaps because of the heat and humidity—reminded me that I was in the south.

We passed villages and 'developments'. I don't know what else to call them. They were not exactly villages, just a string of structures: a small hotel, a few provision stores, pan and cigarette shops, building material shops. We stopped to have coffee at one such development. The aroma of strong coffee seemed to pervade the entire street. I noticed the hoardings. They were all written in Tamil, I couldn't see anything in English. This was what happened as one moved away from the main cities. Later, as these wayside developments were sucked in by the growing cities, the hoardings would be written in two scripts, English and the local language.

There were three restaurants. They all looked like Udipi restaurants, like the ones I used to frequent in Matunga in Mumbai. The owner sat near the entrance, surrounded by large jars of biscuits and sweets. Boys in vests and lungis kept running between the cash counter and the customers. And there was the familiar, heady smell, a mixture of flour batter and spicy sambar and ground coconut and freshly brewed coffee.

As we finished our coffee I saw Hara, Irinouchi and Pierre walk in. Hara was wearing a garland of flowers around his neck. He had removed his shirt and was in his vest. Irinouchi carried half a dozen of the small illaichi bananas and some of the longer Kerala variety. They joined us.

'We stopped at the village,' Hara said, pointing at the flowers and bananas. 'Strange-looking bananas they have. One so small, the other so big. Are they good?' Irinouchi peeled the small one and took a bite. 'Too sour,' he said. He bit into the Kerala banana and frowned.

A boy brought the coffee. He set two steel bowls in front us, the smaller one set upside down in the larger one. 'Where is the coffee?' Hara asked as he peered into the two bowls. I asked the waiter to pour the coffee out for them. Like a deft juggler he lifted the small bowl and coffee spilled into the larger bowl. Then he

poured the coffee from one bowl to another, building up a froth. Hara watched him in wonder.

We left shortly and I noticed that Irinouchi had left behind the bananas. 'Let them be,' he said as I picked them up. 'They taste odd.'

Beyond the restaurant or 'hotal' as the local people called it, there was a bakery. As I walked towards it, I could smell baked flour and butter and the aroma of biscuits. It seemed as if my sense of smell was easily excitable that day. I was smelling things most of the time—the red earth, the muggy weather, the coffee, the batter.

How the smells accompanied the street! They gave the street and parts of it an identity. All along the street, there were flower-sellers. Strings of white, fragrant jasmine and those translucent orange flowers called kanakambaram which Hara had around his neck. There also were cartloads of bananas. Clusters of bananas hung down from every small cigarette shop. This I had seen only in the south. And the smell of all these filled the street, giving weight to all that took place there.

There was a little temple beyond the lane that forked from the main road. Around it were old houses. They appeared to be the remnants of an old village. At the corner was a street market, also a spinoff of what was originally the village market. The shops on the main road were obviously meant to cater to those passing through, like us. It was a place in transition: the older parts, the more meaningful ones, had crumbled; only bits of them were left. The new additions were haphazard, aimless; they were 'in transit'—not belonging to the old village nor quite new and definite, they seemed to be accidental. Such transitory developments occurred on the fringes of many cities and also between cities. Villages were also unplanned; yet they had an inner discipline that bonded them. It was this bond that was missing here. There were only isolated parts, no whole.

I stood before the market and watched the people. There were many women selling their wares, their lips stained with betel juice. They looked several shades more belligerent and spoke louder than their male counterparts. However all wore flowers in their hair; in that there was a touch of femininity.

The street market, the shops, the crumbling village and whatever was left of it, still felt like a place. Or was it because it was so familiar that I felt it so? Like the bananas which seemed all right to me but Irinouchi found odd because their taste, shape and colour were unfamiliar to him. There was more to it than familiarity.

I had travelled to many cities outside the country, unfamiliar places, but they had charmed me. So what was it that made a place? The region, climate, people; their behaviour, culture, history—all did contribute largely in making a place. So did the architecture and the planning, though to a lesser extent. But when all combined together the place became beautiful.

*

As we came closer to Pondicherry, I thought how like a river approaching a waterfall the street was. There was a gathering anxiety of something about to happen, a speed and scurry. All cities had this aspect to them: they were like magnets. This made the city throb, unlike villages, which were placid, undisturbed, somehow timeless. The city began and died easily, quickly. It didn't actually die in its entirety—only a phase died and soon a new one took its place.

One could truly perceive these phases. They were not abstract or even obscure: remnants of the old, the new and current and much more of all that was in between existed side by side as people tried to keep pace with change and growth. In the final analysis, it had to do with people. People changed, and so the cities, streets and architecture changed. Then people tried to keep abreast of the changes.

We drove into the city slowly, but outside, in the street, the pace had picked up. There were many more people around: people walking, waiting, people on cycles, some rushing, even running; they all seemed preoccupied. This was something else about larger cities: people seemed sure of what they wanted to do, yet seemed lost, oblivious of all that was happening around them. As the cities became larger this aspect seemed to increase.

I had felt this in Mumbai, Ahmedabad, Madras and other large cities; they were different from the smaller towns I had lived in when I was younger and the villages I had travelled to. The streets in these cities were just conveyor belts for people. In the smaller towns and the villages the pace was slower yet there was more life. Even poverty, as I saw in the streets and the houses of the poor, seemed different in cities and villages: people in the cities seemed poorer even though they possessed more.

*

Three things strike one about Pondicherry: the sea, muddy and reddish with silt; the influence of the French: wide avenues, planned intersections, french windows, balconies, porticos. And Sri Aurobindo. Or else it could be like what the truck driver told me as we waited behind rows and rows of trucks to get into the city: 'I lived here as a little boy. Some time, I think about the 1950s, that is when my mother died, the French colony was divided into small pieces of territory: there is Karikal in Tamil Nadu, Mahe in Kerala and Yanam in Andhra Pradesh. Because of this, the streets had to pass through various states with different rules, which resulted in a lot of confusion for drivers.'

But neither would be saying much: the city didn't consist of just the sea or the split territory, but the relationships between its spaces and the events of its past and present. The streets that passed from one territory to another didn't belong to a place or people, but were mere thoroughfares and started looking so: characterless and incidental. But the streets in Pondicherry were more legible: they formed a grid and around it was a semi-circular boulevard.

Arun told me: 'There is a canal that runs north-south and divides the town into two parts. In the days of the French, this canal separated the European and Indian areas. Where the

Europeans lived, some streets have a typical Mediterranean look. Between here and the canal are the ashram and its offices and institutes.' Arun pointed out the buildings which I couldn't possibly see as they were set well back from the road.

I never expected waterfronts to be all that different, but the one here was: it was smaller, more intimate than Marine Drive in Mumbai or the Marina in Madras; it related to people more than cars. There were many civic buildings on the street, which gave it a totally different character, as they were more accessible than the

private residential and office buildings on Marine Drive. There were small restaurants here and there and people on the street. Even the sea seemed friendly. I felt I belonged here though I had just come.

We drove through the inner lanes; they were empty to the extent of being desolate: there were people but no crowds. There were also no hawkers. I thought something was missing but it was just that I had got used to crowds, chaos, noise, and walls that stretched on and on. Perhaps that is why these looked so empty, devoid of things.

We drove through a street where all the buildings looked Mediterranean: tall windows, louvred, some painted green, the walls whitewashed and some painted in warm colours, but rather aloof. This was surprising; I had always expected open windows and warm colours to be alluring.

We turned into a narrow lane. The houses here were a part of the street, intimate with it: most had verandas that faced the street. In some of the houses the verandas still had their original wooden pillars and brackets, but in the others these had been replaced by more modern material like brick and concrete. But the plinth height remained the same, not more than six inches.

The houses were small. Mentally, I linked scale to intimacy. It was the rich and the famous who built the largest, the most expensive, the most impressive and the most durable buildings. There evidently was a little snobbery attached to this which was displayed in their aloofness. But it was the vernacular buildings, like the ones I saw in this street—small, intimate, domesticated, without pedigree and with permanent traces of the years spent in the sun—which constituted the major part of a city.

*

Arun stopped before an old house much like the others in the lane. The front of the house was not more than four metres wide and the tiled roof of the veranda was supported on two carved wooden columns. I couldn't see anyone sitting out on these verandas as they did in the pols in Ahmedabad; it seemed more like a space or thing that connected the house to the street.

Standing there I imagined the entire street without these verandas, and the houses with their doors closed. Somehow it made the street appear unfriendly. There are some streets that have the quality of remaining in your memory point by point, in a succession of street-parts, of houses along the streets, and of doors and windows in the houses, though nothing in them possesses a special beauty or rarity. This street was like that. This undeniable quality lay in the patterns following one another; in their rhythmic sequence.

Arun's aunt Saroja opened the door. She was a beautiful women, tall and slim and well preserved. Her complexion was not pinkish but creamy, and this was further set off by the off-white Kerala mundu saree she was wearing. I knew instantly that I would like her; she seemed to like the same things I did.

I had tried to imagine what the house would be like within when the door was opened. I was delightfully surprised. It opened into a large space. It couldn't be called a room—though small and compact, it didn't seem enclosed. In the middle of the space was a glass-covered court which had been filled with pebbles. There were several tree stumps planted in the pebbles on which leather bags were displayed, and several stands around with more leather items.

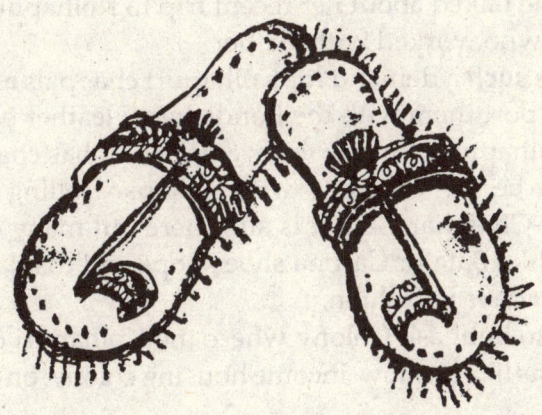

The walls were lime-washed: pearly white but without lustre. I liked them dull and smooth but uneven in the manner of old village houses where the craftsmen used their hands and a minimum number of tools. The flooring was of rough granite slabs, neutral grey in colour, against which the aged wooden columns looked lustrous. The red of the mangalore tiles on the roof, and the white of the pebbles in the court made the place reticent yet inviting.

'It was an old house really, and coming apart,' she said happily. 'When I decided to set up this boutique we went looking for a place. I wanted a traditional place, not a modern shop with glass windows. I don't much care for modern architecture. When we found this place I said no, this is in shambles, but Arun insisted, he said he could do wonders with it, and he did.'

When she had finished showing me around the shop, she gave hurried instructions to her assistant and took us to another house nearby, as though she was going from one room to another in her own house. This intimacy reminded me of the street in Tanjore, the ease with which I ran in and out of the house, or went to the neighbours' on errands.

Saroja's house had a rear court where we sat that evening under the swaying branches of a tree. Dr. Ramakrishna had changed from his suit into a white veshti and shirt He looked more comfortable, as did Arun, having rested after the long and hot drive. Saroja talked about her leather business and her plans to expand. She talked about her recent trip to Kolhapur in search of craftsmen who worked with leather.

'There is such a demand for Kolhapuri chappals and I thought I would export them with the Pondicherry leather bags. I hadn't been to Kolhapur for many years and how it has changed. There used to be a bazaar with shops selling Kolhapuri chappals—Chamhar Gali. It is still there but many of the shops now look like Bata or Carona shoe shops and display the sports shoes nowadays in fashion.

'I went to Subhash Colony where the Kolhapuri chappals are made. It was like any low-income housing colony; only at the back of every house there were craftsmen working on the chappals. Even in a traditional craft such as this they had an assembly line manner of working. Each worker worked on a particular part of the slipper and passed it on to the next worker. The last worker piled the finished pairs in tall heaps. They were picked up by women who worked from their homes and they added gold tassels and red trimmings to the chappals.'

Saroja excused herself and walked into the house. Lights were switched on within. It was customary to switch the lights on, particularly in the kitchen and the prayer room, before it was dark outside. This was a ritual I was used to since my grandmother and then my mother practised it without fail, accompanying the act with a short prayer.

The bulb dangling from the tree under which we sat began to glow as Saroja reappeared. In her hands were small boxes and following her was a maidservant carrying a tray of tall mugs. As I blew on the rasam and sipped it, Saroja showed me the contents of the small boxes.

'These pieces of jewellery are also from Kolhapur. It is known for its gold jewellery filled with lac and silver jewellery that is gold leaf plated. These are old pieces called the Kolhapuri Saz. I bought them from an old shop in a street called Gujeri where my friend took me. This street only had shops selling gold and silver jewellery and moneylenders.

'I have seen this in Mumbai and Madras; there are many banks in the Javeri bazaar. So money-lending and jewellery shops are intimately connected. This street, Gujeri, is also close to the palace and the large wadas where the rich used to live. Have you seen these Maharashtrian wadas? You must see them,' she said.

She carefully put away her splendid jewellery back into the boxes. She rubbed away the sweat that had collected under her eyes. She did sweat profusely, even out in the open where every once in a while the breeze rustled the leaves. I thought of the Maharashtrian wadas, Saroja's house and other courtyard houses. Just as a greater meaning could be read into all these traditional houses with courts and verandas, a greater understanding became possible of all kinds of streets: friendly, intimate, hostile, indifferent, chaotic. The streets told their own story. The city lived it.

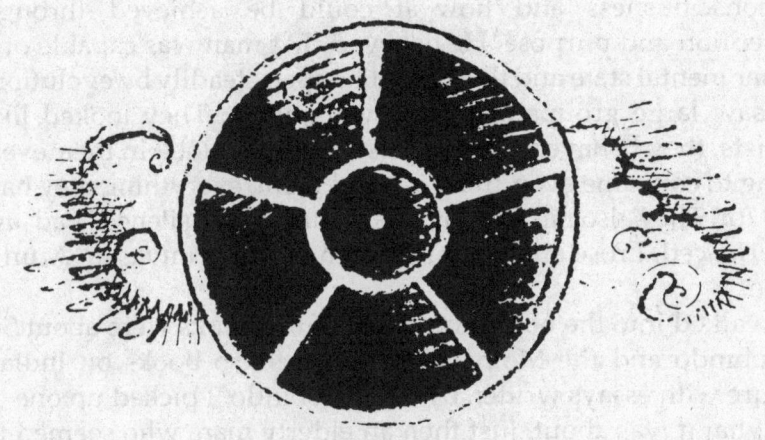

Chapter 10

AUROVILLE: SOME THINGS REMAIN. THEY REMAIN AS THOUGH still, suspended in time through the years. Saroja had dropped me the next morning at the ashram before she went to her shop. It was fifteen years since I had been there. It was still the same: the few buildings in the compound, the large trees and the paved space between the buildings that contained the tomb of Sri Aurobindo. People sat around the tomb in silence, thoughtful, peaceful. Even the rustling of the leaves, the murmur of people talking, seemed a part of the silence.

Space, independent of its size, took on different meanings depending on where it was, how it was used. I remembered a small indent in the street that climbed uphill where I lived in Mumbai. It was a small clearing with a platform in its centre and on it a cross. There were always candles. Close to this was a market and around it traffic, a continuous flow of traffic and people. Yet this little space in the street was quiet. This was the only thing one

143

remembered about the street besides the way in which it went
uphill and dipped all the way to the sea beyond.

As I sat I thought about what Aurobindo wrote about the scale
of consciousness and how it could be achieved through
perception and purpose. He believed that man was capable of a
higher mental state and this would happen steadily by evolution.

I saw large groups of people walking in. They looked like
tourists, they behaved like tourists—with that look in their eyes,
trying to consume everything around them, everything they had
paid for. They also talked a lot; this disturbed the silence I had just
experienced. I rose and went in search of Mr. Srinivasan, Arun's
uncle.

I walked into the bookshop. Most of the books were about Sri
Aurobindo and the Mother. There were also books on Indian
culture with essays written by Sri Aurobindo. I picked up one to
see what it was about. Just then an elderly man, who seemed to
belong to the ashram, walked up to me. The old man eyed me
suspiciously. He had watery eyes and a complexion the colour of
old potatoes. His head was huge and round, unlike the rest of him.
I looked at him and down; his feet were bare. I heard loud voices
behind me and I turned to look. 'These tourists,' he said with
unconcealed disgust. Visibly he didn't like people. I didn't like
him at all, at least at first.

I told him I wished to see Mr. Srinivasan and at once he broke
into a smile. 'I am he,' he said and led me to the end of the room.
He opened a door and, to my astonishment, closed it in my face,
only to reappear an instant later to let me in. He sat down in front
of the window. His hair, I saw now, was white. On the table and
all around him were heaps of books. I looked around me, slightly
mystified. Everything was in order, the furniture, the colour on
the walls, though it was too bluish for my liking. But the room was
curiously without character. This was surprising, as Mr.
Srinivasan appeared to me as someone with character, at least a
peculiar one. This fact didn't seem to have any influence on his
surroundings.

He stood up again to clear the books from the table and I saw
that he was surprisingly tall, well over six feet. I estimated he was
fifty-five years old. Broad-shouldered, slightly balding, with a

trim moustache, sharp features, piercing eyes. Deep voice. Calm, unless provoked. I remembered my grandfather.

As I tried to pick up the pile of books from the only available chair, he glanced at the book in my hand which I had forgotten to replace on the shelf, 'Ah, so you like to read about culture.' So saying, even before I had sat down, he marched me to a small courtyard outside his room. As I walked behind him I noticed the way he held one end of his white dhoti which was rimmed with gold thread. It was just like what my grandfather used to wear and he also walked in the same fashion.

In the courtyard that Mr. Srinivasan promptly led me to, there was a single tree. It was a temple flower tree, not with pink flowers but white. It was not very tall, its branches were fleshy and ugly, but one never noticed this. It was the whole thing that one saw, it was sculptural. While I admired the flowers, Mr. Srinivasan sat down on the brick platform below the tree and said dramatically, 'Culture is a way of life; it is a consciousness; it is the goal that we set for ourselves; this goal is formed by ideas and motives and they become the truth, the ideal. You see this in literature, art and

in other creative fields.' When I told him I was an architect, he said, 'You see it in architecture. Also in the people, their intellect, emotions and sensibilities.'

He said all this with eyes nearly closed, without looking at me. Then he turned to me. 'What kind of architecture do you like?' he asked abruptly. I told him I liked what was modern and innovative and also the traditional. He stared into space, concentrating.

'You like innovative things and also those that are traditional. That itself explains the difference between culture and tradition. Sri Aurobindo wrote about three spheres of knowledge: the sense-knowledge which was what normal people have; the ideative knowledge which was more rare and refined, like the mind of a thinker; and the self-effectuating knowledge which was dynamic and those minds that were illumined had it. There are many ways to perceive, to see and feel; people do it differently depending on the ability of their minds. You must agree that there are some architects who just perform, some think deeply and create and there are a few, very few who perceive far beyond what is obvious and perhaps are not even understood or appreciated by the others.'

He closed his eyes again. But this time, and to my relief, he quickly opened them, touched both his temples with his finger-tips delicately and continued, 'Tradition is like sense-knowledge, it is followed like a habit, repeated over the years and handed down through generations. But culture is different, it doesn't emerge but evolves. It is like self-effectuating knowledge; it is dynamic, it absorbs and changes. What is tradition today was culture before. Culture lives in the present, tradition is something that has passed.

'Truth is most important. Dharma is the basic truth. There are two aspects of dharma—satyam and ritam. Satyam is the essential truth of all that is static, all that is basic and fundamental, but without motion, without change. But the same truth in movement, in things active, is ritam. Don't treat this as philosophy and forget it. It is true of everything, even architecture, but you must try to understand clearly.' So saying he continued even more seriously, 'Satyam and ritam together acquire a form; and when they combine it becomes beautiful. Like this tree, it grows and changes,' he said pointing to it.

'When ritam (movement) acquires a form then form gets an inherent law, and it begins to conform. When a thing is beautiful and has an inner order—in this is contained the real idea. Each form has its real idea.' He suddenly asked, 'Do you have a purpose in life? That is artha. Artha is not just an economic concept, it is what a person is interested in. Artha must be sought with dharma, with truth.

'Do you desire to be something? To achieve something? To acquire something? As we grow we desire at different levels. Every desire is legitimate and has a role to play; desire is kama and it is equally important in life. It is important to desire to acquire things, to explore, to understand one's needs: emotional, intellectual and physical. All the while pursuing your artha, while satisfying your kama, you must have your mind on moksha. Moksha is not salvation from the world; it is the liberation from nature, from falsehood, ignorance and incapacity. One has to free oneself to perfect oneself.'

He also talked about energy: He said, 'Within all of us there is energy. When that is contained and not allowed to diffuse then it becomes tapas—a heat energy. It means a control of the mind, will power. When this energy is preserved then it turns into light—tejas. Here the brain becomes illuminated—this further becomes vidyut, an inner electricity which allows you to function in a masterly way with intellect and will. When vidyut is preserved it becomes ojas. This is the principal power of ether at the creative level. It is the power of creativity. Literature, art, music, architecture—all need creativity.'

Listening to him I learnt many things, some new, or helping consolidate what I had been thinking: I was sure now that beauty was not confined to physical aesthetics, it was the inner truth. There was continuity because of inherent values. They were not ethical values, which change from age to age; not physical or intellectual values which also change; but values of truth which were continuous.

'The chaos we experience is because there is no equality, harmony and unification. You must not forget this,' he said, as I left the ashram. All the way back to Saroja's house I thought of all that he had explained; I tried to link 'equality-harmony-unification' to the city and then the street. I could sense the connection but I failed to see it then. It was much later after my stay in Auroville that I understood the significance.

*

'Auroville was born out of a dream—a dream shared by Sri Aurobindo and the Mother,' Saroja said as we drove there. 'They wanted a place on earth which did not belong to anyone, or any community, or nation; a place where everyone could live together, under one authority. According to Aurobindo and the Mother, what was needed was truth and peace, and overcoming ignorance and incapacities. Belonging was not important. They wanted a place where people's relationships were based on brotherhood, where social, and economic position did not matter.'

It was dark when we reached Auroville. I couldn't see anything but the road in front of me lit by the headlights of the car. It was long and winding, with trees on either side. I did not remember trees in Auroville. The last time I was here, almost twenty years ago, it was barren; I remembered how hot and parched it was.

'You must meet Joss,' Saroja said when I asked her about the trees and forests, and the next morning she took me to meet him. He was bent over a couple of saplings that were growing around a mature tree and he appeared to be engaged in some sort of rapid mental calculation, while his fingers made a number of flurried gestures round the saplings. For all they conveyed, he might have been signalling to the plants to grow quickly. He stood up, taking all the time possible, and said after a moment of agitation: 'Oh yes. Yes, er—Saroja.' He coughed and smiled; he had a charming smile. 'Ah, your friend wants to see the forest,' he said. 'Certainly, with pleasure.' He started walking hurriedly ahead.

'When the first settlers moved out of the Auroville plateau, almost twenty-five years ago,' he said, 'this land was visibly dying. There were the occasional trees—palm, mango, banyan—but the earth was carved and gullied by years of monsoon rains. This was the result of two hundred years of deforestation, bad land management and overgrazing. Previously the land had been covered by scrub jungle with an eco-system unique to these Coramandel plains, containing a variety of species of trees.' He pointed to the variety of shrubs, plants and trees growing around us.

'The region's scrub jungles were cut down to build and develop Pondicherry and other nearby towns. The British accelerated the process of deforestation by allotting parcels of land to anyone who would cultivate them for a year. After a few years much of the land lay fallow, and with the onslaught of the rains, the process of erosion began. In the early fifties the last remaining forest plot on the Auroville plateau was cut down to make way for a cashew plantation.'

Delicately, with finger and thumb, he fished out some seeds from his pocket; his hands were white, small and manicured, despite the fact that he worked with plants and soil. 'These are seeds of very delicate species of trees; they grow here now.' He looked up lovingly at the tall trees below which we stood. 'Auroville has been restored to its greener past. Retrofitted,' he said softly more to himself. I liked the word—retrofitted.

However, through the rest of the day, as I saw more of Auroville, I began to question the word because there were parts that didn't seem to fit. Saroja introduced me to many foreigners who had lived here for several years: they were architects, planners and designers of various things. I talked to them about Auroville, and they told me about Indians and about their native country. They unanimously agreed about 'unity in diversity'; yet they were disparate, not unified and this was obvious. I couldn't get over the feeling that something was missing and I didn't really know what.

I had seen all kinds of houses and buildings here, various styles and various materials, innovative, simple. Some were rather good and original, but it was not enough. I tried to find out by talking to them, by trying to understand them as people. But they all said the same thing, again and again: 'We are experimenting with a way to live together.' It didn't seem like they were living together. There were just a few houses here and there forming communities with various names, but the texture of a community was missing. It was not like what I had seen in Ahmedabad in the pols, in Siddpur, even in the single street.

There was nothing between these designed houses, nothing connecting them: spaces, streets. I looked for them; if there was anything at all it was the large forest. There was so much diversity but no unity; not physically and not socially either. Despite the stylised houses, it looked primitive. There was no main street, a market, a bazaar. There was no chemist, laundry or a hairdresser. Even villages had them. There were hardly any people around. I wondered where they met, where they got together. There must be some place.

Auroville seemed to me like a laboratory, a large ground for experimentation. Each one here was a thinker, with a specific goal. But there were no ordinary people who normally make up a community. A bit petulant, I thought of what Joss had said about

Auroville being retrofitted, and decided he could have meant only
the forest.

*

It was rather late by the time we went to Pierre's house for dinner.
His house was a large assortment of spaces dominated by trees,
shrubs and creepers of all sorts. Strangely, it was called
Strawberry-pink Villa; I could see neither strawberries nor
anything strawberry-pinkish about it. The only such thing was the
front door that had an air of pink-faced determination. The
windows here and there when they appeared were painted green,
cracked and caked in places; they were unobtrusive most of the
time, hidden behind thick foliage of obstinate winding creepers.
The garden surrounded by a lantana hedge had flower beds
worked in a complicated fashion and marked with smooth white
stones. A white cobbled path led to the front door passing through
the overgrown flower beds. Next to the door was a bougainvillea.
The warm air was thick with the scent of over a dozen kinds of
flowers and full of the gentle, soothing murmur of insects. It was
an unusual garden all right: parts of it grew wild, other parts were
carefully worked on to the extent of being decorative; but most of
all I think it created an atmosphere—a feel of space. It was as
though the plants and trees were used to structure the space and
at the same time hide the house. This was the first time I had come
across an architect who preferred to conceal the labours of his
imagination and craft.

Beyond the pink door, to my utter surprise, was a large
meandering space: as it turned into a corner it became a particular
space, like a sitting room, or a dining space, a library or a kitchen.
There were large tree-like plants within the house so making the
difference between the inside and outside largely unfelt. Just as in
the garden, I was struck by the manner in which space was
modulated inside the house. In the kitchen, dinner was being
prepared accompanied by an absorbing discussion on
architecture and architectural appreciation.

151

'Who is interested in architecture, tell me?' Pierre was asking acrimoniously, waving the large knife he was using to cut a loaf of hard bread. 'They are interested in painting, music, in sculpture and literature but not architecture—the mother of all arts it is, imagine!' he exclaimed. 'The columnists devote their time and expertise reviewing a book by Koestler and nobody will boast his ignorance of not knowing a painting by Matisse or a poem by Eliot or works of Bach, but who's heard about architects, who talks about architecture? You can shut off a radio, close your eyes to books, exhibitions, walk out of theatres, but can you close your eyes to buildings, to the city? Such indifference!' he said and with equal vigour switched on the blender to reduce fresh skinned tomatoes to pulp. 'What we need is to build an architectural culture. All this avant garde architecture and ostentatious novelty is all very well, but modern architecture must revive tradition.'

Through all this demonstration, Hara paced up and down between the kitchen and the living space and Irinouchi sat perched high on a stool in the kitchen, almost invisible in his quietness. Sandra, Pierre's live-in girlfriend, cooked spaghetti and Saroja and I offered to cut and toss the salad.

'The trouble is with architects themselves. They busy themselves with the problems of contemporary architecture with profound passion but lack specific cultural knowledge to enter into a historical or critical revaluation,' Peirre said as he poured the tomato pulp into a dish and set it on the dining table. 'We must know traditional architecture; why do we look at the traditional and the modern differently? In an organic culture, I would believe that there can't be two ways to judge modern and traditional architecture. If we were to use the same criteria, the past would surely provide a base and history to the modern rootless person, to the absurdities of the functionalist and rationalist points of view. Don't you agree?' He looked at Hara Sensei for support.

Hara had sat down at the table, a low and long affair hardly two feet in width. Around it were cushions to sit on, very Japanese. Hara didn't reply to Pierre's question but stared at the painting on the wall across, it was a print of a cubist painting. He stared hard, screwing up his eyes. I thought he was trying to look minutely at some aspect of the painting, but realised he had been thinking when he at long last spoke

'What happened in painting?' he said pointing to the painting on the wall. (There were hardly any walls in Peirre's house; wherever there were, they were punctured with windows or large circular jalis.) 'Cubism started as a simplification of the pictorial formula which was what painters were occupied with before, and with cubism came abstract art. The problem with abstract art, as I see it—I may be mistaken—was that content became immaterial: it was eliminated: they went on about line, colour, form, volume, mass, space-time—what do all these words mean? To us, to the painters? They have become, although vague, conversational cliches. Everyone today talks of things being architectonic—that's another thing—what is architectonic? Simple representation is what they mean; everything visual without overstatement and decoration becomes what they call architectonic. Architecture has also become like that—an abstract art. We are all so vague when we appreciate buildings: we talk about truth, movement, force, outline, harmony, proportion, solids-voids, symmetry, rhythm, mass, volume, character, personality—what does all this mean, if it does not make the essence of architecture clear?

'One must find for oneself the essence of architecture,' Hara Sensei said, rubbing his chin slowly. And as though on cue Pierre remarked with enthusiasm: 'I have now begun to think in terms of space; that is the essence. I try to find meaning in words like rhythm, scale, mass, balance through defining space. Unless we are able to see space and understand it, we will continue to look at architecture as we do sculpture and painting.'

Hara looked up, admiration in his eyes, and then at me, perhaps because he had been trying to explain to me the day before about experiencing space.

'How do you define space?' I asked Pierre, since it still seemed ambiguous to me. 'How would you define space in a city, a street?'

'The facade on the street, the walls of a house, however beautiful they may be, they are only the container; the content is

the internal space,' he replied. 'Too often, even in the past, the container has been the object of more thought than the content. It was much later that content became the focus. It was the Renaissance painters who discovered the perspective dimension in painting—they painted the height, width and depth of objects. This idea of the third dimension helped in perceiving architecture—its interiors. Then the cubist revolution introduced the fourth dimension.'

By now we were all sitting at the table with our plates full of spaghetti and Sandra passed the cheese and the grater. As Pierre grated an enormous quantity of Italian cheese over his tomato sauce and spaghetti, he said, leaning towards me, 'Look at this bowl on the table, it looks different from here and from where you are sitting. If you were to walk around the table, it would keep changing, from each point there would be a new perspective. The bowl is not entirely complete in its third dimension, by a single perspective representation; there is essentially a fourth dimension. The "time"dimension—depending on where you are standing and when—what you see becomes different. This explains the plural aspects of an object, its total reality. In every physical structure there is not only an external form but also an internal organisation. The cubist painters saw it this way and that is why they painted not only the external form of the box, but also the box in plan, the box exploded, smashed—this is very important to architecture: the idea of the fourth dimension, the element of time is indispensable.'

He sipped from his glass of white wine. 'This element of time is different in architecture, unlike in painting and sculpture. When you appreciate the facade of architecture, it is like a painting—when you move around it, it is like sculpture, but when you move within its space, the element of time is very different because you are moving in it. That is why space is most important in architecture.

'What is beautiful architecture? It would be one in which the space is interesting, that is what attracts us, not just the facades and form. Look at this house, I put in only spaces,' he said beaming. 'Unfortunately architecture has been described historically only through its decoration and facades and number of columns but this tells us little about its spatial quality—the sense of space is the protagonist of architecture but not the only one. With form and decoration, it combines into a total experience.'

After dinner we sat in the garden. I talked to Pierre about streets. He seemed to be very excited about the subject and plunged into a long narrative of the streets of Europe, then looking at my face which must have seemed rather vacant yet politely patient, he said in a retrieving manner, 'Ah but you know about all that.' I nodded and admitted to him that it wasn't really history of architecture or that of streets that I was thinking about but their form and space. He smiled and said softly so I could just hear him over the cries of the cicadas in the shrubs around us: 'A house or a city, it is the same thing. In both, space is the most important. The street is the main space in the city; and the architecture of this space, its form and character defines a city. A building in a street provides two different spaces: one within it and the other outside it. You can't only look at one of them, you must examine both, only then will you understand the architecture of the street and the city.'

He continued: 'After a century of predominantly decorative, sculptural and non-spatial architecture, the modern movement banished decoration; it expressed volume and space. European functionalism emphasised volumetric values, the organic movement was more concerned with space. But decoration is not an adjective to architecture, it should substantiate it.'

Sandra brought us coffee in black clay mugs. The mugs were beautiful: rough textured and the colour of slate, very subtle. There was an artistic sensitivity in Auroville, in its people. Sandra, who was Dutch, sat down beside me. She told me of her reaction to Auroville. 'When I came here I was so charmed. Coming from Amsterdam, a totally structured situation, the city, the people, the trains, everything, this breath of freedom and creativity was refreshing. So I can understand why people get so excited when they first see this place, there is so much personal expression here. That is very stimulating. Or rather, not personal, that would have made it intimate in a way. No, it is not a personal expression, it is more individualised.

'You know, the Mother's dream for Auroville was not like this, like it is now; it was like a "galaxy". She had wanted an unusual design for the city of Auroville; something that was a promise of new forms, a new community architecture. It started that way, but the first monumental stage of Auroville architecture came to an end after the initial enthusiasm, and then all the exuberance and creativity was directed away from the community to the individual. I understood this gradually. I tried to develop some sort of an overview about this place, its people. Frankly, I realise there really is no overview. My expectations had to be accommodated in a different kind of reality.'

There was sadness in the way she said this; I understood her feeling. I had felt it too—something that was nebulous about the

place, as though it were incomplete. There was no clarity: there were numerous parts that didn't add up to a whole. Sandra smiled at me when I shared my views with her and in a defensive manner, she said: 'Actually Auroville reflects the fact that Auroville belongs to nobody. That it is free from personal demands, and that people are able to live in houses designed for nobody in particular.'

It felt that way—a feeling of not belonging, of not being at home, that one was in transit. Maybe the idea of transition was at the root of Sri Aurobindo's and the Mother's philosophy. Here people had a tendency to cling to their personal needs, personal lives. I had actually noticed a certain 'distance' that people maintained. When they were together their behaviour was cultivated, not spontaneous, but carefully structured. Looking back on this conversation with Sandra now, I can see the difference between a place that belonged to nobody and one that was for everybody.

*

The next morning Sandra managed to procure a bicycle for me and we cycled our way to Matrimandir, the central place for meditation. It was a long time since I had been on a bicycle, which made it somewhat exciting. The road was only a muddy track and I slipped, falling headlong into the slush. It must have been in a frantic attempt on my part to get over the embarrassing situation that I asked her how she managed for money. She answered seriously as she helped me pick up the cycle, 'I came here eleven years ago,' she said. 'In those days the Aurovillians were supported by a central fund. But soon the money was not enough. So some of the members left for a short period so that they could earn money and bring it back to Auroville. But that was not enough. Then we were asked to fend for ourselves. I left then because I couldn't manage. I wrote to my parents to send me money for the ticket. I went back home and worked there for a while. But eventually I returned. Now I do some work here and get paid for it. They don't pay much. One can earn so much more outside.'

We reached a wide, open space with beautiful lawns and clusters of boulders. In the centre was a huge sphere; this was the Matrimandir. All around it was space, and the mandir looked like an architectural monument: the space had yet to become a place. It required people, activity, ritual to make it one. I understood then that space by itself, as Pierre had assumed, was not the essence of architecture. It was something more than that. We climbed the helical ramp leading to the meditation hall.

The hall was white. Gleaming white. Pure white. It was covered with a circular dome on top of which was a tiny skylight. The sun's rays streamed down through this and hit a large crystal ball in the centre. Exactly, precisely, the centre. There were a number of rounded columns forming a circle in the middle of the circular room. They reached nowhere; they were free-standing, arrested in space. And the space itself was awesome. All that Pierre had explained the night before came back to me. Here form and space were both powerful. It was without decoration, without a sense of minuteness, larger than life. Yet everything was so precise. Even the silence. It was rather frightening. More frightening than peaceful, disturbing.

We came out and sat under the beautiful banyan tree, more beautiful than the building in front of me. Sandra told me the banyan tree was the geographical centre of Auroville. But a centre was made of many other things: people, activity, living; it was more than a physical centre. Perhaps it was wrong on my part to look for a city in Auroville; it wasn't there. Neither was there any street or centre. 'Something may be beautiful in itself, but its meaning comes from its context—from being the right thing in the right place at the right time,' Mr. Srinivasan had told me. In Auroville, context was absent.

Auroville was an experiment in self-sufficiency. But self-sufficiency beyond a point could be dangerous, it led to isolation. I had experienced it in Auroville. Mr. Srinivasan had talked about truth, about satyam, the truth of the object, and ritam, the truth of motion. In Auroville, I found satyam, objects, but the ritam was missing: there were no patterns: no movement of objects, activity. There was no feeling of a community, no intense participation. I tried to understand the element of beauty in Auroville; it had some beautiful architecture, beautiful forests; they were all like beautiful objects. There had to be some pattern that gave it an identity, continuity: the patterns of events, activity, people—they were translated into the patterns of space, and when this happened, space became a place, the place became beautiful.

Mr. Srinivasan had also talked about equality, harmony and unification. I wondered whether this was possible in such diverse circumstances as existed in Auroville. It was made of disjointed parts, there was no energy to form a whole. There was only satyam, no ritam, and without both there was no dharma—the idea of truth, the whole.

*

The sun suddenly disappeared, and huge rainclouds cast a shadow on the ground around the banyan tree. The coming of the storm was evident in all the events that preceded it: the big raindrops that stippled the dust, the water that collected here and there in puddles. I thought of peace and silence. Peace was full of serenity. Silence was an absence of sound. Then I heard the thunder as the rain came down in howling darkness. Defenceless against the fury of the wind, the tall trees rustled like heavily starched silk. As I walked away, I carried with me the impression of an embryonic village, of a community still trying to make a beginning.

Chapter 11

GOA: THERE ARE DIFFERENT KINDS OF EMPTINESS. A place may be empty because of a lack of symbiotic exchange, like it was in Auroville. A street is empty without spatial coordinates, a framework for determining distances, vertical accent, focus, landmarks, all of which make a place. Space is empty when the objects in it have no influence on it and in which people feel isolated: nothing relates to them, they do not respond to anything. This lack of binding destroys people's sense of identity and belonging.

*

I returned to Mumbai alone. Hara Sensei and Irinouchi stayed back in Auroville. I was in time for the cartoonist Mario Miranda's exhibition of cities. He drew archetypal images of people. Almost always his backdrops were buildings and houses; he captured through his sketches the gestures of people and flavours of

161

architecture. 'There must be things in a city which are readily identifiable by people. People must identify with the place,' Mario said to me.

We met again at his flat facing the sea. He had invited me for tea, which he served from a thermos. 'I hope the tea is all right,' he said. 'My maid prepared it in the morning.' It was cold. I was curious to talk to Mario because he had seen in the cities that he had sketched precisely what I was attempting to see: our intent

was similar. Mario talked about New York, Paris, Jerusalem; eventually he began to talk about Goa to which he belongs. His dog licked my feet and his two turtles circled around where we sat in the balcony; below the surf gently broke on the shore.

'I come from Loutolim. It is to the west of the Zuari river. It really is a village, in fact all of Goa is villages; except for a few towns. My family were like the English squires for generations. I lived there as a child. I remember the priests in cassocks and berets, elderly spinsters who liked to gossip, drunkards at the local taverna, and farmers. I liked sketching all this: the village, the street, the church—there was always a church in the village although there are more Hindus in Goa than Christians. I liked to sketch people. There was also a barber shop where men sat and gossiped, and a taverna where you could hear a lot of tall tales told over large quantities of feni. I have heard so many stories as a small boy. Goa is beautiful in the rain. I always go there in the rain.'

*

When it rained I went to Goa. I drove from Dabolim airport to Loutolim. It was a long, pleasant drive through a wet and very green landscape. Here and there were small houses, their boundary walls of undressed laterite stone, red, crumbly and porous. And everywhere the palm trees, tall and exuberant.

We stopped at a village for a cold drink, in a busy market place. Women shouted at passersby, holding up their catch—fish, crab or mussel. There were other women selling cane baskets, pineapples, bananas, bread, earthen pots; and pigs, goats, chickens, dogs ran all over the place.

'First time to Goa, madam?' the driver of the cab asked me.

'Yes,' I replied and asked his name.

'Joey, madam, Joey D'Souza. I live in Santacruz; its a village, but becoming like a town now, lots of builders are building there,' he said, waving to another cab driver who passed us.

We passed a village and then another. Goa was like this: groups of houses linked together by a road. According to a legend, Parsuram, an avtar of Lord Vishnu, fought many wars and wanted a place to rest. He shot an arrow from the Sayadri hills into the sea. The arrow fell at Banahalli, now called Banaulim. That was the beginning of Goa.

Goa had been for centuries a collection of marshy and possibly unimportant islands, part of various Hindu kingdoms, then of Muslim fiefdoms on the mainland. These rulers did not recognise Goa's potential as a harbour. The Portuguese who captured it from the Muslims in 1510 did. They made it the greatest of Asiatic ports and imported Christ and the Inquisition. The Portuguese were thrown out in 1961.

'There is a famous church dedicated to Our Lady of the Mount and it is built on the highest hills,' Joey said. 'It is full of dust and dead insects now,' he said sadly. 'Then there is the cathedral called Bom Jesus in the great square of Velha Goa. You want to see? In it is the casket with the body of St. Francis Xavier. He was a great saint. Dona Isabel de Carom, a Portuguese woman, wanted to posses a relic of the saint, and she bit off his big toe. They say that the blood flowed and the woman ran away scared with the toe in her mouth.'

*

Mario's house was a large villa with its own chapel. 'We have documents from 1700,' Mario claimed as we sat in the veranda and watched the evening change to night. Mario was enjoying his feni. He had had several; I was still gingerly sipping my first diluted with generous quantities of lemonade. 'It was built by a family called Gomes, then the Mirandas came,' Mario said. 'It has been modified through the years. Most of the buildings were whitewashed. Colour was added here and there. Teak was used, as it was termite resistant, otherwise there is a lot of termite problem. Even the local matti wood is good. We put tobacco leaves in trunks and book cases to keep out the termites.

'When I took over the house I reduced the size,' he said. 'The bathrooms were just pits in those days and below them were a whole family of pigs.'

'Pigs!' I said, and he laughed. 'Don't be so shocked—they were like scavengers, they ate all the muck, but it frightened many foreigners who came to stay with us. There was an American lady who would drive all the way to Margao to use a toilet. The old bathrooms were large, I broke them down. They were built in a row and had six sections with a corridor connecting them. The men would sit with their cigars, papers and even have a conversation with the neighbours. Women had separate toilets. I changed many things in the house. The old house had too many big halls. You see in those days there was no corruption as such and people didn't pay money. They only had big banquets for officials who needed to be pampered for some service in return. Also these old houses were built for large families and many servants. It is difficult to maintain them without servants.'

He went on: 'Before the Portuguese came this was a big Hindu city—Lotle, it was called. There was this bandit Kustabha. He was like Robin Hood, he robbed the rich and helped the poor. So all the houses had secret chambers and dungeons and there were bars on the doors. My great-grandfather, he was an administrator and

his soldiers tried to kill Kustabha, but they killed the wrong person and the head was sent to the viceroy. The viceroy sent a letter sacking my great-grandfather. In the meanwhile Kustabha's mistress betrayed him and he was killed by my great-grandfather's soldiers. They treat him like a hero.' He smiled.

'I am basically from the Sardesai family,' he confessed. 'I was always attracted to the Hindu temple—Shantadurga temple, that is our family temple. Have you seen it? You must go and see it, it is very different from other Hindu temples outside Goa. We still have the tradition of giving oil and rice to the temple. This temple has helped me—I have faith in it.' He told me about Frank Simoes and his experience of housebuilding. 'Frank Simoes came back after living and working in Bombay for many years. He and his wife Gita built a house here. After a lot of exploring he got land in the village of Candolim. Then after finding an architect they tried many contractors but they were not willing to build the house. One of them agreed but later gave up with a crazy explanation that Shantadurga would not permit him to build the house because a spirit lived in his cashew trees and she had to be appeased by shedding the blood of a cock on the land. No one will build even a shed without performing a special puja to the goddess. The brass idol of the goddess has ten leaves on either side. The pandit performs the puja, then soaks a bunch of tulsi leaves in a vessel of holy water and places one green leaf on each brass one. When a question is asked of the goddess, if she responds, a leaf falls to the ground. If the leaf falls from the left, the answer is yes, if from the right, no. So each of the contractors went and did this puja before they considered building Frank's house. After that Gita went and did the puja and three leaves fell from the left. Finally the pandit did a havan for an hour with offerings of fruits, holy oil and ribbons, kumkum, mirror, agarbatti and all these were placed under the cashew tree where the spirit resided in order to appease her.

'Another puja had to be done when the actual construction started.' Mario was enjoying the story. 'When the foundation was dug, the pandit performed an elaborate puja on the site and there was a parish priest who blessed the stones. A cross was carved on one stone and a small gold cross was laid in it. A swastika was inscribed on the other and it was inlaid with the five precious stones of the zodiac: pearl, coral, sapphire, emerald and ruby. Then Frank had to climb down into the pit and sprinkle holy water on the bricks and break a coconut. Poor Frank.'

The next morning Joey took me to the Mangeshi temple. It was the most unusual temple I had seen. We went up a ramp. Beside it was a large water tank with a tulsi-dan in the middle. Near the temple was a dipmal—a lamp pillar—in white, seven storeys tall with arched openings and bands at the base of each storey which, I was told, was a feature in all Goan temples. There were no carved pillars or vimanas in the temple; its front portion had a domed roof painted white and its walls were painted ochre. The central hall had a sloping roof and over the garbhagriha was another, higher dome. There were smaller domes on the sides. I could have never imagined a dome over the garbhagriha. It was a fusion of Hindu, Christian and Muslim forms. The interior also was very different: it had large chandeliers and lamps hanging from the ceiling and the walls were painted in a bright blue enamel paint. Large round columns supported the arches. The ceilings had plaster of paris mouldings, some of them painted or gilded with gold. The Shantadurga temple we went to next was not very different.

The churches were huge, cavernous, monumental. They were not architecturally brilliant, more like fortresses, though the interiors were profusely decorated. The light came in through the high windows in pale shafts, revealing on all side baroque decorations. The enormous walls were covered with elaborately moulded and recessed plaster panels and studded with wooden and metal frescoes. The altars were carved out of wood and layered with gold leaf. It was the woodcarver's art known as the Indo-Portuguese, I was told, and the Goan carpenters were known for their expertise in carving wood for altars, screens, chairs and other furniture.

*

After my tour of the churches I went to meet Chico Fernandes. Chico is the proprietor of the Mayfair hotel in Panjim and a genial sort of person.

Mario had asked me to meet Chico who could tell me more about old Goan houses. The next morning, reinforced with a list, and a guide-cum-photographer in Chico, I set out in search of old Goan homes. The first on the list was that of the chief minister, Dr. Wilfred D'Souza, in Saligao. 'Dr. D'Souza is a surgeon and his wife, Grace is English; he met her in England where he went to study. Very nice woman,' Chico informed me. We left Panjim and drove through what seemed like pleasant countryside: winding roads, trees, their leaves softened by the rain, and houses nestling in folds of the landscape. When we reached the house, Chico stopped at the rear gate. 'Let's go through the kitchen,' he said. 'Everyone goes through it. The front is only for strangers but all those who know us enter through the rear of the house.'

The kitchen opened into a veranda of sorts In fact it was part of the driveway. There was a large dog in it and in the garden was another pet, a shaggy donkey which I later learnt had been presented to the surgeon but loved his wife Grace. We walked through the kitchen into the dining room which was equipped with an old dining table and equally old chairs. On one side was a modern staircase with its wooden treads supported on a central joist. The living room when we walked into it was full of old furniture. Dr. D'Souza sat in one of the carved sofas talking to a guest. Grace came in with a tray laden with cups of coffee which she gave to each one of us.

'It is a very old house,' she said.

I asked her about the staircase in the dining room. 'That is new. When I removed the old staircase, people said, why are you removing it. You have ruined it. But it was very narrow and inconvenient. Like there was a mud floor, so we put in tiles. Every year we made changes. It is not so easy to live in these old houses, but we tried not to change much. There was no plumbing, the bathrooms were outside. We couldn't use it that way. So we built two bathrooms near the bedrooms. There was no electricity, no lights, no fans, no phones, so we put those in.'

I asked her about the old furniture. 'It's all very old—a hundred and twenty years,' she said. 'If you go to old Goan houses you will find the same motifs on the chairs. It is as though they were mass produced.'

'Who did that large white and blue mansion belong to?' I asked Chico as we drove past it a few minutes after we left the chief minister's house. It was a beautiful mansion with wrought-iron brackets and railings, and shell window panes. The walls were painted white and there were bands of turquoise blue around the doors and windows. There was a balcony in the front.

'That belonged to the landlord of this village. He owned a lot of land around this area. He went abroad,' Chico explained, and added, 'Did you see those glass windows? They are from Macau. Only the rich could import them. The others used nacre, mother of pearl shells which were inserted into wooden battens. There were many beautiful mansions even before the Portuguese came to Goa. People think they were all influenced by the Portuguese. Not so. These old mansions were all constructed around a central courtyard and the main building material was laterite stone. The

roofs were tiled. In fact these mansions had some influence on the houses the Portuguese built for themselves and which eventually became the popular Goan style. The converted Goans adapted some of the Portuguese features which were largely Italianate in form and style. The original Hindu courtyard became the Iberian patio. The Christian Goan mansions were hidden behind wide verandas. They were not so rigid as the Hindu Goans and their houses did not have orthodox divisions—their bedrooms were anywhere and they opened directly into the dining or living room. The exterior of the house had balustrades and wrought-iron work of European origin though much of the interior was oriental.'

Chico explained about the Goan master builders who had, even before the Portuguese came, learned to build with baked clay roof tiles and laterite stone, termite resistant wood like matti, oyster and other seashells for window panes. They had perfected the curing technique for stone and wood. They exposed stone for one or two monsoons and wood was seasoned in salt water. They used mud from termite and anthills to bind the laterite stones because it was fine. They used vegetable dyes for colour, kendu leaves for buffing wood and lacquering techniques—a blend of hot and cold processes that the painters used.

'When the Portuguese came,' Chico added, 'there was a development of new house types. For example,' he said, 'they were concerned about the heavy rainfall and so they introduced elaborate cornices. However, the heavy tropical rainfall always left an indelible imprint of slimy green moss on the walls, particularly on the base of houses and other buildings. So the municipalities and the local bodies enforced a strict rule which was imposed in the cities of Goa: the owners had to whitewash their homes after the easterly monsoons were over. In fact the big churches still follow this rule.'

*

After lunch in one of the shacks along the beach, Chico took me to Fontainhas which he decided I must see. 'Fontainhas was the Latin Quarter of Goa and it was so called because of the fountain in the residential district,' Chico said as we walked through the narrow winding lanes. 'It supplied water to Cidade de Goa, as Panjim was known. Water spouted from a lovely female bust.' Fontainhas was unlike the Goan villages. It was dense and very urban: the huddled buildings, winding streets and small squares, and the warm colours on the walls reminded me of the pols of Ahmedabad. It had life. Abounding life. Because of the undulating land there were different kinds of streets; there were ramps and stairways and there were intimate links between buildings and spaces. As we walked we could look into people's homes through the windows. Each house stood out, yet blended with the total sequence. The entrance to the houses was emphasised, and was coloured in earth pigments, each different and vibrant with a band of white around the doors and windows. The external wall was broken by pilasters, cornices, mouldings and the intervening spaces were coloured. Windows, balconies, railings, brackets were all ornate.

'There is not much carving like in traditional Hindu houses,' Chico said. 'The interior is plain and simple, only painted.' When I asked Chico the reason for this he said, 'The laterite stone is soft

171

and porous and is best painted. Before the Portuguese came all the houses were of exposed laterite; it was the Portuguese who taught the Goans to apply stucco to their houses.

'They used to cure and prime the plaster in pits filled with water mixed with jaggery and jute waste for better grip and smoothness. The plaster is washable with soap water.' I asked him about the shell windows and he explained: 'These shells were used as they kept away the heat and the glare of the sun.' I looked at the flooring of one of the houses whose doors were open; it was patterned and colourful. 'They are original Italian tiles,' Chico told me. 'They were laid on plaster made of calcinated local seashells. You saw the railings on the steps?' he asked me. I nodded my head. He said, 'The Portuguese introduced all that and the Goans learnt to make a ferrous base, a kind of distemper which acted as an anti-rust coat.'

*

The next day Chico drove me to Pernem, which was a long way away, to meet Devendra Deshprabhu. He lived in a large house which Chico said was a Goan Hindu house set in a large garden of eight acres. We entered the house through a pair of old wooden doors into a parlour all in blue: blue upholstery and large oval shaped windows stained blue. It contained the most exquisite reclining chairs, old Portuguese, carved in wood and laced with matted cane. This room opened into a corridor which had another set of carved furniture in wood and cane. Outside it was a large courtyard with a tall chameli tree, its flowers spreading their fragrance through out the house. Devendra took us into the living room which was a storehouse of old furniture—all beautifully sculpted into elephant heads and tusks, one of which tore my saree as I attempted to sit down.

Devendra was a short and thin man, one of two brothers who had returned from Bombay to live in Goa. 'My family came here maybe at the end of 1500,' he said. 'We had some land, we were small landlords in the old days. This house was built at the end of 1600. It was built like a small castle with four towers at the corners. Every generation then went on adding to it. Initially they only added what was necessary, then when the family became powerful and rich they tended to become extravagant. We come from a kingdom nearby, from Samant Kudal, and then when there was some problem we took shelter here. We were here when the

173

Portuguese came. My ancestors bought land from them. My great-grandfather was very powerful; he was given the title of Viscount.'

He took us around the house. 'This house is very large; it has eleven courtyards with rooms around it,' he said. 'I think as the family made additions, they kept connecting the rooms with corridors and courts. In that sense it is badly planned, there is wastage of space. There are a hundred and twenty rooms, and only three families live here. Every wall is a load bearing wall, no reinforced concrete is used. The walls are made of laterite stone and the mortar is of fine mud and jaggery to which the juice of apta leaves was added. This makes it termite-resistant. All the rooms have motifs on the walls.' He pointed to the brown floral motifs above the door and along the wall. 'This was a kind of fresco work. This fresco work in Portuguese was called cao; it was used in all the Hindu temples. Of course here we have painted over it. Originally it was not brown in colour, more terracotta.'

Chico asked him whether he could take one of the chairs out in the veranda to photograph since it was very dark inside.

The road from Pernem to Siulim seemed unending. We even had to cross the river, swollen with the rains, to cut the journey short. On the way we passed fields with lush green paddy and coconut groves oscillating in the breeze. We passed clusters of houses and amidst them temples which had popular Hindi songs blaring from them. '*Tu cheez badi hai mast mast*' was one scintillating song that played at a small roadside temple before we turned into a lane which took us to Remo Fernandes's house.

'Did you know he was an architect?' Chico whispered to me as we walked to the house. 'He is now a popular rock singer.' I was admiring the columns in the front veranda: they rose out of a lotus-like base. The house was typically Goan with large glass doors with pointed arches fixed with glass. The living room had modern cane furniture besides old Goan furniture. 'We have to modernise these old houses, we can't live in a museum,' Remo said almost apologetically and immediately even before he was asked. Remo looked Goan, suntanned and lean with a musical drawl in his voice. His long hair was secured into a pony tail. His wife was French and largely instrumental in renovating the house, making it more livable.

'It belonged to my grandmother,' Remo said about the house. 'At that time no one wanted to live in it, so it was sold to a German chap. About that time I came back from Europe and asked my parents not to sell but they had taken an advance so they sold it to him. Two and half years ago we bought it from him at a price three times higher. In those days many people sold their houses; it is only now that the trend has changed. This place is like a village; the builders have not yet come into Sivolium. There are some people here who have returned from the Gulf and they have built what they think are modern houses. Atrocious houses.'

He showed us around the house. The dining room had been changed into a family room. 'Earlier they cooked on a wood fire so the dining room had to be away from the kitchen,' Remo explained. The dining room now was adjacent to the modernised kitchen; it opened directly on the back garden. There was a tall chikoo tree in it. 'It's so quiet here,' Remo said. 'I am happy I came back.

As we drove away the evening was ablaze with a rich, multitudinous range of colours. *'Yeh kali kali aankhen'*, another popular Hindi song, thundered from the temple as we passed it; it grew fainter, then there was a cacophony of chirping and buzzing of insects and birds in the fields. As we passed a few houses, people standing outside them smiled, the children waved out. I had noticed that in Goa, people smiled a lot; friendly trustful smiles. Smiles that were unwary of the future.

I had dinner by myself that night. In Goa I had seen what was missing in Auroville—the kinds of spaces that the environmental psychologists call territory and orbit. The villages in Goa were loosely connected but within, the villages had strong ties; they formed territories and orbits. Territory is a space which a person—or a group—identifies as his own; this forms distinct locales. The orbit is wider and contains two or more territories and all the spaces in between. The territory is intimate, the orbit, formal and the combination of the two gives texture to streets.

As I drove to the airport the next morning, Joey waved to several drivers. 'We all know each other, madam,' he said as he stopped to read an address scribbled on a piece of paper which the driver of another car showed him. He gave him directions to reach the place and added, 'We live in different villages—Calangute, Margao, Colva, Santacruz, Ponda, but we all know each other.'

Chapter 12

KOLHAPUR: NAINA HAD BEEN MARRIED TO ASHOK FOR OVER a year. I knew her from the time she was teaching at Sir J.J. College; she had shifted to Kolhapur when her husband had started an architectural practice in that city. 'There is no work in Bombay,' she had said to my surprise. 'And anyway my parents are there and I lived there when I was a small girl.' She and her husband now lived with his parents in an old wada. She wrote to me from time to time asking me to visit her, and ever since Saroja had told me, when I met her in Pondicherry, about Kolhapur, I had wanted to. I eventually went a few days before the Ganpati festival.

Naina was at the station: she was tall, slim and fair. She had cut her hair short. 'My hair falls so much. Must be the water of Kolhapur,' she said as she took me to the wada. It was dilapidated; the entrance wall was being rebuilt and without the hewn-stone-and-brick wall which gives the wadas the appearance of small forts, the wada looked vulnerable.

As we entered the wada we walked into a number of schoolchildren in blue uniforms in the courtyard. 'Part of the wada is a school now,' Naina explained. 'Before we shifted here Ashok's parents were alone and there is plenty of space.' We climbed up the stone steps to a veranda which had a table and few chairs. Naina said, 'Ashok's father is a retired lawyer. He used to sit here and work and meet his clients.' I looked around. On the first floor, there were colourful clothes and towels hung out to dry on the decaying wooden balustrade and behind it, a succession of rooms. Large padlocks hung on the doors of each room.

'Those rooms are rented,' Naina said. 'They have been given out to college boys; it's like a hostel. The men of the family used to live in those rooms but they have all moved out now. Even we are thinking of shifting into a flat, but Babuji wants to stay here.'

She took me to the majghar to wash up after the journey. We went through a corridor into a rear court. The majghar was dilapidated, desolate except for the parijat tree in the centre which was in full bloom heedless of the decay around it. 'This is where the women did all their chores. The kitchen is here,' Naina said pointing to a room. 'This is where all the family functions took place.' On the first floor was a large hall which was now used as a living room. There were two bedrooms on either side. Both were painted a pista green. The paint had peeled, the wood had rotted, the broken furniture had been crudely fixed, the flooring had cracked. It was a collision with a past now spectral. Later, as we sat in the front veranda drinking sugary tea and eating batata wada and chivda, Ashok's father told us about Kolhapur. 'When Shivaji died, there was no one to take charge of things. For three decades things were in limbo. Finally the elder son settled for the northern territory and the capital Satara. The younger son opted for the southern territories with Panhala as the capital. But later he shifted his capital to Kolhapur. When Shahu Chhatrapati came to the throne, Kolhapur became a known city with public buildings and a palace. The palace is a strange combination of Hindu, Muslim and European styles. Parts of it look like Rajasthani architecture. It was built by the architect Charles Mant. He liked local architecture. You must also see Pangu's wada. He is my friend. Tell him I sent you,' he said suddenly, breaking away from history and Shivaji.

We left in a rickshaw. Naina asked the rickshawallah to take us to Kumbhar wada. 'I want to buy a Ganpati,' she said. 'The Ganesh festival is only a week away and I have to make a lot of arrangements. All the relatives come to our wada. I hope you don't mind. You will enjoy seeing how these idols are made,' she said. The Kumbhar wada had a single narrow street full of mud as it had rained through the night. The houses had narrow fronts, just about six feet wide. Their doors were open and I looked into them; they were deep like long corridors and most of them had a small court at the end which acted as a light well.

Naina walked into several houses and while she inspected the idols and held long arguments over the sanctity and usefulness of the clay idols compared to the mass-produced plaster of paris or even cement versions, I wandered through the houses and talked to their occupants. It was dark inside and the men and women were busy making the idols. We walked very carefully, avoiding the clay and the idols on the floor in various stages of completion. The houses were full of idols, including the upper rooms and the loft.

In the houses that I saw, invariably the first two rooms were

used for making the idols. Behind these rooms was a small kitchen and space to eat. There was a small open court with a washing area on one side. Then there was another room which in most cases was also full of idols and in some houses this room opened into another court. So from the street you could see a long shaded corridor of rooms with two wells of light. All the houses were tucked close together; there were no windows, only the two doors on either end and the two courts. From the street, as it was narrow, the houses looked single-storeyed but they all had more than one, sometimes two or three floors. Since the upper floors were set back and not visible from the street, it was difficult to judge their height. A staircase behind the kitchen climbed to the first floor. From the landing above the kitchen you could see the tiled roof of the house-front. Another stairway climbed to the next floor which occupied a space half that of the room below it. Over this was another pitched roof.

Naina took me to meet Tukaram Wadangekar. 'He is a very good artist. He has done GD,' she said which meant that he had completed the Government Diploma in Arts. He was the seniormost potter, and quite old. He was seated in front of a gigantic Ganpati which he was painting. He proudly showed us drawings of several Ganpatis he had shaped. Over tea he told us more about the craft and the potters. 'We now have a cooperative society,' he said. 'The society buys the clay for us; it mixes it with jute fibre for reinforcement and then we buy it from the society. It is subsidised.'

After buying a small Ganpati we left the Kumbhar wada. On the way Naina asked the rickshawallah to stop and pointed to a shop selling milk. 'Would you like some flavoured milk?' she asked. Kolhapur is known for its milk products and ice-cream.

'This is the Dudh Tekdi,' she went on. 'In this street cows and buffaloes were brought to be milked in the morning and evening. The cows would be standing in groups here and there down the street and people would wait with pots and pails. This was the main activity in this street. I remember coming here as a little girl; it used to smell of cows, dung, dust and fresh milk. Now you'll find only three or four cows. People have got used to packaged milk.'

We passed through a street full of jewellery shops, some with

the traditional low counters and mattresses to sit on. 'This area is called Gujeri. Chipde here sells old Kolhapur jewellery. It's very good,' Naina said and took me inside the shop to meet its owner. He was an old man wearing thick-lensed spectacles. He was carefully scrutinising an old piece of jewellery when we entered. He held it out for me to see. It was a beautiful piece. 'You won't find such intricate workmanship now,' he said in a gruff voice. 'People today, they don't understand anything about craftsmanship; they want cheap imitations of the real thing. We sell them too. What to do.'

Beyond this street was Pangu's wada. It had high walls and three stone steps led to a doorway made of wooden shutters and metal strips. Pangu himself opened the door when we knocked. He was a lean old man dressed in white pyjamas and a bush shirt. He invited us in and gladly showed us around. He had also rented out the rooms around the front courtyard. The veranda had been enclosed with grilles and converted into a living room. On one side was a television set that contrasted with the older ambience of wooden pillars and roof beams. There was a temple at one end of the veranda and a large wooden swing at the other. Pangu led us to the back. He pointed to a grey modern structure and said, 'I was forced to sell the rear portion of the house. They have built this modern house.' Seeing the disappointment on my face he said, 'Why don't you go to the Gurumaharaj wada. That's a good wada.' He gave Naina directions.

The Gurumaharaj wada, despite the reconstruction of a large

part of it, captured the spirit of a traditional wada. It had a front chowk with two tiers of verandas facing it. There were decorative patterns on the beams and paintings of religious themes on the walls. There were recessed altars outlined in red and gold. The wood on the ceiling was painted a bright blue and the floor was in warm brown stone. But the special feature was a secret grain store built into the pillar near the entrance with a shutter at the bottom. From there we went to the Sankracharya wada, the only wada that has survived, as we were told.

The Sankracharya wada, a very old two-storyed structure, was built around large chowks. There was a tulsi-dan constructed in the centre of the entrance court and a well in the rear court. The feel of the wooden structures, the sloping tiled roofs, the smell of cowdung used on the mud ground, the pinkish brown stone—all were typically traditional except for a few modern intrusions like the tubelight.

I had seen enough of wadas, or rather, whatever was left of them; they were no longer the vibrant living units of the past but desolate shells. Before we returned to Naina's wada, she insisted that I try Kolhapur's famous misal. We went to Bhavda misal shop which she said was well known; people from Bombay particularly frequented that shop. The eatery seemed a typical wayside hotel painted in a bright cobalt blue, with a glass showcase displaying the crisp sev and papdi. Photographs of famous patrons—movie stars and cricketers—were displayed on the walls. The misal turned out to be a pungent and delicious mixture.

Back in the wada, we sat in the veranda with Ashok and his father. 'You should go and see Nana Phadnavis's wada,' Ashok said. 'It is very beautiful and old,' he said. 'Of course it is not as good as the Vishrambagh wada in Pune or the Raste wada in Wai,' he added, hurriedly assuming I had seen them or at least heard of them. I hadn't. 'It is in the village of Menavali. Nana Phadnavis is a legendary Maratha leader who received the village as a jagir. He built a complex of a wada, ghat and temple. You see, there are four features in traditional Maratha architecture. The gadhi, wada, ghat and temple. The wada was usually built at the highest point and the ghat and the temple at a lower level. The gadhi is actually a fortified castle though this is missing in Phadnavis's wada.

'This wada is built around square chowks and it is surrounded by pillared aisles and is raised on a high plinth. There are many rooms around the aisles. All this was encircled by a high external

wall—the tatbandhi. There were many courtyards and these were the nerve centres of the house—everything happened there. They also had different names. There was a haldi-kumkum court which was used by the women to celebrate festivals. This court was decorated with paintings and the wooden panels on the ceiling were intricately carved with floral motifs. This court was close to the tatbandhi so that village women could enter directly. The kandangali was the service court; it was used by servants to grind masalas and to store water and grains. The pangatticha chowk was used by friends and relatives and the Tulsi-Vrindavan chowk was meant exclusively for the family. There were also semi-open courts on a high plinth which could be used during seasonal floods. These courtyards separated the wada into private and public spaces.

'The wada was made basically from bricks on a high stone plinth. The bricks were bonded by mortar containing hemp and bamboo fibres. These bricks were raised in the trabeate system around a grid of timber beams and columns. The wall had a short horizontal timber plank every few brick courses which helped to distribute load evenly over the wall below it. It also prevented vertical cracks. The walls were thick for protection and to keep the interior cool and they were corbelled at the top as a decorative element. The doors and windows were not hinged but they pivoted around a pin which fitted into a mortice on the wall. The floor was made of many materials: wood, brick, cowdung. And the roof was supported on wooden posts; it had rafters, split bamboo which supported clay tiles.

'The ghat was a flight of steps to the water which was an elaborate arrangement of platforms and steps with separate areas for washing, fishing and rituals. The temples in Menavali are plain, without much decoration. There are three temples—' Ashok's explanation was interrupted as Naina came back from the kitchen. 'Come, let's eat dinner,' she said.

*

As the train travelled back to Bombay, I thought about all the changes that had happened in the city of Kolhapur, its streets, its wadas and how people faced this change. I thought of how the architect and what he did was responsible for at least a part of the change. The old wadas were not built by architects but by master builders. In Sanskrit, stapathi, the word for architect, means a master builder; and in ancient Greek the architect was the chief carpenter. They both suggested that what architects did was 'build'. But today architects didn't build, they 'designed'. The change from 'build' to 'design' had taken many years, and it was this change that was partially reflected in cities like Kolhapur.

At the beginning, people lived in natural shelters or adapted to them, instinctively. They gradually learnt the method of building with local and natural materials and they built their own houses. There were no builders or architects then. It was only after the method of building was established that craft (which is nothing but repetitive art) came into the picture and with this came carpenters and master builders who built for people. Stone was cut, bricks and roof tiles were made, stone jalis were carved, wood was shaped and the house was built; it was not designed. After craft came art, a higher plane of evolution, and with it came the patrons of art; they had money and vision, they also travelled. They wished to build palaces, towns, citadels, temples. To do so they needed architects, people who knew the method of building, the crafts involved in it and the art of making it beautiful.

Since the very root of art lies in its not being repetitive, architecture was not repetitive; each example excelled in being original. Architects became great masters like artists and like them began to create, not just build.

The Industrial Revolution changed this. With it came mass production and standardisation and also a new advanced technology and a whole new breed of engineers. The art in architecture took a back seat; it was replaced by technology and the architect teamed up with hi-tech engineers and built intelligent buildings that cooled masses of people at optimum temperatures, conveyed them vertically in shafts, protected them from heat, fire, rain—and individual thinking. The builders crept in and with them the real estate brokers who set up shop in bloated suburbs selling homes: a set of walls and one and a half bathrooms. Homes became a product, a merchandise. The end user became a calibrated unit, not too tall and not too broad, each one alike and predictable. It was the age of consumerism: everything was bought and sold at a market price.

The relationship between man and his house changed. Many more relationships were consummated: man and the broker, broker and the builder, builder and the architect. Architect and the user? No, they didn't get to meet. Architecture which started as the act of building became an act of design and then became the act of selling. The only difference was that in the past, people were involved in the act, and today everyone else except the one who is going to use it, is involved. So architecture changed from a shelter to a work of art, and then to a dwelling unit.

Change. That was the moot point: the freedom to change and the freedom of choice that followed it and how people used it.

Kolhapur is a small town, and mine had been a short visit, but its desolate wadas were examples of how the freedom to change and the exercise of choice had led to an immense, an almost immutable sadness, within which the death of the past had become definite.

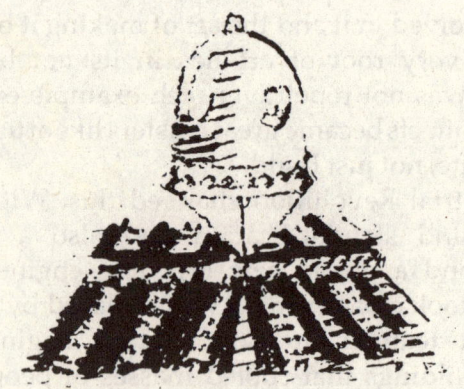

Part III
Journeys

Chapter 13

JAIPUR : BEGINNINGS ARE FRAGILE MOMENTS. THE BEGINNINGS of villages, cities, streets, communities, friendships—they are all delicate and indefinable. My study of streets seemed to have had many beginnings and many more pauses. Tokyo, Mumbai, Ahmedabad, Siddpur, Madras, Pondicherry—in these cities, in their streets, I experienced all kinds of beginnings, seeing not just the city and its people but also learning about the processes that made a city. Hara Sensei had made me see beyond all that was obvious, perceive that the street was also natural and organic and grew in response to requirements as the city began to grow. The 'chaos' in the street therefore was not a deformity but a spontaneous response to a given situation; the street was a reflection of a complex society. As there were different contemporary societies, so there were different streets: the small streets in small towns were different because they maintained the natural limits and the organic balance. But this limit was forfeited

189

by the streets in the city which were expanding their economic power and sustainability, because they were boundless. Compared to the village street, the urban street should necessarily have been successful. But the very success of the urban street, because it was open and adaptive, encouraged its habits and demands, and this nullified all its benefits. So, the self-contained urban street which was imposing in its dimensions but fragile in proportion to its size was quite unlike the little town street intimate in size but full of resilience. The urban street lacked an inner cohesion, and being under pressure to continue to expand, it destroyed itself.

*

Hara Sensei had explained all this and returned to Tokyo. I waited for other beginnings.

It was the first day of January. For me it carried excitement for another reason as well. I was keyed up about the plans I had for the next few months. We were sitting in Samovar, a small restaurant adjoining the Jehangir art gallery, and while Prakash was cutting his stuffed paratha into small wedges with a fork and spoon (I wondered why they always provided a fork and spoon and why Prakash couldn't use his fingers), I sipped from a glass of cool watermelon juice spiced with chat masala.

The first time I had met Prakash was in a publishing house where, besides all the other things I was doing, I was also editing an architectural magazine. He was a photographer and he had done several assignments photographing architecture. We had worked together and I had got to know him and his capabilities better, but I wasn't sure how he would fit in with what I had in mind. That was indeed the trouble with Prakash, one was never sure what he was all about, a fact that I was to be reminded of frequently in the coming months.

He was all 'in-between' as could be: neither tall nor short, thin nor stout, dark nor fair, young nor old, and could never get terribly excited or agitated. All these were remarkable attributes for an assistant and especially since I was exactly the opposite, I believed he would do very well as one.

As briefly as I could I told him about the villages and their street patterns and all the streets in Tokyo and Mumbai. I told him about Ahmedabad, Siddpur, and Pondicherry and Auroville. I told him about Hara, Dr. Srinivasan, Ramakrishna and Pierre. In fact I told him all I could possibly say within three-quarters of an hour. He looked interested, smiled frequently and listened without uttering a word. 'I want to go to Rajasthan,' I told him. 'I want to go to Jaipur, Udaipur and Jaisalmer. Would you like to come? Would you photograph the streets?'

His eyes looked like a camera with its shutter open, remarkably passive, recording not thinking. He looked beyond me at the other people who were in the restaurant, and after what seemed to me well over ten minutes, he blinked his eyes and said, 'Sure. When do you want to leave?'

It was almost the middle of March when we did leave. In the intervening months I had rushed to Delhi, requested Hudco to fund the trip, procured an advance without much difficulty, met and discussed with various officials of the cultural and tourism departments of the government. But really providential were two introductions that Naina had provided when I had written to her about my travelling plans. 'When you are in Jaipur,' she wrote, 'you must meet Krishnan. He was in Chicago with me. He is now a professor at the Jaipur college of architecture. You must also meet my aunt, Urmilla Chaturvedi. She teaches history at the college there. I will write to both of them.'

I received a letter from Krishnan. He wrote in Rottering ink, black and bold, confirming the dates and that he had made arrangements for us to stay at the college guest house. He would meet us at the bus terminus, he said, and gave a short description of himself.

We left by train for Delhi. It was an overnight train with seats in place of berths, to my discomfort. Promptly at ten, almost an hour after dinner had been served, the lights were switched off in the compartment. It was the signal for the fat man sitting behind me to start snoring. I am allergic to snoring. I can never sleep if I hear snoring. 'Will everyone start snoring?' I asked Prakash nervously.

'Don't worry', Prakash said kindly. 'People don't really snore when they are sitting in uncomfortable positions.' But he was wrong. Soon I heard a lively chorus of snores.

'Let's get out of here,' I said to Prakash, and that is how we came to travel in the foyer for most of the journey, standing and talking while the train rattled and whined to itself, swiftly shedding villages and towns and large bits of countryside in its wake. Prakash said, 'So you want me to shoot the Hawa Mahal, the Jantar Mantar?'

'I want you to shoot the streets,' I said.

'How exactly?'

'It's not just the buildings on the street,' I said, 'or the traffic. I want you to photograph the street's character.'

'What character?' Prakash asked. 'The streets look the same to me—they have buildings, shops, traffic, people and a lot of muck.'

'You have to look at the street differently; you have to see its architecture,' I explained. 'What do you feel when you look at architecture?' I asked him.

'You mean a building?'

'Okay, a building. Let me tell you. Whenever I look at a building I experience two kinds of feeling. One is physical and visual which I can easily describe; it is more direct and immediate. But there is also something that is psychological and this is inexplicable. You

192

can sense it not just intellectually but emotionally: this, I think, is the essence of architecture.'

Prakash, seemingly unconvinced, said, 'So?'

'So,' I went on, 'the streets are also like that, like architecture They have a personality and essence and this is what forms the their character. And that is what I want you to capture through your camera, Prakash.'

'You want me to shoot the street's personality? What is its personality?'

'The architecture of the street, that is to say the buildings on the street, the historic monuments, the character of the terrain, people and the environment.'

'So I can shoot the Hawa Mahal and the Jantar Mantar? Both are monuments,' Prakash laughed. 'On the other hand,' I continued seriously, 'society, its traditions and aspirations are responsible for the street-essence.'

'Whatever is that?'

'It is like the ritual in a temple; it is to do with custom and how people behave in the street, collectively. You must admit there is a hidden code.'

'And how am I to photograph all this hidden stuff?' Prakash smirked.

'Possibly you can't. I don't see how you can photograph the essence of things. You can possibly document the history and tradition through the monuments. Also possibly the symbols, rituals; but there are also non-apparent things like attitudes, philosophies, religious sensibilities and aesthetics and lifestyle. How will you photograph these?'

'I like to shoot beautiful things: beautiful buildings, streets,' Prakash paused. 'I would love to photograph the European streets, they are so pretty and organised. Why not go to Europe? Indian streets, they are chaotic.'

'Yes, Indian streets may be chaotic, but there is something very organic about them. Do you know anything about organic phenomena?'

I looked at Prakash. He was looking out of the window. Then

he said in utter incomprehension, 'Can you tell me simply what to look for in the street?'

I said to him as I would to a roomful of architecture students: 'First we look at the street's configuration—straight, curved, meandering and so on. Then we estimate roughly its age. We look out for the major events that mark the street; identify the symbols and see how permanent they are. We study the architectural character of the buildings and the character of the spaces and seek out the relation between the buildings and the street. Also the relationship between street-form and the topography. We study the heights, proportions, scales, shapes, symmetry, materials, colours and the relation between the old and the new. We observe the activities in the street, formal and informal, and see how the street adapts to changes over the day and through the seasons. We study the functions of the street and seek out the changes over the years.'

'Is that all?' Prakash asked sardonically.

'No,' I replied, 'that's not all. This is only the basic. The main thing is to find out how people use the street, about the houses they live in and how they relate to the street.'

*

We took a luxury coach from Delhi to Jaipur. On the way, watching Sridevi on the video, Prakash suddenly asked me, 'What is all this mandala business? Jaipur was built on some cosmic diagram?'

'Yes. That is what is believed.'

'And what is this yantra bit?'

'When I was a little girl, my grandfather in Tanjore would tell me stories about the Vastu Purusha. I was fascinated by this Purusha. It seems the gods saw something blocking the sky from the earth. This creature had a hump and a crooked shape. The gods then pulled him down to earth and trapped him in a square and that became the Vastu Purusha mandala. This is the magic diagram or what is called yantra. Vastu is the site of residence. Purusha is the cosmic man and the mandala is a closed polygon.

194

Then they made more squares in that square in which this formless creature was held.'

'What good is all this? Why trap an inculpable being and build squares around him?'

'I don't know, but when a city plan is made according to this mandala, it captures the Purusha which is nothing but the primordial energy in its bhumi, the earth. This, I presume, is good for the city.'

'Go on.'

'There was this model of the cosmos in the Shilpa Shastras. This was used to plan the old Indian towns. The surface of the earth is demarcated by sunrise and sunset into east, west, north and south points and these points defined the mandala, or cosmic square. This square did not represent the outline of the earth but the primary pairs of opposites.'

'So the cosmic model was a square,' Prakash laughed.

'So the cosmic model for a city had an orthogonal plan with a regular grid. There was strict orientation and formal elements: there were axial streets, defined enclosures and gateways. Up was more important than down and big was better than small. The centre was sacred and there were different meanings given to the cardinal directions and their relation to the sun and the seasons. Everything was arranged in hierarchy using two-sided symmetry, contrast and duality.'

'All this was scientific or just superstition?'

'Scientific essentially, but the manner in which they were propagated became the basis of superstition. There were five rules—about orientation, plan, the system of proportions, the formulae and the science of rhythms and metres . . . .'

I had indulged in a bit of serious reading about the Shilpa Shastras and the mandala before the trip and I summarised the five rules in my mind:

The mandala was used to derive the plan and orientation. It was divided into smaller squares and diagonals with definite direction and width. They

intersected at the 'soft' points (nadi) of the site which could be damaged if built over. The mandala could consist of sixty-four or eighty-one squares. The houses of the Brahmanas, palaces of the kings and the temples were built on the eighty-one square mandala. The sixty-four square mandala was used for villages and towns.

The mana was a system of proportionate measurement. It was believed that if a temple was built according to perfect measurement then there would be a perfect universe. Every creative activity, architectural or sculptural, had to have perfect measurements because they were metaphysical. The cosmos could only be built with order.

The varga consisted of the six formulae to which the perimeter of the building had to conform. If three of these were maintained the building construction would be auspicious. Anything less would not. The mansara provided nine different lengths, nine breadths and five heights for a building. So the length, breadth and height were selected according to this and the six formulae were used.

Chanda was about rhythm; it was a science of metres that was used for the plan and the vertical section of the building. The chandas of the ground plan were derived from the Vastu Purusha mandala. These chandas were like the ragas in music: there are six primary chandas which multiply into thirty-six secondary chandas. The old temples were built according to these chandas.

As the coach turned into the terminus at Jaipur, I got up to spot Krishnan. It was crowded outside and dark as we had reached late.

'What does he look like?' Prakash asked.

'Tall, thin. Striped shirt.'

'That's hardly a description.'

'And curly hair.'

'Any Malayali will have curly hair.'

I saw him, tall, lanky, his body bent in several directions as he looked about him. His moustache, unruly and long, curled over his lips in swirls and his teeth protruded, giving him a permanent pout. He was not handsome at all. But I was to know later that he was warm and kind and helpful, apart from being very intelligent. He grew on people.

Even as he introduced himself I would have guessed, had I not

197

been told, that he was a Malayali although he spoke with an American accent: nasal and with a drawl. But he had not been able to get rid of the way the Malayalis roll the 'L's: I quickly noticed the way he said 'whole', 'simple'. As we struggled with our luggage, of which there was a lot as we carried with us photographic equipment and books besides other personal items, he told us, 'The guest house is being used for a wedding and all the rooms are occupied, but I have managed to talk to the hostel warden. I hope you don't mind sharing a room with the boys,' he asked Prakash and then turning to me he said politely, 'Madam, you will have to share a room with the girls.'

Since it was late and I was too tired to dispute all these arrangements, I agreed. Krishnan promptly announced: 'We had better eat something here, the canteen will be closed by the time we get there. We will have to take a vikram to the campus. As we crossed the street to a fast food restaurant I asked him doubtfully, 'Vikram? Who is Vikram?' At which he laughed and replied, 'That is a vikram,' pointing to a large-sized auto-rickshaw. 'They call it vikram here.'

Seated at the restaurant he asked us what we wished to eat and I said I wanted to eat something that was locally available, a Rajasthani dish. 'Yes,' Prakash agreed, 'in Jaipur, I want only Rajasthani, or,' he nodded a bit confused, 'Jaipuri.'

'The onion katchoris are famous,' Krishnan said and enquired about their availability.

'No,' said the bearer, 'we can give you pav bhaji or idli sambar, vada chutney.'

'Don't you have anything that is typical of this region?' I asked again, to which he replied with pride, 'We make delicious south Indian food. Better than in Madras or Mumbai.'

Eating the idli and sambar I looked at the street. What was different about it? It looked like any street in any town. Were all the stories about the mandala true? Across was the railway station and bus terminal; they looked like any other station and bus terminal and even the food was much like what was available anywhere. I wondered what the other streets of Jaipur would be like. With mounting apprehension I awaited the morning.

I awoke in the morning, scratched the mosquito bites I had

acquired during the night and wondered where I was. It was a small room with four beds arranged around it and two narrow windows. Through a window I could see a bare patch of ground. Unlike the powdery red earth of the south, the soil here made me think of the colour and folds of an aging camel's skin. Two skinny girls, my room-mates, walked into the room with wet towels and wetter hair and informed me that it would be a good idea to finish with the toilet and bath since all the girls would be waking up and there would be a tremendous rush. 'Breakfast and tea is served only till nine o'clock,' one of them said. I had never been in a hostel before. The one I had lived in Tokyo was more like a number of private rooms. Krishnan and Prakash arrived while I was eating my breakfast of boiled eggs and buttered slices of bread.

'I was telling Prakash that we will meet at four in the afternoon in front of the palace. I have a lecture until three. For lunch go to this restaurant.' He handed me a piece of paper. 'I have not been there for some time but I am told they serve a good Rajasthani thali. So, why don't we go to the city first.'

Prakash hailed a vikram at the gate of the campus.

'It's full,' I said. 'He won't stop.'

He stopped. Prakash smiled as we squeezed ourselves into the already crammed vehicle. We stopped at Suraj Pol, the imposing pink gateway to the city. 'It's like a prop,' Prakash said looking through the camera lens, 'so light. What is it made of?'

'Stone and plaster possibly.'

'It looks as though it is built of papier mache or plaster of paris, like the gateways erected at fairs. Pink City,' he went on. 'And it really is pink.'

The main street was wide and on either side of it rose pink buildings four to five storeys high with shops below. A terrace ran along the entire street on the first floor, making the street appear even wider. Prakash disappeared up a stairway and I followed him; it led us to the terrace. There were a few shops here too, possibly trading offices, as they lacked the liveliness of the shops below.

From the terrace I had a better view of the whole street: a strong frontal horizontality created by the almost flat facades, the line of the terrace, the shops below and the continuous row of buildings on either side. They also created a powerful perspective because of the series of parallel lines as the street converged towards the chaupar—a square at the intersection of streets. And within this framework of horizontality and parallel lines was an unanticipated variety: more terraces, balconies, jharokhas, windows, Greek pediments, trompe l'oeil windows with louvres of stone, jalis, brackets, domes, turrets, none of them disfiguring the building form or disrupting the perspective, but becoming a motley, a masquerade painted the colour of terracotta combed with white festoons.

'Prakash, shoot the details, the pink jali, white motifs and that green window. Shoot close-ups and long shots.'

'Not now. I have loaded a black and white film,' he said.

'Black and white? It's all pink here.'

'Sure. But just look at the grain, the texture of the walls.'

At first look what seemed to be a uniform pink was actually various hues of pink, and the walls were not smooth but textured like the mud-plastered walls in villages. Prakash shot the walls, parts where the plaster had peeled off, signboards, each shop. The shop floors were almost level with the pavement, complementing the open, accessible look of the street. There were bazaars and more bazaars. Possibly the first city I had seen where the pleasures of shopping became a planning priority. The Kishanpole Bazaar, Gangori Bazaar, Johri Bazaar, Sireh Deori Bazaar, Tripolia Bazaar, the Ramganj Bazaar. After a quick walk through the markets which were the quintessence of Indian bazaars and so nothing different, we walked back to the chaupar. It was full of people, traffic and hawkers; though meant to be a large open space, there was no space in it. The shapeless mass of its activity was counterpoised by the buildings surrounding the chaupar, by the definitiveness of their domes and jharokhas. Beyond the chaupar, facing the street, was the Hawa Mahal, at a location as inexplicable as one could think of. The focus of activity, view and vista, space—all were at the chaupar. The Hawa Mahal did not face it, nor was it visually connected; it stood beyond adding one more brocaded pink face to the horizontality of the street.

Prakash loaded a colour film and stubbornly exposed half the

film on it. The Jantar Mantar, part of the street and yet distant from it, took up the remaining half.

By noon we were seated in the restaurant eating masala dosa and wada. The waiter had told us that they had discontinued the Rajasthani thali since everyone wanted either Punjabi or Madrasi food. 'Also it is fashion,' he confessed.

Having eaten what we didn't want to eat, we parked ourselves in the sweltering heat outside the restaurant wondering what to do next.

'Why don't we go and see Urmilla Chaturvedi,' I said. I showed the address to a shopkeeper. He pointed to a lane across the street. The lane, though narrow, seemed to swell as we entered it. Maybe it was because it was suddenly quieter, or the absence of the sun's glare in this silent meandering lane.

I turned to tell Prakash about how quiet and cool and therefore how spacious the lane was. Perhaps he could capture this through his camera, impossible though it seemed. But I saw that Prakash had perched himself on top of a Bajaj scooter parked alongside a building. He had carefully covered the seat with his handkerchief. His camera was stuck into his face, the lens cap was off, and with one eye shut and nose puckered, he was busy shooting. I didn't know what he was shooting. The street, houses, people? Would he capture the silence and the shade?

Urmilla Chaturvedi's large haveli was all of two floors and a terrace. I had noticed the other houses had enormous walls that segregated their interiors from the street. But Urmilla Chaturvedi's haveli was different. It had no such wall but the entryway turned after the main door, what in Hindi is called a 'modh', or turn. The purpose was the same: it was a threshold which kept the inside private by isolating it from the street.

Urmilla Chaturvedi was a white-haired old lady with skin that was creased like crushed paper. But the eyes were intense and full of energy, and her stride when she took us within the house was enthusiastic and swift.

We walked through the various rooms and into a large central courtyard. Prakash who had been passive until now went to every corner of the court focusing his camera. Perhaps it was indicative of how photographers react to light. He had been unable to take any photographs within the house since it was so dark.

'It's cool here, even though it is open to the sky. I thought the rooms were cool because they were dark?' Prakash said.

'It is the haveli design. Their walls are thick so the house is cool. Moreover, there are very few openings.'

'That is why the rooms are so dark.'

'There are only small openings in the outer walls and they stop the hot summer winds.'

'Unlike the large windows in modern houses?'

'Yes. They may be good for cross-ventilation but they do not suit hot dry climates. And these small windows have deep sunshades and screens so the air is compressed as it flows through.'

'This cools it,' Prakash judged.

'These old havelis are not cooled by direct ventilation. There is a passive circulation of air through the shaded small openings and inner courtyards.'

'So why is the courtyard cool?'

'Because,' I explained, 'it is enclosed by thick walls and rooms and it is protected from direct sun and hot winds.' The courts worked by trapping cool air in the night. The trapped air did not get heated during the day because of the size of the court and its proportion compared to the height of the building, which meant that it was normally in shade. In larger havelis, instead of one big court there were invariably a series of smaller ones. As the air in

203

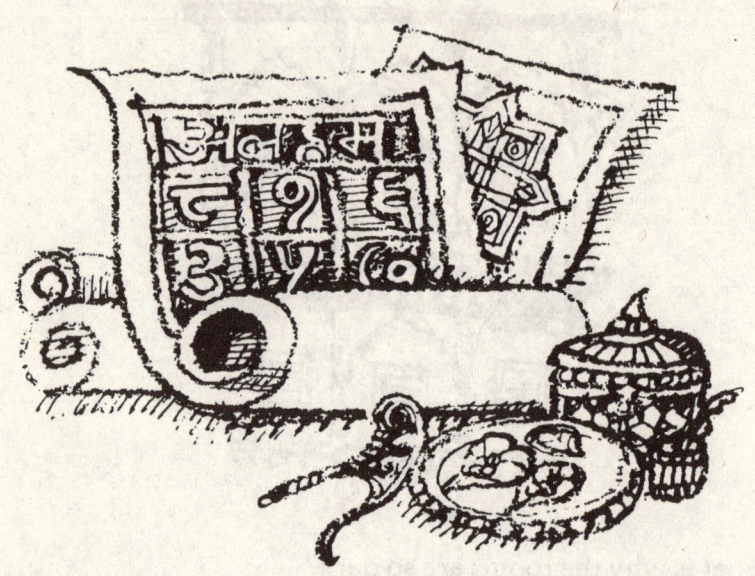

the court became warmer and lighter, it rose and fresh cooler air blew in through the screens. It was this circular movement of air currents that formed a special microclimate within the haveli. The fact that the houses were built next to each other also helped as it reduced the area exposed to the sun. Even the spaces between the buildings and the lanes were narrow and therefore cool.

Urmilla made us sit in one of the rooms facing the inner court while she disappeared into one of the rooms beyond. The walls were painted the colour of pink guava. There was a swing in the middle of the room and a bed with mattresses piled on it, a study table and small cupboards against a wall.

Urmilla reappeared carrying a tray with glasses of tea. A short man with a pronounced belly walked in behind her. I presumed he was Mr Chaturvedi. He sat down beside us and picked up a glass of tea that his wife offered him as she said to us, 'My husband.' I later learnt that he was a Sanskrit scholar, an astrologer and an authority on Shilpa Shastras.

Then sitting down and wiping her face and neck with the end of her cotton saree she said without a preamble and as though she was continuing a history lecture: 'Did you know Vidyadhar was a Bengali?' 'Vidyadhar who?' Prakash asked.

'He was the architect of Jaipur,' I said.

Urmilla added, 'Sawai Jai Singh engaged him to design Jaipur, the new capital. Before that the capital was Amber.'

'Where is that?' Prakash asked.

'Close by, on a hill,' Urmilla continued. 'When the Rajputs migrated into Rajasthan, they fought many battles, built many capitals. One of them was Amber in the Aravallis. But Jaipur was the first one they built on the plain.'

'Why?'

'Because although the Amber Kachhawahas became friendly with the Mughals to protect Amber, Bahadur Shah invaded the capital anyway and threw Jai Singh out. When he was in exile, he thought of the new city. Jai Singh was a mathematician, he was the one who built the Jantar Mantar. He wanted to build a capital that reflected the universe.'

She paused, 'There is a story. Raja Kedar who ruled over Jessore, now in Bangladesh, had thrown a black slab of stone in which Goddess Kali was trapped in the sea. When Mirza Raja Mansingh of Amber set out to conquer Bengal, Kali came to him in his dream and extracted a promise that were he to win in battle, he should remove the sacred slab from the waters and release her

205

from the stone. When the raja did so, it seems the goddess came before him. So he carried back the stone, the image of her, back to Amber and made her the supreme goddess of his kingdom. The Bengali priests also went with the raja to perform the various pujas and started to live in Amber. Vidhyadhar belonged to one of these families. He designed Jaipur according to the cosmic diagram—the Vastu Purusha mandala.'

Mr. Chaturvedi had finished his tea; he unwrapped a couple of pans and put two in his mouth.

'You know about the mansara?' he asked me.

He went to the adjoining room where I could see him standing on a stool retrieving something atop a steel cupboard. When he came back to us he had in his hand an old Air India attache case, the one they give to first-class passengers. 'My son lives in America. He travelled first class and they gave him this, free,' Mr. Chaturvedi said proudly. He then removed more papers and charts from the attache case and said, 'You see, Yama, the god of death, presided in the south so that direction was always avoided.' Of course a simple explanation for this would be that the sun was too hot on the south side and the soil too dry. Moreover the prevailing winds and rains were from the southwest and this would expose the site to them.

'The mansara said that the site had to be fit in colour, smell, taste, shape, direction, sound and touch. Ground sloping to the east was good. It also got the full benefit of the morning sun. A good site had to produce a hard sound. It would have a stream running left to right; its water must not smell bad. The site also should produce water when dug to a depth which was equal to that of a man with his arm raised. The ideal climate was one with moderate temperature.'

The mansara documented many kinds of towns with a distinct boundary, form and street layout. They were classified according to their form, location and function. For example, the Sanskrit word for a city was pura. There were many kinds of puras: The nagara was an ordinary commercial town with four gates in four cardinal quarters. The rajdhani was the capital town with the royal palaces, gardens and shrines. Pattana was a large commercial port and durga was a fortified town. A labour town for local industries like mining was called kheta and kharvata was a larger version of this. Sivira and senamukha were military towns. Sthaniya was a mofussil town near a river or hill, dronamukha a market town, kotmakolaka a populous settlement in a hilly or wild tract. Nigama was an artisan town and matha or vihara was a university town.

Towns were classified according to number and direction of the streets and were encircled by a path (mangalvithi) which was the auspicious path. The street running east to west was called the rajapatha and the street passing through the centre was called the brahmavithi. The street pattern was used to divide the town into wards for different social groups. There were different street patterns:

Dandaka was rectangular with straight intersecting streets and wide central avenues. Sarvatobhadra was an oblong or square pattern with four streets of equal length; the nandhyarvarta one where the street began from the northeast corner and ran south. The padma was octagonal or circular with seven or more east-oriented streets. The swastikas had the shape of a swastik and the prastara was like a conch; the karmuka, like a bow, semi-circular and ideally suited for sea ports; and the chaturmukha was square or oblong with four large streets on four sides and two large ones crossing in the centre.

Urmilla Chaturvedi had been in the kitchen and now she came back. A young girl followed her carrying a tray with plastic plates. 'I fried some hot katchoris for you,' she said and passed the mint and tamarind chutney around before sitting down beside me.

'You really think Jaipur is built on the mandala?' I asked her.

'I don't know about Jaipur, but this world is made from imbalance.'

'You mean gravity, force?'

'No, the imbalance between the being and the non-being. There are many myths about creation which explain how chaos was converted into order.'

Order was very important, she explained. Every principle, even in building, was about order. The diagrams that were used to order the built forms formed a relationship between the cosmos, time and man. It was important to maintain a balance between the physical and the metaphysical and that is what these magnetic diagrams did. If they were not followed, or if there was a mistake, then it would be inauspicious. But there were also remedial measures and at every point the construction of a building had to be checked to make it auspicious through a number of rituals.

'The modern architects use these diagrams, but they are only form generators, they have lost their meaning. Such static copying of the old models is not right, I think,' she said.

We left. But what she had said remained in my mind: there was meaning and purpose in the magnetic diagrams, which came alive through rituals. Without meaning, purpose, and ritual, re-inventing old forms was futile.

*

We were half an hour late for our meeting with Krishnan, and when we reached the palace he was standing in the shade of a tree, covered in sweat.

'So you want to go around looking at streets in different cities?' he asked me as we sat down under the tree. 'You know, I saw many Indian cities before I started my study on Jaipur.' He drew a series of squares in the mud and said, 'This is Jaipur.'

'Looks like a packet of cigarettes to me, Four Square,' Prakash said.

'Not four squares but nine,' Krishnan corrected him. 'The figure 9 was very spiritual because it connected man to the universe.' He took out a cigarette packet and wrote some numbers on it. Prakash peered over his shoulder.

'Look,' he said thrusting the packet under my nose, '9 is a number that always adds up to itself: 9x2=18 and 1+8=9.' I looked at the other numbers he had written: 9x3=27 and 2+7=9. 9x4=36 and 3+6=9.

'So?'

'So people believe the nine-square theory about Jaipur but no one seems to be definite about it. It is supposed to be built on a three-by-three grid, on the prastara plan, with two major roads running east-west and north-south dividing it into nine squares. But one road is missing because there is a ridge where the road should have been. And the ninth square that fell on the Nahargarh hill on the northwest was shifted to the south-east. So it doesn't accurately follow the nine-square plan.'

As he talked, Krishnan drew squares on the ground with a stick. The nine squares he had drawn at first became seven squares.

'Two squares of the nine are not clearly demarcated, also they are of unequal size. But how can anyone force a rigid pattern on the site, however magnetic the pattern may be? Architects always have to compromise. So Vidyadhar compromised. Okay, Jaipur is more or less flat but there are hills. Then there were also the problems of defence and water. He had to juggle all this and produce a workable plan. Maybe he started with the nine squares and ended with seven.'

'It is like any modern Western city with straight streets,' Prakash said.

'Some historians believe that Jaipur was built to a modern plan and had nothing to do with the mandala. Historians have written about the connection between Jaipur and Europe and whether the plan could actually be European. There is a plan of Christian-Eriang in Brandenburg which was rebuilt after a fire; it had a palace precinct and gridiron streets and Jaipur seems just like that.'

It was rasping hot as we walked down the main street connecting the two main gateways, Suraj Pol and Chand Pol, which were the two ends of the plan. There was a marriage procession right in the middle of the street preceded by a band playing film songs. The heat, noise and dust made it even hotter.

'The layout of roads,' Krishnan said as we squeezed through the marriage party, 'suited the climate of Jaipur, as the city's east-west axis is located at a fifteen-degree deviation from the cardinal directions. As a result, people in the streets do not face the low angle of the sun in the morning and evening. It brought in the early morning winter sun and the wind flowed through the streets.' Despite the angle and the breeze it was hot.

'According to a recent theory,' Krishnan added, 'the fifteen-degree deviation is attributed to the line of the sign of Leo which is not only the central sign in Jaipur's horoscope, but also signifies birth in Jai Singh's own horoscope.'

We had reached the chaupar. It was crowded with more people and more hawkers. Krishnan said, 'Chaupar is a game they played, like ludo, and because the crossroads looked like the game board they called it chaupar.' A little girl selling packets of rubberbands and pins ran up to me. Prakash bought a plastic comb from another girl. 'Jai Singh had attended many durbars in Delhi,' Krishnan said. 'The Akbari style of architecture was popular but the red sandstone and marble quarries were outside Jai Singh's kingdom. He did not think much of the grey Jaipur stone, finding it dreary. And he wanted to build Jaipur fast. So he decided to cover the walls with a coating of red earth from a village nearby to make it resemble red sandstone. But not every house in Jaipur was pink—there were many white houses. Later Maharaja Ram Singh tried colouring each street in different colours—green, yellow, pink. The entire city needed a facelift when the Prince of Wales was to visit. So it was coloured pink.'

It was close to five-thirty. We had been walking for an hour, and I suggested a break. We walked into a small ice-cream parlour. I ordered a cold coffee topped with vanilla ice-cream. When Prakash had consumed every trace of his yellow, pink and green ice-cream, he signalled to me. 'I must go out and shoot some photographs,' he said. 'The sun will be setting soon.' We accompanied him into the main street. Prakash took many shots of a potter's stall and its gigantic heap of pots.

'The city was designed for grand processions,' Krishnan said. He pointed to the terrace above the shops. 'They become viewing galleries and stairs lead up to them. As you can see, there were many ideas behind the plan of the city.'

One of the ideas behind the plan was also the mixed land use adopted in order to save energy. The idea of zonal land use was in fact introduced by the British. It not only opposed the urban lifestyle and economy of the people but also wasted energy by dispersing activities. A town house often had a shop below and residences above. Spaces and buildings were often used for a number of activities and not for specific functions alone. Where you lived, provisions were available next door, vegetables down the street. The doctor's clinic was next to the jeweller and the school was a ten-minute walk away and the temple around the corner.

Jaipur is a combination of the complex and the simple, which is good. Even better is that the complex and simple are interchangeable: the main streets with the imposing gateways dissolve once the marked thresholds of the city are crossed. What is complex becomes simple; it is further simplified by the routines of activities, predictable and repetitive, which soften the imperial scale of the town. On the other hand, the lanes in the mohalla appear simple but contain a complexity that is mysterious. Like the complex and the simple, there is also the connection between the part and the whole. The street corner therefore becomes a whole, and the street, a part. These aspects give rise to different scales which give the city an urban character: the large regular streets feed the smaller streets of the mohallas and the chaupars formed by intersecting streets. Indisputably the layout of the streets regulates the plan of the mohalla and town, the street ultimately testifies the shape of the town in which only the major axes are marked and the residual spaces develop spontaneously according to the social hierarchy and the topographical constraints.

In Exodia, Italo Calvino's mythical city, a carpet preserved its true form, the coloured threads led one from one kind of street to another. Alleys, steps, hovels, bustle, confusion and smells: despite them all the streets were woven according to the geometric scheme of the carpet on land.

Jaipur reflected the myth of constellations and primordial power; but when you stare at the stars above you see the difference between absolute patterns and life. The pattern then lives, changes, deforms according to its fate and inclination.

Chapter 14

SHEKHAVATI: 'ONE THOUSAND AND TWO HUNDRED RUPEES, saab,' the taxi driver said. I continued to bargain with him as he looked appealingly towards Prakash and then at Krishnan who stood at a distance from us and was rapidly devouring a banana. Then with an air of one in charge I said, 'Let's go by bus. It will be nice to mix with the local people.' 'Yes boss,' Prakash said as he winked at Krishnan. We marched into the terminus and climbed into a bus that was proceeding towards Sikar, in Shekhavati.

We found comfortable seats. I sat near the window, Prakash sat next to me and Krishnan sat two seats behind us.

Just five minutes before the bus was to leave a large crowd of colourfully dressed villagers charged in. They carried with them large bags and tins; some even had gunny sacks, one of which was promptly stuffed under my feet. It seemed to contain onions or potatoes; I could feel their rounded forms with my toes. Two

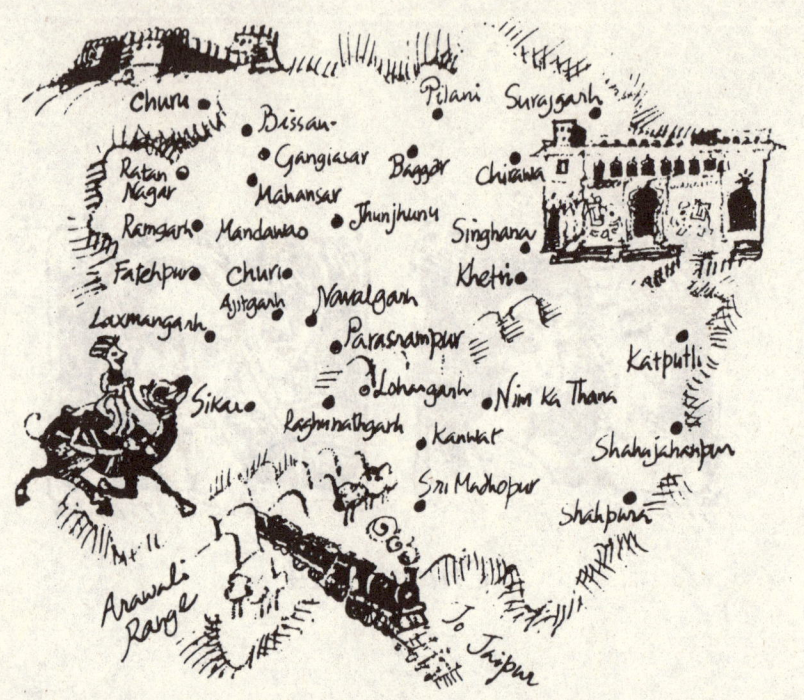

couples got in, the women with children in their arms. Seeing them Prakash and Krishnan got up and the two men sat down in the vacated seats. The women then deposited the children in the men's laps and the bags that they were carrying were dumped in front of my seat. Prakash and Krishnan shrugged their shoulders and grinned as they watched me struggle to settle into a comfortable position. I tucked my feet under me all the way to Sikar.

'How long will it take to reach Shekhavati?' Prakash asked Krishnan. 'Shekhavati is a region, it is not a town,' Krishnan said. 'We will have to go to Sikar, it is the main town. But there is nothing much to see in Sikar. From there we can go to Laxmangarh, Fatehpur, Ramgarh. These are all small towns in the Shekhavati region. All these towns have havelis whose walls are painted.' Krishnan sat down on some luggage in the aisle and told us a legend about Shekhavati. 'You know, it was all because

214

Shekha was not bathed in cow's blood that he did not become the ruler of India.'

'What Sekha? What cow?' I asked him.

'Mokul Singh, the ruler of Barwada, bathed his son in goat's blood instead of cow's blood.'

'Why?'

'Because he did not have a son and wished he had. His guru granted him his wish and asked him to go back and graze his cows. He also gave him an idol of Krishna and taught him a mantra. Later Mokul Singh met a Muslim fakir called Sheikh Burhan. This fakir was trying to propagate Islam amongst the Kshatriyas. The fakir told Mokul Singh that a son would be born to him and when that happened he must bathe the child in cow's blood. When his son was born, since he couldn't kill a cow as he was a Hindu, he bathed the child with goat's blood. He called his son Shekha after the sheikh. It seems because he did not use cow's blood Shekha never became the ruler of India.'

However Shekhavati was founded and the Shekavats became powerful in Rajasthan. Shekhavati is not known just because of these Rajput rulers but also because of the Marwaris, who brought a lot of wealth to Shekhavati. They built huge havelis for themselves. Many migrated to Bombay and Calcutta where they made their fortunes. The Birlas are one of these families.

The bus passed through a narrow road to emerge in a square thick with dust. We had reached Sikar. As we got down a number of men came towards us shouting, 'Fatehpur, Laxmangarh, Jhunjhunu.' We followed one to his jeep. The only problem was that nine more people got in and we were packed so tight that we

215

couldn't move.

I sat huddled in a corner looking at the road shimmering in the heat. On either side of it was bare ground cracked like unburnt pottery left too long in the sun. I sat listening to the other passengers talk in an unfamiliar dialect, and the occasional clicking of a woman's bangles. Suddenly the jeep screeched to a stop. I could see a sandy track disappear into the distance. We had reached Laxmangarh. We ambled into town on a horse cart, its bells jingling in rhythm with the cart's movement.

The streets of the town were straight, unlike any of the small towns and villages I had seen in Rajasthan. The Bhil villages were built around small hills and they were organic in pattern. They had evolved bit by bit and were not planned. But Laxmangarh seemed to me totally preconceived. When I asked Krishnan about this he said, 'Of course it is planned. In fact it is planned according to the Jaipur model.'

The shilpis (artisans) who had worked in Jaipur worked here and in the other towns of Shekhavati. Thus what they knew became a local tradition. In the eastern part of Shekhavati, primogeniture was not followed and when the thakur died, his thikana (kingdom) was divided between all the male successors. The younger ones built their own forts and the new villages that came up were planned. Moreover, the wealthy Marwaris became patrons of art and architecture and they built many buildings, gardens and squares in the town.

We came to the Ramji Lal Kedia haveli. I stepped back to look at it. Every bit of the wall was painted. There were floral motifs in blue and brown over windows and doors on the first floor. Under the brackets of the balconies in front of these doors and windows was an intricate rendering of what looked like an army camp. On the left were musicians and soldiers, although I didn't quite understand what they had in common, and on the right were camels, bullocks and horses carrying cannons. But the rendering with a touch of humour to it was a painting of a man riding a bicycle in Baridas Vaid's haveli. It looked like a circus-man riding a bicycle. Only he wore a typical merchant's cap and a dhoti. In Balmukund Bansidhar Rathi's haveli I saw a painting of a woman dressed in a blue gown. It looked like a gown made from a silk saree. Her hair was tied in a bun and she wore bangles on her wrist. She also wore boots, which made her look rather funny. And she was listening to a gramophone of the early type, with a large funnel-shaped speaker. The gramophone sat on top of a wrought-iron stand covered with a pink cloth with flowers on it.

Krishnan had ready explanations for everything. About this lady in the blue dress he told me: 'In the early days, Englishwomen in India got bored and lonely. So they occupied their time with housekeeping, sewing, supervising the gardens and maintaining a retinue of servants. This painting is of one such Englishwoman.'

Krishnan led us to a tea shop at the end of the street. As we sat on the benches there, I watched the shopowner make the tea. He had an old aluminum kettle into which he poured water and as it boiled he added enormous quantities of what looked like tea-dust. Then he poured large quantities of milk into it from a brass pot and heaped spoons of sugar. The tea was poured into another pot through a deeply stained rag used as a strainer. He gathered the cloth with his fingers, twisted it and squeezed every drop of tea from it and threw it aside.

While we sipped the tea in small glasses, Krishnan looked at the measured drawings of Nawalgarh, Laxmangarh, Ramgarh and Fatehpur that he had brought with him. All of them had more or less a planned street pattern. 'There was nothing historical or natural to preserve,' Krishnan explained. 'And the land belonged to the thakur, he could plan the town with the help of astrologers. Basically they needed two things: they needed a small hill on which to build a fort for defence and a superficial vein of water. The construction of the fort, which was usually in the south, was in itself a ritual. Also part of the ritual were a number of wells, a temple for Lord Krishna who was the protector of the Shekhavats, the ramparts and four gateways along the main cardinal directions. When all this was ready the thakur built himself a court and courtiers and servants were given buildings near the palace. Then, the thakur invited the merchants to settle in the new town by offering them concessions and economic advantages. The merchant's havelis were located to the north or northeast of the fort and along the main axis which linked the eastern and western gateways. To the west were the houses of the artisans. The Muslims also lived here.'

After the tea we walked to Ganeriwala's Char Chowk haveli.'The word haveli is Persian,' Krishnan said. 'It means a surrounded or enclosed space. It is more than just a form of architecture, it implies a way of life. In Mughal times it was used for a residential block, three to four storeys high, around an open courtyard. Many families lived in it together, sharing some of the facilities. In it was a common well, a space for washing and a place for children to play. A joint family was the smallest economic unit; the haveli was the smallest social unit.'

He went inside the haveli. It had four open courts surrounded by rooms. It was not the size of the haveli that was impressive but the spatial detail, and the fact that every space and element was differentiated. Khura was the ramp; darujo, the doorway; mori, a small door within a large door; tibari, a three-arched veranda; deodhi, entrance to the ladies apartments; gokha, a place for sitting outside the entrance; poli, entrance hall; rahose, inner balcony; sal, room inside the tibari without windows; chandni, roofless room and so on. It laid open a highly developed indigenous building tradition.

A very tall man, old but erect, appeared before us. Adding to his impressiveness was a bright yellow turban. I looked for Prakash; I wanted a photograph of this man with the haveli as a backdrop. Prakash was never around when I needed him. I found him crouched behind a column zooming in on a painting above the doorway. I looked at the painting. There was nothing unusual about it since all the havelis were painted. Then I saw a huge beehive and I looked at Prakash. He smiled and winked. I returned with Prakash and asked the old man if we could photograph him. After his picture had been taken he invited us to his house behind the haveli. He told me he was Rambir, the caretaker of the haveli.

His house was small but had two courts: there was a forecourt immediately after the main door and an inner court beyond the room in between the courts. This room we entered was dark after the glare of the sun in the court. It had raised flooring on one side, a cot and a reed chair. Sitting here, over glasses of buttermilk that his wife served us, we listened to him talk about life in the havelis. 'My grandfather used to tell me all about the havelis and what happened in them. Most havelis have two courtyards, one at the entrance and an inner courtyard where the ladies remained. When a male guest entered the house, the women would retreat to the zenana and peep out from the fretted windows. The haveli was full of activity. The women of the house would get up very early, before dawn and worship the tulsi and then milk the cows in the nora. They churned the butter, cooked and stored water in the parinda, which was a small but airy room.'

'The women kept their faces covered (as his wife's had been

when she served us) even when there were no men around. Young girls were not allowed to go outside the inner courtyard of the haveli until they were married. So the haveli was the whole world to them. It was built that way. The maidservants went to the bazaar to shop for them and vendors came to the haveli to sell their goods. The street outside the house was a separate world, and their familiarity with it was only because of the stories they had heard; havelis were a beehive of gossip. The men either worked in town so left early or held office in the baithak which was a special area in the haveli. So the haveli was built in the way that people lived.

'The life of the rajputni was one of hardship. In each stage of life death awaited her. Why, I have always wondered, but I accepted it because it was the way of life. Many an infant girl was killed at birth; then there was the jauhar or mass immolation following defeat in war, and, of course, sati.'

All the havelis were of a typical design, only some were larger and more ornate. What was typical in them was that the rooms did not connect. Instead all the rooms opened into the courtyard or, if they were on the first floor, on a balcony overlooking the courtyard. Some of the rooms on the first floor were roofless and were used to sleep in the hot summer months. Krishnan pointed out the special design of windows. 'It is such a well thought out system of ventilation, look,' he said as he pulled me back from the haveli to be able to see its entire height. 'There are three levels of windows. The lower ones are louvred or fretted. You can look out through them but people from the street cannot see inside. The second level of windows are higher and let in light without glare, often through coloured glass. The last level and also the highest are small windows which help to circulate the air. When the air in the room gets warm, it rises and fresh air through the lower doors and windows replaces it,' Krishnan told me, enthusiastically tracing the motions of air currents with his finger.

He told us about the love paintings: 'Some were specially commissioned and are very erotic. Some could be seen only in privacy, while making love.' We came upon one such painting on a strip of a wall behind the door which could not be seen unless the door was shut. Yet I saw that it had not escaped Prakash's attention as he was standing close to the wall taking a close-up shot. All this room had was this tiny painting and a large bed. 'There was very little furniture in the rooms,' Krishnan said. 'The concept of furniture did not exist. There were only mattresses with bolsters and platforms like the arcaded tibari. It was only when the British influence spread in Rajasthan that the havelis began to be furnished with copies of heavy European furniture, ornate mirror frames, chandeliers, glass paintings and imported lace curtains.' He looked at his watch. 'Let's go if we are to reach Fatehpur.'

*

221

Fatehpur was different from Laxmangarh. It was more like a mohalla with winding streets with spaces that changed from large to small and streets that culminated in cul-de-sacs. It reminded me of the pols of Ahmedabad. Krishnan took me to see the Nand Lal Devra haveli saying, 'You must see the fresco on the ceiling.' I noticed, when I stood under it, that it was a square ceiling with another square in the centre patterned with mirrorwork. Krishnan pulled me to a corner of the room from where he said it was easier to see. 'It is the square version of the Rasa mandala,' he said. He pointed to the border which had painted on it numerous Krishnas and gopis holding hands and dancing around the square in the centre. 'You see those pointed skirts? It shows the influence of the Jodhpur school of art. The gopis found Krishna's flute irresistible and danced around him and Krishna multiplied himself so that he could be with each of the gopis. Lucky fellow,' he said and led us away to show us something 'interesting'.

At the Motilal Bhotika haveli, there was a large elephant drawn on the wall. Elephants were like an obsession here. There were a number of things painted on the wall: a woman with a yo-yo, another one with a veena, a camel rider and a horseman. The colours were earthy—reds, browns and greens. At the bottom I noticed impressions of painted hands. 'That is what I wanted to show you,' Krishnan said. 'These are called thapas. They are present-day symbols of the practice of sati. Those widows who jumped into the funeral pyre of their husband were remembered by their handprints on the wall.'

We sat in the veranda looking towards the forecourt. It was cool and quiet, and each was engrossed in his thoughts. I remembered once more the quality of silence in the Aurobindo ashram. That was more spiritual; here it was restful, like a pause. The call of a peacock could be heard at a distance. Krishnan said, 'The Italians used water with the pigments because the lime surface acted like an adhesive. In Shekhavati, the colours were mixed in lime water or lime plaster and then were made to settle into the plaster by beating, burnishing and polishing.'

He stretched out on the floor. 'Do you know how these colours were made?' Then with an air of one who is about to tell a secret he said:'They used natural pigment.'

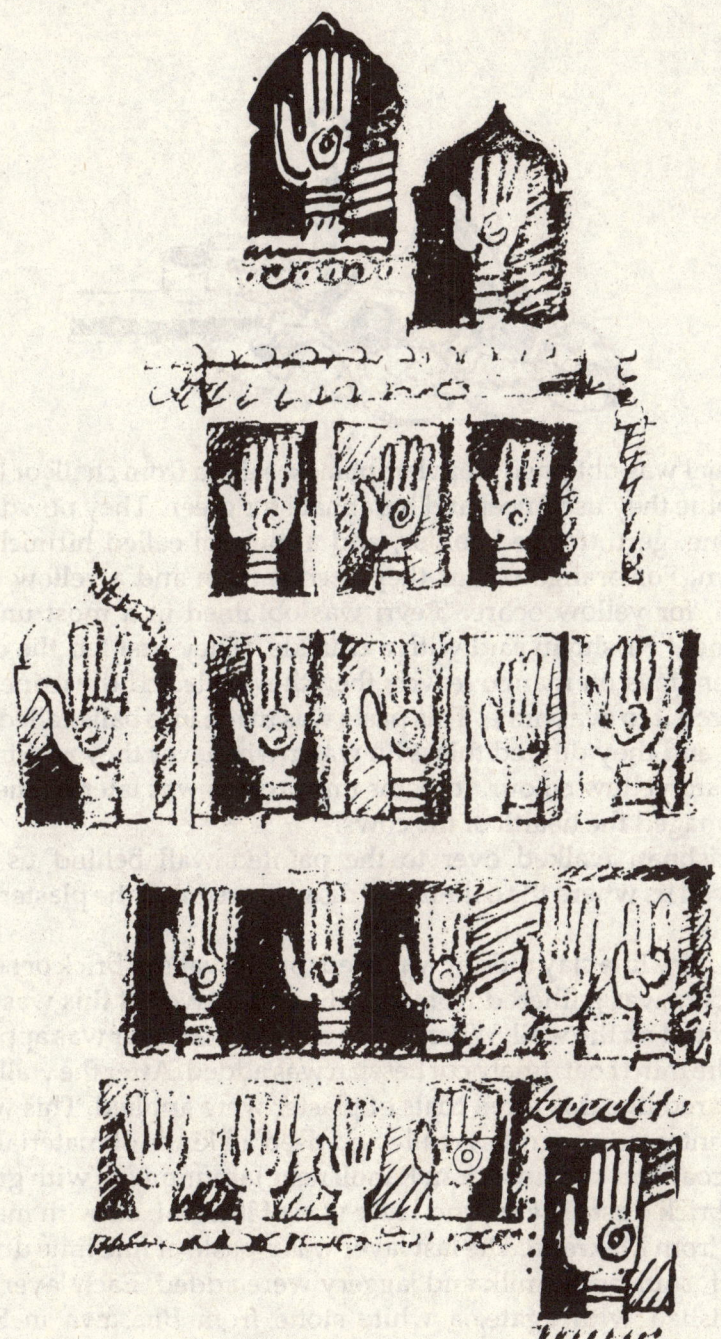

223

Kajal was obtained from lampblack, safeda from chalk or lime. For blue they used neel and harabhata for green. They powdered a stone, geru, for red colour, and a mineral called hirmich for brown. For orange colour they used saffron and a yellow clay, pevri, for yellow ochre. 'Pevri was obtained in a most unique manner,' Krishnan said with a chuckle. 'They first fed the cows for ten days on mango leaves; then they collected the urine and allowed it to evaporate. This paste was made into balls called gau golis and they diluted this with water whenever they required a brilliant yellow colour. It seems this process was later banned as it damaged the health of the cows.'

Krishnan walked over to the painted wall behind us and showed us where the colour had disappeared and the plaster was visible.

'A very fine clay mortar was used for the walls of brick or stone. The clay was gathered from anthills and a layer of this was first plastered on the wall. When it was dry another layer was applied. For the third coat, finely cut hessian was added. After the wall was prepared like this three coats of plaster were applied. This was a very interesting process really and used all kinds of material: the first coat had kali lime from Ranoli near Jaipur mixed with gravel and brick dust. The second layer was of lime mixed with marble dust from Makrana. The last layer was a paste of fine lime dust to which sour buttermilk and jaggery were added. Each layer was burnished with agate, a white stone from Bhasawa in Sikar district. The designs were painted on this last layer when it was still wet. Owing to a chemical process, as the wall dried the pigments became sealed into the plaster, which is why these frescoes have lasted so many years. A quick rubbing of agate fixed the colour and crushed coconut or its oil was applied with a soft cloth to seal it. Later when synthetic dyes were introduced from England and Germany this technique was abandoned because these dyes could not be used over wet plaster. So another technique called the frescosecco was used. This was like tempera, painting on dry plaster.'

During the next two days we travelled to Ramgarh and Nawalgarh. We saw more streets, havelis and frescoes. They had popular themes and some had humour to them and it was this aspect that surprised me most. The painters, Krishnan told me, had a free hand to explore their fantasies. Their paintings did not have to be ideological or biographical; the illustrations were invariably about local legends, animals, portraits, hunting and wrestling scenes, and glimpses of everyday life. Floral and geometric designs were used often as space-fillers. In some places the frescoes were elaborate and thematic, like the complete Ramayana painted on the ceiling of a chhatri (cenotaph) in Ramgarh. Krishna being the patron deity of the Shekhavats, the Krishna-gopi episodes were very popular.

The later frescoes, unlike the earlier ones that dealt mostly with traditional themes, were different: they were influenced by oleographs, lithographs and photographs from England and also, in particular, by the work of Raja Ravi Verma of Travancore. 'When oleographs came to Shekhavati, they became fashionable

because they were so glossy,' Krishnan told me. 'The artists were also seduced by this and they painted the contents of these imported oleographs in their frescoes. Then when photography came to India, artists painted from photographs. The queens and kings, ladies and gentlemen, warriors and merchants—all were painted. What started as a decorative art became a status symbol and the wealthy Marwaris began to emulate the British and their havelis began to appear garish. Everything changed then and the original identity was lost forever.'

*

Although the frescoes bonded all the towns of Shekhavati, Laxmangarh with its straight streets and formal composition stood out as being different. In it was the idea of the whole, making it monumental. It lacked spontaneity, unlike the other towns which were not ordered. On the other hand, there was often the danger of excessive variety in the others; it became difficult to experience a hierarchy. In Jaipur I had seen the 'whole' break into parts and in the towns of Shekhavati, the numerous parts did not define the whole.

We drove to Jaipur from Nawalgarh in a press jeep, the driver of which was kind enough to give us a ride. My thoughts went back to the havelis. It was hard to believe that they once had been full and resonated to the bustle of a large joint family. The rows of portraits of ancestors on the walls seemed grim, prepared for a life of solitude. But the streets lived on, revealing images of their history with every step through them.

Chapter 15

UDAIPUR : IT WAS ON THE WESTERN LAND ROUTE TO INDIA, and it was not so much a matter of destiny as much as prophesy that Rajputana became a conglomeration of belligerent races—the Aryans, Huns, Scythians, Turks, Afghans and others. Some of them were purified by fire to become Hindus, a conversion that was to lead to the Rajput chieftains, pledged to the protection of clan and dominion by the sword. They delighted in festivals and fairs, kept their women in purdah lest the Mughal kings kidnap them, and built for their pleasure and defence palaces, gardens, forts, citadels and towns on hills with winding streets that rambled and twisted, not just to accommodate the slope but more importantly to snare the enemy in the web of lanes.

*

It was late evening when we had arrived at Jaipur from

Shekhavati. On the way Krishnan told me about Mr. Goel. 'You must meet Goel saab,' he insisted and fixed up a lunch meeting with him in his house the next day. His house was in an old and crowded area of Jaipur. The breeze that blew through the lane smelled of wet earth, sodden leaves. It smelled of village-rain, in the groves and fields, and the same breeze had travelled into this lane, bringing news of showers in a far-off place. It was the spraying of water on the walls to cool the house that brought out the earth-musk, I later learnt.

Goel shepherded us into the dining room minutes after we arrived. The table was already set for four. When we were seated, Goel's wife entered the room from the adjoining kitchen. She almost filled the doorway; she was enormous. She wore a starched cotton saree, the pallu of which was pressed into neat folds and secured by a dazzling gilded pin, and an embroidered handkerchief was tucked into the saree at the waist. She gave us a friendly smile and soon she was filling our plates with sweetened dal and vegetables and paper-thin chapatis dripping with home-made ghee. As we ate, Goel told us about Rajasthan.

Rajwara, later called Rajputana, stitched together the states of Mewar, Udaipur, Marwar which is Jodhpur, Amber, Jaipur, Jaisalmer, Haraoti which is Kotah and Bundi, Bikaner, Kisangarh and the Indus desert. It is a land of mountains, rivers, plains and desert: the Aravalli range raises its knuckles, Mewar—the medpat—extends its flat belly; the desert plains hold the towns of Bikaner, Jodhpur, Jaisalmer; there are the river basins of the Chappan and Banas, and the salt-river, Luni.

'Did you know that ar means a hill,' Goel said. 'I recently read a book about places and names. But ar is not Sanskrit; it must be Hebrew or Greek. That is how Aravalli got its name, it means the hill of strength. And Ajmer and Jaisalmer got their names from the word meru which means a hill in Sanskrit. Jaisalmer means the hill of Jaisal and Ajmer, the hill of Ajaya. Pat is a flat land, a tableland and Medpat was the flat land of the Med tribe. The desert is called marusthali, the region of death. The Rajputs believed that they were the descendants of the sun, sea, moon and fire and for many years they were constantly engaged in battle. First they fought with other Rajput kings and then with the Mughals. But they didn't win with the Mughals. The Mughals and

Rajputs because of their wars and friendships gave birth to a hybrid culture of arts and crafts. You can see it in everything in Rajasthan, from miniature painting to architecture.'

The dining room was actually a long veranda which had been enclosed with low walls and windows. Through the door I could see the rear courtyard and an elderly woman sprinkling water from a small bucket. The way she did this was delicate, rhythmic, and it was soothing to watch her. I blinked as my eyes adjusted to the brightness after the dark of the veranda. I smelled again the sweet odour of moist earth, the most natural and unpretentious of all fragrances.

'She is Lalita, my sister,' Goel said. He called out to her. 'Lalita is a folk singer. She sings for All India Radio and gives stage performances,' Goel said with pride. 'Tell us that story about Padmini,' Goel asked his sister.

Her voice, when she spoke, bore him out. It was guttural, but musical; the raw, pulsating voice of the hill people.

'She was a beautiful queen,' Lalita said. 'Lotus faced, doe-eyed, and everyone had heard about her beauty.'

When Alauddin Khilji heard of her, she told us, he wanted to see her. He told the Rajput chief that he would retire from Chittor if he could only have a glimpse of Padmini. The Rajputs agreed to let him look at her in a mirror. But Alauddin laid an ambush and kidnapped Padmini's husband whom he promised to release in exchange for her. So Padmini set out in a veiled palanquin accompanied by maids who were actually the bravest of Rajput men. When the time was right they threw off their veils and attacked Alauddin's men and released Padmini's husband. Alauddin attacked the fort, and the women, realising the hopelessness of their predicament, decided on the ritual of jahar. The women dressed in all their finery and jumped into a huge fire. That is how Padmini and her husband Rattan Singh died and Chittor was captured.

'The Mughals were always eyeing the Rajput women,' Goel remarked. 'That is why they were kept in purdah.' Then on Goel's persuasion, Lalita sang a song for us in a gutsy voice.

It was about Pushpavati, the queen of Vallabhi. When she was offering prayers for her unborn child, she heard that Vallabhi had been attacked and that her husband had been killed. So she hid in a cave where she gave birth to a son whom she called Guhil, meaning cave-born. Then she gave her son to the maidservant, ordered a funeral pyre and walked into it. The Bhils looked after Guhil. Soon Guhil became the chieftain and his men were called Guhilots. The Guhilots moved to the plains of Mewar and called themselves Sisodia after the name of a village they had come across on the way. Rana Udai Singh was one of them. One day when he was six years old the fort was attacked and the rana was killed. Realising that the boy's life was in danger, the nurse put the sleeping heir in a fruit basket and asked the servant to take him out of the fort. She then put her own child on the prince's bed and he was killed. The entire household believed that Udai Singh had been murdered. The nurse carried the prince across the Aravalli to Asa Sah of Depra. He grew up as his nephew but because of his princely behavior people became suspicious. Rumours spread about him and the nobles of Mewar came to see him. Then the nurse told them that he was indeed the son of Rana Sanga and everyone was overjoyed.

When Akbar attacked Chittor, the capital of Mewar, Udai Singh ran away into the Aravalli hills. One morning when the rana was out by Pichola lake he saw a sage. He told him about Chittor and its fall and asked where he should build the next capital city. He was told to build it at the very spot, and that is what Udai Singh did. He dammed a mountain stream. On a cluster of hills near this he built a small place called Nauchauki around which many other buildings were built. It became a city, which he called Udaipura, the city of the east, from the word udaya—the point of sunrise.

'But it was Jagat Singh who eventually occupied the throne and who built those magnificent buildings in Udaipur,' Goel

230

concluded.

Lalita sang another song about the Ganghor festival. The tune was infectious and the rhythm throbbed in my mind hours after we had left Goel's house. When we climbed into the bus to Udaipur that night, Prakash was still whistling the lilting melody. I thought of what Lalita had told me about the festival.

The Ganghor festival was celebrated with particular fervour in Udaipur. It was the festival of Gauri, the goddess of abundance, like Isis of Egypt or Ceres of Greece. In the joyful month of Phalgun the young girls went to a spot outside the city and brought earth for the image of Gauri. With this earth they shaped the form of Gauri and a smaller one of Iswara and placed them together. Then they dug a small trench and barley seeds were sown in it. A day before the festival, the rana distributed to all the chiefs and servants either a dress of green or some portion of the dress. The women gave the barley shoots to the men who wore them happily in their turbans. The women waited in the private hall. In the palace courts, people waited expectantly for the astrologer to fix the hour to slay the boar for Gauri. The boar was the enemy of Gauri and its killing brought good fortune.

'Gauri,' Lalita had told me, 'means yellow, like ripened harvest, the colour of ripe corn. In one hand she holds a lotus, that represents birth. And in the other a warlike conch. So she is both life and death. But during Gauri puja she is only seen as Annapurna—the benefactress. That is why we must pray to her for the safety and prosperity of our men.'

When the hour arrived the men gave the signal and the guns on the castle summit announced that Gauri had commenced her excursion to the lake. The cavalcade assembled on the magnificent terrace, and the rana surrounded by the nobles led the way to the boats. The procession came winding down the slope, the goddess gorgeously arrayed in yellow robes blazing with pearls and gold. On her arrival the rana and his chiefs rose and remained standing till the goddess was seated on her throne near the water's edge. The women formed a circle around the goddess and sang and danced to drum beats and clapping of hands. The goddess was bathed and after the ablutions were over conveyed back to the palace.

Prakash gently pulled at my sleeve and I woke from my dream.

My legs were cramped and my neck hurt. The bus had stopped and a few people were getting off. 'Are we there?' I asked Prakash.

'Its another two hours to Udaipur,' he said. 'Would you like some tea?'

*

Even as we got off the coach, an auto-rickshaw drew up to me. 'Where would you like to go, sister?' the driver enquired. He was

dressed in an immaculate white shirt and trousers and seemed educated. I asked him to take us to the tourist hotel. I was tired after the overnight journey and he offered to show me around the city once I had rested. A couple of hours later we started off through the narrow streets of the city. I asked him his name. 'Girishbhai,' he said. 'Everyone knows me here and I know every place in the city. I was once a government guide but they don't pay much. I took a loan from the bank and bought this.' He looked affectionately at his shining vehicle. 'I earn much more now and because I know the history of this city, my passengers are happy with me. They tip me well.' I made a note of this.

As we swerved through the winding streets, I peered out. The buildings crouched all along the vein of the street which rose and dipped with the terrain. The street though narrow was the focus, the impression of its space intimate. The buildings along it were painted white, with colourful paintings of elephants and other motifs on the walls. Curved brackets held stone sunshades over the windows. Their form matched the undulations of the street. I learnt later they were part of what was Mewar architecture. The brackets and sunshades broke the white mass of the building and the darkened openings of windows helped the building's 'solid' form blend with the 'void' of the street.

At one moment the old city appeared like a backdrop for a historic drama which was about to unfold; at another, the enfeebled houses seem to exude a life different from what they were meant for. And on the roadside the uneven lines of small shops and wayside stalls selling vegetables, books and fashionable clothes at a discount spoke of present needs and times.

Music blared from radio sets in tea shops: the new Hindi film songs at once familiar because they were playing in every city, in every street established the changed ways, and the occasional old song harked back to older times and memories of films seen long ago. History was not absent in these streets but washed up like driftwood: barring the palaces, some of them turned to hotels, brass-studded doors opened upon messy courtyards, braced stairways led nowhere, graceful arches housed cigarette shops and neon signs dangled from brackets encrusted with pigeon droppings. Propped up forts, the skewed walls of houses, chipped mosques, crumbled mansions, forgotten lanes and rotting gateways served as signposts to the city's past life.

There were more reminders. The old city was encircled by a six-mile long bastioned wall which had eleven gateways, of which only five remained. The Suraj Pol was the main entrance to the city and the Chand Pol was the gateway from where the rana used to sight the moon. The elephant gate, Hathi Pol, at one end of the main street, was the main gate to the palace. Beyond it, Jagdish Chowk linked the palace to the rest of the city. Badi Pol and Jagdish Chowk, the first gateway to the palace, in the old days,

accommodated a hundred elephants, the rana's infantry, cavalry and artillery for inspection. From Badi Pol I could see glimpses of the Tripolia, a triple gate of marble arches. Above the Tripolia was the Hawa Mahal where the women of the palace would come to watch the street from the windows. Beyond the Tripolia was the Manek Chowk from where the high broken facade of the palace was visible. What were these gateways and courts for? The relationships between them sustained the city's life, fastening the city's parts into a pattern.

The patterns were repeated within the palace. As in the street, there were a number of chowks: Moti Chowk, Ganesh Chowk and some others. They became spatial tools of organisation of a large complex, whether a palace or a city. The chowks became gathering points during festivals and functions, they helped cool the palace, and they formed a spatial hub around which the various rooms were organised.

'They used local stone,' Girishbhai said. 'The spanning system was 8'x8' to 12'x12'. As they were using stone they had to follow definite sizes.'

Girishbhai talked about decoration and murals, marble columns, coloured glass and mirrors. What was of particular interest to me was what he explained about the walls: there were setbacks in the walls, gokhalas he called them, and the columns broke their monotony.

Girishbhai knew his history well, as too the palace. I wondered whether he had read or learnt all that he explained or whether it was just that he was very observant, a trait that I wished Prakash would display more, as all he did in the palace courts was walk behind the pigeons with his camera aimed at them. He also made pigeon sounds to placate them as he photographed their smug gait.

Whatever the pols and chowks were meant for then, today, stripped of function and history, they had become dormant landmarks on the street, and that was their new function. They turned the idle spaces in the street into places where people could stop before proceeding further. This 'place-making' was particularly needed when the street pattern was chaotic and with a hidden hierarchy which was not visible but sensed: the broader streets became main streets for this reason and for the fact that

they connected the gateways to the palace. The main bazaar and temples were located on them. They were connected to lanes which had both shops and houses and then to more private lanes which had houses alone. No street was parallel to another; they followed each other like the branches of a maze. In such a situation the pols and chowks in Udaipur, which had in the past performed various functions which no longer existed, became focal points giving the street a distinct identity, not physical but psychological; important because then people were familiar with the street.

Off the Bazaar street, the Kalash Marg which was where the kansara (coppersmith) and the soni (goldsmith) communities resided, the street was narrow, dense with three-storeyed houses sharing spaces and common walls, some with shops on the street, others with a platform. We stopped at one such house; Girishbhai had to pick up a copper vessel for his mother. There were two rooms at street level. Both were workshops. A common room, a private room on the first and on the second floor, another room and a terrace called chandni—moonlight—used in the summer months for sleeping out at night, and in winter serving as a living space, for sitting, cooking, meeting people, comprised the rest of the house.

There were two other streets: Dashora and the Chitrakala Marg. Girishbhai's friend lived on Dashora Marg.

'He is a Dashora Brahmin,' he said. 'So are most of those who live on this street.'

It was a corner house and fairly large. Girishbhai introduced us to his friend Gopinath and together with him we did a quick circuit of the house. The otla—the platform facing the street—opened onto a small space formed by a baffle wall, a modh like the one I had seen in Urmilla's haveli in Jaipur. Beyond it was the chowk from where a staircase led to the upper floor and the rooms above. One room on each of the floors had a large jharokha overlooking the street; the other rooms had no windows and opened into the chowk.

Girishbhai and Gopinath took us down the street. It was quiet, unlike the Kalash Marg where the houses opened into a bustling lane. There were hardly any people here. No doors were open and even the few windows that were open did not have people watching the street with idle curiosity. Why were the two streets so different? In appearance they were alike—narrow and winding.

'The Brahmins who live here prefer privacy,' Gopinath said.

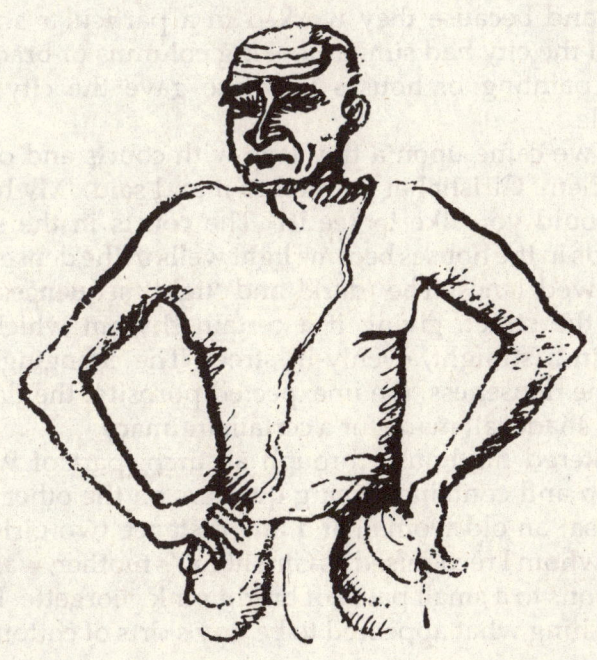

'Though they live together they do not like to mingle with people. So they build their houses inwards and not towards the street. Here people won't sit out; they prefer to sit within their houses.'

Turning into Chitrakala Marg Gopinath remarked, 'Look, this street is different. It is more open.'

It was. People sat on platforms outside their houses, many windows opened into the street and most houses had their doors open.

'The artisans live here; they like to be with other people and they are not very private,' Gopinath said as he waved to a man sitting outside his house.

He introduced us to him. 'This is Ramesh. He is a painter; he paints buildings.' Ramesh's house was small and somewhat artistic: the columns and doorways were carved out of stone and painted white, and the spaces were uncluttered.

'Most houses here were built of stone. It is used even for the floor,' Ramesh said.

He also talked about the stone parts of columns, lintels and brackets which were often carved and put in place during construction. There were only a few stone carvers and cutters who did this and because they worked in a particular style, many houses in the city had similar looking columns or brackets. This and the painting of houses in white gave the city a certain monostyle.

When we came upon a tiny lane with courts and old houses around them, Girishbhai pointed to it and said, 'My house is in there. Would you like to see it?' The courts in the street and courtyards in the houses became light wells in the dense backdrop of shadowed lanes. The 'dark' and 'light' sequences pulsated through the street, giving it a certain rhythm which is often missing in a straight, evenly-lit street. The changing width of streets, the denseness, the unexpected porosity, the dalliance of light and shade, all made for a certain intimacy.

We entered his house through an arch, part of which was walled up and contained living quarters on the other side. In a veranda sat an old woman and at a distance two girls. The old woman, whom I recognised as Girishbhai's mother, was stitching gold ribbons to a small patch of bright pink georgette. His sisters were stitching what appeared to be tiny skirts of cotton and silk.

'They make dresses for Rajasthani puppets,' Girishbhai said as he introduced us to his family.

Girishbhai's mother said, 'We have been making puppets for years. When I was a little girl I used to go to Bapu Bazaar which is close by. It was full of toy and puppet makers and the street was festooned with their products. You could see them busy working at their toys inside the houses. I knew most of them. Now they have all gone.

'In other streets there were craftsmen decorating silver and copper pots and plates. Many jewellers did meenakari. Women made tie-and-dye fabrics and pichwai paintings. Streets were working places then, now they are only choking with traffic. Times are changing.'

Various aspects of Udaipur filled my mind: its history, much of which I had gathered at Goel's house, its culture, arts, crafts and architecture; and its people who lived in white and aged houses. Now, as Girishbhai drove us up a hill in the gathering dusk, I contemplated the natural aspects of the city. The noises of the street had faded and I could hear the cicadas in the bushes, and the squawking of birds that hadn't yet returned to their nests. The sound of the leaves when a breeze stirred them sounded like the rustle of a little girl in a starched skirt running. From the top of the hill I saw the city of Udaipur. The palace looked like a fortress on a lake. It served a different purpose now. In its streets I could see the imprint of its people: how they lived and worked, their requirements and needs, immediate and current, imposed on the old.

*

Several cars were parked outside the large haveli of Ramdas Sethji. The doorman, who was in a white uniform, announced our arrival to another man and then shut the door in our faces. Sethji when we encountered him after some twenty minutes was sitting in a secluded courtyard of his sprawling haveli. He sat in a chair, a towel around his shoulders, while a young and robust man, also in uniform, applied copious quantities of oil to his hair, thick and lustrous despite his age—he must have been over sixty.

Sethji owned a prestigious antique shop in the city. He was also involved in some kind of an export-import business; he was very rich. Girishbhai worked for him in his spare time and decided that it would be profitable for us to meet him. Sethji's enormous haveli, of which we saw a lot during a guided tour that lasted almost an hour, was like a museum: all its walls were adorned with

240

miniature paintings and pichwais, swords and shields.

The library was a small room in the quietest corner of the haveli. It had a wooden floor which was carpeted here and there. There were bookshelves in teak and the smell of wood and old books lingered like nostalgia. Light came in through a single window. The wall opposite it was covered with paintings. They were all pichwai paintings of Nathdwara similar to the one I had seen in Girishbhai's house in Ahmedabad. Brilliant in their colours, some were adorned in gold and jewels. A bearer brought us some tea spiced with cardamom. We sat around an antique table near the window sipping the tea.

'What does pichwai mean?' Prakash asked.

'Pichwai literally means something at the back,' Sethji said. 'They were used as a backdrop to the idol of Krishna in Nathdwara.'

The pichwais depict scenes of worship or events in Krishna's life. In the late fifteenth and early sixteenth centuries there were many sects that worshipped Krishna. The Hare Krishna movement, now very popular in the West, was one of them. The founder of this movement was Chaitanya. He was a Bengali mystic and he preached that Krishna should be intensely worshipped, adored. This the sect did through ecstatic dancing and singing. But the sect of Vallabhacharya followed the Pushti Marg (way of grace)which believed that salvation came from God alone. He did not prescribe such display as a form of worship. Another aspect of this sect which made it different from that of Chaitanya's was that the worship was done in private temples which were designed like rambling havelis with many courtyards and shrines. They were quite different from the normal Hindu temples. The temple was considered God's household and every luxury was bestowed on him. The whole idea of worship in this case was directed toward aesthetic enjoyment, rasa. The meaning of rasa is sap or juice but it also denotes ineffable bliss. That was the sole idea of Vallabhacharya's preaching.

Amongst all the pichwais on Sethji's wall the most colourful was the one showing the Rasalila, the festive dance. It was Sethji's favourite. It had eight Krishnas, each with a gopi dancing beside him. There were twenty-two panels around the painting showing the adornment of Srinathji during the seasonal festivals. There were many variations to the Rasalila and Sethji explained some of those that adorned his library wall. Then over another cup of cardamom tea, he talked about the Rasalila and the Rasa mandala.

When Krishna was growing up, he played many pranks on the gopis. They were in love with him and to win Krishna, the gopis decided to bathe in the month of Aghan which is auspicious for washing away one's sins, and ask the goddess Gauri for a boon. Krishna of course stole their clothes while they were in the water. He promised to return them if they met him in the following new year. When this reunion took place, it was late autumn, and Krishna danced with all the gopis in a circle. He used the magic of maya to duplicate his image several times. This was the Rasa mandala and Krishna's various games or sport with the gopis was the Rasalila.

'It's only thirty miles from here. Why don't you go to Nathdwara?' Sethji suggested as we parted.

*

We went to Nathdwara the next day with Girishbhai. He told us the story of Nathdwara: 'The Hindus in Mathura were very scared because Aurangzeb had prohibited idol worship. As you know, Mathura was the home of Lord Krishna. They asked the maharana of Mewar to look after the Lord's idol. He agreed. So the idol was put on a chariot and sent to Mewar. On the way, at Sihar, the wheel of the chariot sank deep into the ground. They believed that Lord Krishna wanted to stay there. This is how this unknown village of Sihar became the home of Srinathji and it is since then called Nathdwara.'

Nathdwara struck us as a dusty, decrepit town. There was more dust as busloads of people rushed towards the street that led to the temple. There was only this one street. All along it were shops selling pichwais or silver and gold jewellery. In some shops you could see the artists at work. People walked along the street incessantly, like a river flowing downstream. It was as though a magnet at the other end of the street pulled them along. I was eager

243

to see the source of such force.

When we reached the temple at the end of the lane I was disappointed. It was like any other haveli. It had a number of halls and courts and elephants painted on the outer walls. There was no grand doorway or steps or shikharas. In other words it was not like a temple at all.

Next to the temple was a little lane. It branched into many more lanes and like capillaries they spread into the town encircling the temple. Each lived its own life and pace divorced from the main street that led to the temple. The houses followed the contours of the hill. Steps and platforms announced their presence; windows, brackets and sunshades pierced their facade. Some of the houses were made of mud. In the quietness of the inner lanes I could hear the murmuring of pigeons. In one of them was a marriage procession in progress: Orange, yellow, pink, blue—the bright colours of skirts and turbans danced against the white of the walls. Suddenly the local band burst into music. The quietness faded, the lane became a pulsating river of sound and colour, and in the distance the bells of the temple called.

'Let's go,' Prakash said, 'there's nothing much here.'

'Only the temple,' I said, 'but this town exists because of it.'

'So what is surprising?'

'Remember what Chaturvedi said about different kinds of towns. This is a temple town and there is nothing else.'

People travelled from afar to worship the idol of Srinathji and in a few hours left, as we did. By dusk the streets emptied of visitors; buses and cars took them away. The shops closed their shutters and the owners of the few restaurants called out to their last customers before they also closed. When all had left, and the rest had shut, the rhythms of life in this small temple town remained, and in their slowness was a promise of permanence.

Chapter 16

JAISALMER: FEUDALISM WAS AT THE ROOT OF THE NOBLEST DEEDS and deepest crimes. Kingdoms were won and new capitals built at the behest of ascetics living in the forest to whom the superstitious Rajputs went for guidance. Such were the ascetics who recommended Jodha to erect a castle on the hill of strife and Jaisal to construct his on the triple peaked hill; one recommended for its impregnability, the other linked to a legend that brought Lord Krishna and Arjun to the site to attend a great sacrifice. The castles were built but the former was condemned to have only brackish water and the latter, it was prophesied, would be sacked two and a half times.

*

It was over ten years since I had last met Lila. She was my cousin, daughter of my maternal aunt. When she opened her tresses they would bounce up, like a bunch of tiny springs, into little curly strands that engulfed her small head. That and her pock-marked face was what had stayed in my memory.

Lila's parents, my aunt and uncle, were orthodox Tamil Brahmins, and though Lila was allowed to go to college (she was a double graduate) they were eager to get her married from the day she turned nineteen. She had married Sunderam after their horoscopes had been carefully matched. He worked for the tourism department and was posted in Calcutta. They had been transferred to many other cities since then and now they were in Jodhpur.

Lila's mother, when I informed her about my likely visit to Jodhpur, had sent me parcels of foodstuffs from Madras through a friend who had visited Bombay; she also insisted that I should stay with her daughter during my visit. So after Prakash had checked in his belongings at a small hotel we made our way to Lila's house. Two boys playing outside started shouting as soon as our rickshaw reached her bungalow. Hearing them, Lila appeared at the door, looking much thinner than before. She was wearing a pink cotton blouse and a blue nylon sari that did not match. She smelt of soap and talcum powder and on her forehead was a smear of vibhuti (ash); she seemed to have just finished her puja. She enquired about her mother and mine as she led me in. Prakash followed, gallantly carrying some of my luggage along with his own heavy camera bag while the gardener carried the rest, including the bag of foodstuffs.

The house was a typical northern house, the kind I had seen in Jaipur and Udaipur. It had a central court around which various rooms were arranged. It also had a backyard with a service gate at the end of it. Besides the living room everything about the house was typically south Indian: the tall pedestal brass or gun metal lamps, rolled-up reed mattresses and naked bulbs (in many houses of the middle class in the south the bulbs and tubelights never have shades, unlike in the north).

Beyond the formal living room was another long room that connected to the kitchen and the bedrooms on either side of it; it also opened into the central court. This room had no furniture except for two aluminium reclining chairs with seats of striped nylon. It also had a washbasin over which was a small broken mirror and a shelf with comb, toothpaste and toothbrushes on it. There was a green plastic soap dish in which were the gooey remains of Lifebuoy soap, and a thin cotton towel, damp and stained, hung from a rack near the basin. The room was painted a flashy blue and on the wall were hung framed pictures of Lakshmi, Saraswati, Shiva and Muruga, the last a favorite god of south Indians.

The living room of Lila's house, unlike the rest of it, was typically north Indian in decor: it had a divan with a phulkari bedspread and mirrorwork cushions. There were carved Kashmiri tables and chests. The TV was covered with a beadwork cloth; the walls displayed miniature paintings on silk and blue ceramic plates of Jaipur. Puppets in Rajasthani costumes hung from hooks in the ceiling, and, to complete the picture, at one end of the room was a swing suspended by brass links from the ceiling. It was as though the south Indian identity was being camouflaged to conform to a culture that was very different.

Sunderam walked into the kitchen just as Lila was frying the papdams. He was fair and tall and had a large bald patch which he covered with long strands of greying hair combed back to front. He had smeared ash right across his forehead and like Lila smelt of soap and talcum powder. He wore a white full-sleeved shirt and a white veshti. The latter he kept opening, wrapping and tucking often as he stood in the kitchen talking to me. He would lift his shirt, hold it with his chin and tie his veshti tighter. He talked about himself, his job and his new passion—conservation. He was a member of a committee working on the conservation of the old parts of the city and he was full of fervour about it. 'Jodha built Jodhpur on the recommendation of a jogi,' he said. The jogi told Jodha to erect his castle on the hill of strife, Jodhgir. It was good for defence, but neither Jodha or the jogi realised that a good water source was also needed besides all the defence plans. Everyone blamed the jogi and not Jodha because he was a popular king; and the ascetic swore that the castle would have only brackish water. Many sons of Jodha tried to obtain better water by blasting the rock, but failed. Eventually they had to construct an apparatus that lifted the water from the lake.

After lunch Sunderam took us in his jeep to see the fort. I was not keen on seeing it but relented because he was so excited about taking us there. In the distance I could see the rugged stone walls of the fort and its tower like bastions. All forts appeared more or less the same to me: large, rambling and formidable with large gates which invariably had a smaller gate within them. The big gate was meant for a large royal or festive procession and the smaller gate was meant for people to walk in one by one. I had marvelled at the sense of scale and proportion of the ancient builders and how they had built a single gateway to accommodate both the individual and the crowd.

As we proceeded uphill I saw a couple, a man and a woman, who seemed to be gypsies. The man started to play a tune on a stringed instrument and as we stopped the woman began to dance to the music. Her glorious yellow skirt swayed with her movements. Prakash spread out his lenses and rapidly began to shoot the couple. He also made me take a photograph of him with them. As he was about to jump into the jeep the woman caught him by his shirt and demanded a hundred rupees for the photographs. After much haggling and abuses in a dialect unfamiliar to us, Prakash paid her fifty and she happily tucked the note into her bodice and marched away. 'The women here are ferocious, you must be careful,' Sunderam advised Prakash as he started the jeep.

As we skirted a corner I saw thousands of houses huddled below the hill. They were all painted a bluish white and glinted in the afternoon sun as would a lake. 'Brahmpuri,' Sunderam said as he slowed the jeep. I was more keen to see it than the fort and tried to convince Sunderam to take us there. After much protest he consented, on condition that we went to the fort later. 'Mainly Brahmins live here; it is one of the first areas to be built in Jodhpur.

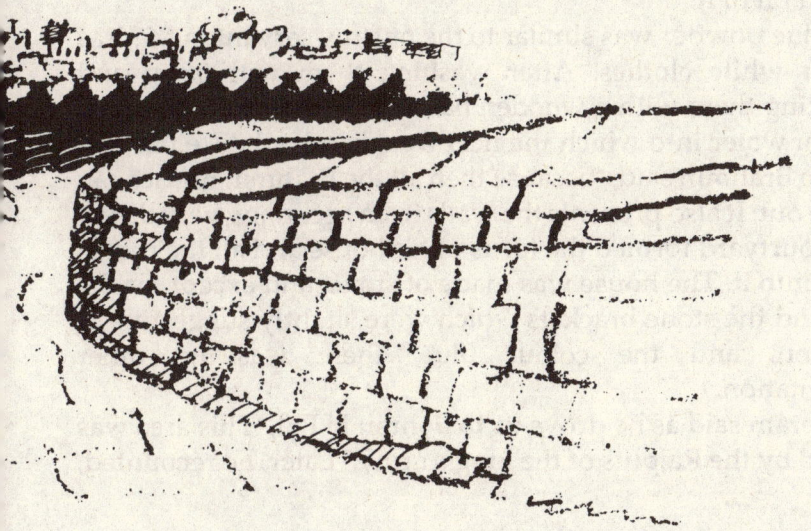

'I know some of them. We donate food and money to them for my father's devasam (death anniversary),' he told us.

The streets were narrow and sloped through most of their length; here and there they folded into steps to negotiate an abrupt change of level. People sat on a platform under a spreading neem tree. Near them, children played marbles. Opposite was a small temple. A Brahmin with the sacred thread across his bare chest came up to Sunderam with folded hands. The dhoti didn't look very clean and he looked in need of exercise. He quickly took us into his house after Sunderam had explained to him the purpose of our visit. We climbed a flight of steps that reached a platform onto which the main door opened. He dusted a chair for Sunderam while we sat down on a mattress on the floor.'It is because of the colour code,' the Brahmin said when I asked him why all the houses were blue. 'Many Brahmins live here, there are also others of different castes, but all Brahmin houses are washed with blue,' he said.

He went into the house and shortly returned with a newspaper packet. He dipped his hand into it and showed me the blue colour in his hand. 'This is neel,' he said. 'When we whitewash the walls we add a bit of it.'

The blue powder was similar to the one my servant in Madras used for white clothes. After washing them with soap and hammering them with a wooden bat, she would soak them in a bucket of water into which the neel was dissolved. 'We use this neel,' the Brahmin said, 'because then all the Brahmin houses can be made out. It also prevents the walls from becoming very dirty.'

The courtyard formed the focus of his house and all the rooms opened into it. The house was made of stone, and except for the arches and the stone brackets which were slightly suggestive of decoration, and the colour blue, there was no other ornamentation.

Sunderam said as he drove us to Bohran ki Pol, 'This area was occupied by the Rajputs of the king's army.' Later, he recounted,

Shivji, a moneylender, helped the king and the king asked him to come and live in Jodhpur. Shivji sent his son and his family and they were given the Bohran ki Pol area as a gift. They lived here for years; their family grew and they occupied the whole area. 'Only people of the Bohran caste (moneylenders) live here,' he said. 'Some of the houses are three hundred years old.'

The houses were densely packed, which I presumed was intentional and necessary given the nature of their profession and work. There was a single entrance gate from which two streets led into the clusters of houses. The streets were not exactly streets; they were more like courts connected by a corridor.

As we drove around the city, here and there I saw the broken walls of the fort. There were gates, but the city had expanded and the gates were denied their hegemony. Flanked by massive bastions and surmounted by battlements, they were built keeping in mind the small population and their mode of traffic. Today they couldn't accommodate either.

The inner streets were full of turns. One could never look down the entire street. They contained bazaars, the Aada Bazaar and the Ubha Bazaar. As the names suggested, one ran through the city and the other across it. There was no vehicular traffic in them as often there were steps to negotiate the uneven climb. They were stone paved and had trees, otlas, wells and temples, shaded by the buildings along them. All this gave them a strong community structure, private and confined. At the Chudi Bazaar, steps from the road led to the shops which were narrow and long like passageways. Separate flight of steps led to residences above. It was fine for the streets that were to be viewed from afar to be geometric, but those that were to be experienced needed texture and detail. I found it in these streets: buildings, the distances between them, boundaries, symmetry and asymmetry and the relationship between the inside and outside. Nuances were necessary. The asymmetrical streets, like those here, were spontaneous; they grew in any direction and the parameters then shifted to topography: steps, parapets, ramps, turns, which formed the nuances.

They were old and beautiful, the gates, the mohallas, the houses and streets with their fistfuls of history. Overused, abused and

out-of-use, parts of them were in ruin. They confessed their sins in a secretive murmur to an ancient sky, and it, raising its arms, absolved them with its silent gaze.

*

'I must tell you about Lodurva,' Sunderam said while Lila brought us filter coffee. 'It was a capital town some fifteen kilometres from Jaisalmer ruled by the Lodra Rajputs. In the end Jaisal became the ruler of Lodurva. But later he decided to build another capital. A hermit, Eesal, told him about the triple-peaked hill that overlooked his hermitage. So Jaisal built Jaisalmer there and all the people left Lodurva and built their homes in Jaisalmer.' Lila and Prakash had stepped out of the dining room and into the courtyard. Prakash was taking a photograph of Lila as she posed beside a tall plant. As I looked at Lila, she waved out to me to join them. Sunderam and I walked into the moonlit court. Prakash took some more photographs; the camera flash startled the little dog tied to a chair. The desert breeze dried the sweat on our faces. In the distance a peacock cried; another one answered its call. The crickets stopped their chirping for a moment.

*

We set out early in the morning, Prakash, Sunderam and I. The jeep made its way through miles of sand and dust. Once in a while a thorny tree appeared. Prakash shouted frequently, 'Look, look there, a peacock!' He persuaded Sunderam to stop the jeep to photograph one of them, but the bird stared at Prakash, turned and waddled away.

The Jaisalmer fort, when we reached it after several hours, looked yellow and weathered like an aged lion. Like one, it wore an air of magnificence. Its meandering walls bulged here and there into large bastions. Sunderam had told me it was made without any mortar and now I could see this. A second wall ran parallel to the main wall. This, Sunderam told me, was built later to strengthen the main wall. It was interestingly called ghaghranuma, which meant skirt-like, and was only fifteen feet high, half the height of the main wall.

In the main market square, Manik Chowk, village women sat with baskets of parched vegetables as wrinkled as their skins. Beside them were a number of rickshaws and jeeps waiting for passengers. The Ganesh Pol announced the fort, the sun emblem on the Suraj Pol greeted the morning rays of the sun.

Large mansions towered over the Royal Square. The Hawa Pol, a gateway to the royal palaces, meandered to the main enclosure—the court of public audience and spectacle. It was here that jauhar was committed. There was a well. 'There was a rivulet here,' Sundaram said. 'Lord Krishna and Arjun came down to attend a great sacrifice near the rivulet. Krishna on seeing the place said that in some distant age a descendant of his would build a large castle. Arjun, who was thirsty, drank the water and told him that the water was brackish. Krishna hit the rock with his chakra whereupon a sweet spring flowed.'

We walked down a lane from the Royal Square. A few of the houses had been converted into shops selling local crafts and paintings. Embroidered or tie-and-dye bedcovers were hung across the walls. There were gypsies in the street. They chased the foreigners, thumping their chests confidently and saying 'Photo, photo.' Seeing Prakash with his camera they came after him. A bit wiser now, he shook his head violently. Instead he focused his attention on a woman who was standing outside her house. She

looked kind and docile but as soon as she spied Prakash focusing his camera on her, she yelled at him and shut the door with a bang.

'Come, this is where Muniji lives,' Sunderam said to me. He wanted me to meet an old Jain muni who was, according to him, a very learned man. Inside the house it was dark, cool and bare. To one side of the main passage was a raised area and sitting in a window there was girl in a faded pink blouse and blue skirt. Her long hair was secured in two long plaits that reached to her waist. The living room had no furniture. It had a small kitchen on one side and a trapdoor to the basement on the other. As we stood in the passage, the little girl went in and fetched Muniji.

'I was born here. My father was a muni in the temple,' Muniji said as we sat in the nook off the passage. 'I started learning the scriptures as a little boy and now I look after the temple. Many Jains come from all over the country to pray here,' he said.

Someone called out from the street and the girl ran out. She returned and told Muniji what their neighbour Hiralal Jain had said. 'My neighbour wants me to go to his house. He has a visitor who wants to see the temple. I have to take him there. Why don't you come with me?' We walked across the street to Jain's house. Intricately carved stone pillars marked the doorway into the living room. Within was a large court, larger than the living room. The rooms facing the court had beautiful jalis fixed below cusped stone arches; there were no windows. Above and looking into the court was an exquisitely carved jharokha in stone. Hiralal Jain's house was very large compared to Muniji's house. He was a wealthy man.

We walked to the Parsvanatha temple. 'It is the Solanki architecture from the Vaghela school of Gujarat,' Sunderam explained. 'In Jain temples, although they are so decorative, it is the serene atmosphere within which is more important.' We removed our footwear and had to deposit our camera bag and all articles of leather. It was fragrant and quiet inside. 'It is the smell of sandalwood and flowers and the delicate aroma of dasanga dhupa, the incense made up of ten fragrant ingredients,' Muniji said. Blending with all this was also the smell of ghee from the burning lamps, and the repetitive sounds of bells ringing and the reading of psalms.

The visitor wanted to look at the ancient Jain manuscripts that are kept within the temple. The Muni took him inside while Hiralal waited with us. 'This temple was constructed by Jai Singh, an Oswal Seth,' he said. 'The deity here is Parsvanatha which was brought from Lodurva after it was captured. This temple was built by an architect called Shilpi Dhanna.'

Sunderam added, 'There is a prescribed plan that most Jain temples follow.'

'The entrance to the main temple complex is through the mukha-chatuski which is a pillared porch. The toranas which are like inverted festoons form the arches. There are three types of torana arches: illika which looks like a crawling caterpillar, the mandala-tilaka which is serpentine, and the double twisted mandala tilika. There is an oblong platform, the jagti, with a stairway in the centre. A little distance from the stairway and on the central axis is the mulanyaka, the main deity. The place where the mulanyaka is kept is the garbhagriha. There is a decorated hall in front of it where the devotees assemble for prayer. This whole arrangement forms the main temple, the mulaprasada. There is another hall, the gudhamandapa. It is enclosed within walls and is attached to the main temple. In the same line as the gudhamandapa and connected to it is a pillared vestibule, mukhamandapa. It leads to the rangamandapa, the dancing hall. The rangamandapa in this temple has eleven bejewelled pillars with mouldings and human figurines.'

Back at Hiralal's house for lunch, we sat on low stools outside the kitchen. While we ate, Hiralal's wife serving us deliciously-prepared dal and vegetables, Hiralal told us about the

rich traders of Jaisalmer. 'There was a Patua clan in Jaisalmer who used to deal in zar and badla (silver and gold threads) ornaments. One Patua seth called Dev Raj had a son, Guman Chand. He was very shrewd and made a lot of money. He had five sons, one of whom became a successful moneylender. He was so successful that even the maharajas, Marathas and Britishers sought his help. He finally settled down in Indore and at that time he had business in over three hundred places. His four brothers also made their fortune and fame. Guman Chand built for his five sons a row of enchanting havelis.' Hiralal went on all through lunch to describe the wealth and fortune of many Rajputs and the havelis they built in Jaisalmer.

The Patua havelis were six-storey structures. A flight of steps led to the main gate which was on a plinth about seven feet high. The high plinth, Hiralal had explained to me, was because of the dust-laden lanes. There were cells below the plinth on the street side. These cells were ventilated by star-shaped skylights and were meant to store merchandise. On the first floor and above were the halls and rooms which were richly decorated. There were small and splendidly ornate niches for oil lamps—ala. There were also separate lamp stands moulded into the wall. There were in all sixty-six jharokhas in the haveli. In the first and second floors they were provided with wooden shutters but on the upper floors they were covered with beautiful stone arabesques.

In the Patua haveli as in the others in the fort, sandstone was used with the screens or embossed panels inserted into the grooves cut for them. The havelis were distingiushed by the balconies, galleries, deeply carved bangaldars (Bengali bowed roof), cusped arches, baluster colonettes and floral panels. These formed a style of architecture which was a blend of Hindu and Mughal architecture and, much later, that of the British Raj.

*

I woke the next morning at five. I opened the window which I had shut the previous night to keep away the desert insects. The air was cool and smelt of crushed nuts. I wanted to go back to the fort again, to see it in the morning light, in its everyday routine,

without the tourists and foreigners who thronged its winding streets. I put on my shoes, picked up my camera and stepped out of the house. I took pictures of the rising sun and wild desert flowers. I also took pictures of the new buildings that were built of the same yellow stone, but they lacked the rhythm that rippled through the walls of the fort.

There were gaunt bushes by the road, sparsely decked with pink and yellow flowers, and in the distance, a few trees. The dawn made a soft leap out of the sky and enveloped me with light before I reached the fort. Within it there were sounds of waking up. It was as though an entire town was awakening, bit by bit: there was the noise of water as little children bathed next to the open drains in front of their houses, and the sound of vessels being scrubbed. People were out on the platforms, in the street and at windows, talking animatedly. I had not seen as many women and children the day before.

Although public spaces demanded formality and required a definite outline, this restricted growth and use. It also affected the behaviour of people and curbed individual freedom. The streets of Jaisalmer changed from morning onwards, not physically but in the way that people used them. Freedom is an important dimension of the street. With it comes spontaneity, recycling of use, participation. Without it the streets become culture-free.

A woman called out to me and I walked up to where she stood, outside her house. After some inquiry she led me in. There was a horse-head over the door. Sunderam had told me about the houses and the various rooms in them. I walked into the mol, the living room; it had exuberant trellis work with leaf and floral motif. As I walked through the various spaces I recollected what Sunderam had explained. He had told me that the houses were planned to keep out the dust and also to be cool. The front space outside the mol was called moda and the back, pathiyal. The mol on the first floor was called medi. In the balconies there were bed rolls and people enjoyed opium together. He had showed me a contraption in Hiralal's house which was used to smoke opium.

He had also told me about stone-carving. The Sanskrit texts explained the art of latticework. However it was in the Mughal times that this art developed and spread to reach Jaisalmer. The jalis in the houses were not exactly perforated screens but the motifs were cut deep into the stone. He had told me about the geometrical patterns and motifs that were used in the latticework. The most popular were the chaublas (checkers), chhayas (hexagons), athas (octagons) and khatarvas (arcs).

The woman in the blue saree took me to the terrace. A ramp

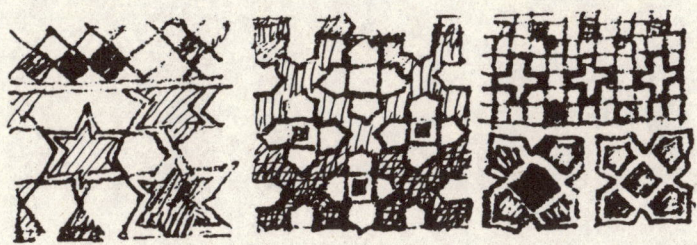

from it led to the fort wall. 'There is an old cannon at the top and from there one can see the entire fortress town,' she said.

I climbed to the top and saw the houses and the winding streets harnessed within the fort walls. The sun shone on the terraces and paved lanes and its light danced off them. Its brightness hurt my eyes. I closed them. When I opened my eyes, for a moment I could see large black patches and through them I saw the silhouettes of the havelis and palaces like blurred images . In my mind, though, the picture was intact: Jodhpur with its torturous optional routes that connect one place to another not by a straight line but by a temperamental zigzag conceived for defence; Jaisalmer built by rich traders who abandoned their ornate havelis for more riches and modern villas away from the heat and dust of the desert. Now only the walls remain like bones of the dead, trapped in the web of history that links one street to another, one haveli to another, while the sandstone that carved the city yellows.

Chapter 17

LUCKNOW: WHEN THE FAR-SIGHTED MUGHALS WERE NOT manoeuvring for power or engaged in hostilities, they were connoisseurs of art, music, dance and architecture. They perfected a manner of courtly behaviour known for its delicacy of language and gesture. The Nawabs of Oudh further refined it and the city of Lucknow is described as the last example of courtly grace. The architecture—what remains of it—affirms this character: filigreed palaces, fringed windows, fancy balconies. Though the crammed alleys, the houses that crumble upon one another amid clouds of soot, the dust and filth under the feet speak of a reality quite different.

*

Prakash's friend, Ameena, was a pretty woman. They had met when she had come to Bombay to study journalism at the Xavier

Institute, after which she had returned to Lucknow where her parents lived. While I was making arrangements for us to go to Benaras he decided he must see Ameena, and here we were. The train had been eleven hours late and whoever had come to fetch us had presumably left.

We were in the prospect of being swindled by the rickshaw driver when Ameena and her brother pulled up in a Maruti van. The rickshaw driver hurriedly reduced his price and, still unsuccessful, dumped our luggage from his vehicle onto the road. Prakash looked a little perplexed, but then he always did. He loaded our luggage into the van and we hurried down the darkened streets towards Farangi Mahal Mohalla.

Luckow, called Lakshmanpur before the Mughals established their rule, has an interesting history. Aurangzeb was dying when Saadat Khan, a Persian from Nishapur, came to India. When he learnt that Aurangzeb's successor was a Shia he decided to be employed at the Delhi court. He became a faujdar or superintendent of a district in Agra, and later the governor of the province of Oudh. At that time Oudh was ruled by many feudal barons and Saadat Khan had to fight his way into Lucknow, which he made his headquarters.

Safdar Jang, Saadat Khan's nephew, became the governor after his uncle's death. In fact the relationship between the Mughal court at Delhi and the nawabs of Oudh was a tenuous one, despite the fact that the very title 'nawab' in Persian meant deputy. After Safdar Jang, his son Shuja-ud-daula became the governor and his forceful governorship attracted the attention of the English East India Company. Initially Shuja-ud-daula resisted the British efforts to gain control. However, the British defeated him in battle and later magnanimously reinstated him as the Nawab of Oudh. Then came two more nawabs: Asaf-ud-daula and Wajid Ali. It was during this time that Lucknow flourished and became a city-culture of ostentation and refinement.

In more ways than one, therefore, Lucknow was a Muslim city and looked it. Islam played a dominant part in the development of the social, cultural and economic aspects of the city. The Muslims who came to India for the first time had established themselves in Sind and Multan. They had come as traders to south

India much before this. However, actual contingence between the Muslim and Hindu culture began not with the occupation of Punjab and Multan but when the Delhi Sultanate was established. Prior to this the country was a complex structured society determined by the religions of Hinduism, Jainism and Buddhism.

As a result of this contingence a stylistic development of Islamic architecture occurred: it was a hybrid style wherein true Islamic architectural forms were blended with Hindu architectural and craft traditions. Out of this fusion were born many formal relationships of building elements, particularly the pillared arched verandas and introverted chowks.

A small side street brought us to the Farangi Mahal Moholla which was a cluster of old and newer houses. Upon entering the quarter and immediately to the right was the main building of the mohalla which I learnt later was the Farangi Mahal Madrasa. It was very similar to the other houses in the mohalla, but much larger. Ameena's house also was very large. 'Abbajan, Prakash and his friend are here,' Ameena called as we entered through a side door into a veranda. Ameena's father emerged briefly to greet us before going back to sleep. He was an old man with bright eyes which matched the henna tints on his beard. When we met him later in the day, he told us about himself. He was a cloth merchant and business was not so good. He had five daughters and a son who was married. One of his elder daughters was to be married soon. Ameena was the youngest and she would have to wait till her sisters were married.

We were sitting in an enclosed veranda; actually the whole house was made of such enclosed verandas called dalans around a large central courtyard. We sat on a divan. Behind us, shelves in the wall contained photographs. A calendar with pictures of film stars hung nearby. It was bright and glossy, in fact it was the only bright and glossy spot in the entire house. On the table was an album of wedding photographs of his son, film magazines and a jar of home-made biscuits. In one corner, a money-plant flourished in a large glazed ceramic pot. An arch opened into the branches of some sweet-smelling foliage; there was a harmonium and a tabla on one side. Near the divan were two cane shatranjis to sit on. From the ceiling hung huge bulbous lights. I noticed the objects one by one; they were numerous enough to be noticed and few enough to be counted and remembered. But what registered most was the sense of space—contained within the dalan and spilling into the courtyard, it imparted composure, an accommodating presence to the partially enclosed room.

The private rooms beyond the dalans were bare but in a way that conveyed austerity rather than poverty. It made me remember what I had read: that poverty meant displacement as well as lack, while austerity meant being poor in a rooted way, within a tradition of culture of sparseness and restraint, which transformed even the absence of things into a kind of being. Seeing this house I could understand the difference. The entire house and the people in it were in a state of 'being', which made it all right despite becoming worn with the years.

Over cups of hot flavoured tea Ameena's father told us about the mohalla. 'This is an unusual part of Lucknow and if you were walking down the chowk you wouldn't even know such a place exists. This area is called Farangi Mahal, the Frankish quarter or the European quarter,' he said. 'The East India company had sent two employees to live here and buy bales of "dereabauds", a kind of muslin made in Hasangunj in Lucknow. In those days goods were being sent from Lucknow to Surat. Many more people were sent later to cure and bleach the muslin in the Lucknow factory.

However because more people were needed and the cost of transport was becoming excessive, the factory was closed. Initially the Farangi Mahal was a cluster of buildings but later the name came to mean the entire mohalla. You can see it even now, or whatever is left of it,' he said. 'It is a mixture of old and new walls. There is a large central space around which the pre-nawabi houses are built. A large gateway on a side street leads into it.'

When I saw it later in the day I found that the houses were no different from the typical Lucknowi house with rooms around a central court, only they were larger. Some parts of the Farangi Mahal were typically European but essentially the Mahal was an eclectic mix of architectural styles, both imported and indigenous.

After a rushed breakfast which consisted of parathas and mince meat and potatoes left over from the previous night, Ameena took us to the Chauk Bazaar where her uncle had a cloth shop. 'It is one of the oldest streets in Lucknow,' Ameena said. 'All these mohallas came much later. At the beginning there was nothing but two hills and the Brahmins who were the first settlers built a shrine on one of them. It was later replaced by a mosque by Aurangzeb which still stands on the hill.' I watched her as she spoke. She was short and slim and her curly hair was neatly drawn away from her face and plaited. Her skin was pale and the eyes had a tint of grey in them. She had perfect features: soft and baby-like. That and her voice that matched her features made her very likable. She was dressed in a blue kurta and a white salwar. A white chiffon dupatta draped her shoulders. As we walked through the lanes Prakash frequently ran in front of her with his camera, imploring her to stop as he took a picture of her. She posed but shyly.

'The main bazaar road runs parallel to this lane, but it is very noisy and crowded. It is better to go this way, though it is filthy.' I could faintly hear the hum of traffic; we were very close to the main road. Yet the lane was much quieter. This kind of street structure with winding lanes, courts and cul-de-sacs acted as a baffle to noise. I had noticed this in other cities as well.

Most of the doors to the houses were closed. No one sat outside on the platforms or peeped from balconies or windows. In fact none of the houses seemed to have any balconies; at least not the bigger mansions. But it was not unusual to find, on entering an insignificant doorway in these narrow and dirty alleys, a splendid courtyard with decorated rooms, gardens and fountains.

From the inner street we turned into a short lane which brought us abruptly into the Chauk Bazaar. The two ends of the street were marked by the Akbari Gate which had replaced an older gate, and the Gol Darwaza, a circular structure which stood in the middle of the street. There were shops with verandas abutting the street and residences above them. Ameena's uncle's shop lay midway along the street. On one side of the shop were mattresses covered with white bedsheets. Ameena's uncle and other salesmen sat on them. Behind them were glass shelves with all kinds of chikan work cloth and sarees. In front of them was a low counter that ran the shop's length. There were low stools for the customers to sit on, and more glass cases with merchandise on the opposite wall.

Ameena's uncle was much younger than her father, around forty-five and stout. He looked as fresh as someone just back from a haircut and massage. Yusufbhai stood up to greet us. Then, seeing that Prakash was struggling to untie his laces, he said, 'No, that's not necessary. I have done up my shop now. Look, we have counters and stools. Like, modern shops.'

Yusufbhai procured bales of cotton muslin and fine silk. These were bleached or dyed and cured in a factory. Then he had the cloth embroidered. He showed us around the place. It was basically an old house converted into a workshop and shop. In the large paved court, women sat fixing buttons to the embroidered kurtas. He took us to the first floor, which served as the residence. One could look down through the iron grille that roofed the courtyard and see the women working. Prakash scampered across the grille on his toes, taking photographs of the women below.

Yusufbhai's wife was sitting on a swing in the veranda, cutting french beans into a plate. She was plumper than her husband and rosier. Her teeth were stained with pan and even as she worked she opened a silver domed box beside her and took out a fresh pan. She called out to a boy to bring sherbet for us. With it came an assortment of biscuits and sweets. The sherbet was green in colour and very sweet. Yusufbhai drank it with relish and started to tell us about Lucknow.

In old Lucknow there were three kinds of areas: one where the merchants built their houses along narrow and dirty lanes that criss-crossed except where there was a market place which broke the network of these lanes. Then there was a quarter which housed the palaces of the kings and their ministers. This area was almost entirely built during Saadat Khan's time. It had wide streets with bazaars and market places. The third quarter had mosques, palaces and gardens.

Yusufbhai bit into two biscuits at the same time and said: 'Saadat Khan also developed many gunjes on either side of the chauk. Do you know what a gunj is? It is a common feature in most north Indian cities. Here in Lucknow there is the Saadat Gunj which was built by Saadat Khan, the Loha Ganj where the ironsmiths live, the Gola Gunj where an early arsenal was established.'

A gunj was an enclosure of masonry, earth or wooden planks which contained small houses and stalls and where essential goods were sold. It was like a caravanserai. They were either constructed for a charitable purpose or they were rented out.

A book about Lucknow describes the town gunj as a square built round a crossroad with two main gates and two smaller ones at the end of each road. The shops with verandas faced the main roads and there were houses at the rear. Bastions marked the four corners. The nullahs or streams which ran through the older parts of Lucknow became natural divisions between these gunjes which formed the backbone of Lucknow. Nothing of them remained now, except for the term and the central crossroad.

Yusufbhai's wife had finished cutting the beans. 'Would you believe that in the nawabi days there were more Hindus than Muslims here?' Yusufbhai said. 'They lived in different areas but their houses were not very different. Even though the Muslims followed purdah and the Hindus didn't, their houses were similar. We had an old ancestral house. My father sold it because it was too expensive to maintain. It was typical of the times. I remember there were two courtyards. My grandfather, father, my uncles and I used the rooms around the larger courtyard; it was the mardana, the men's quarters, and it opened on the street. The smaller courtyard formed the zenana and this could only be entered through the mardana. The rooms did not have windows but there were ventilators. There were no interconnecting doors. There was a big gate, with a guard room above it. There was also the naubat khana above the gate. A man there used to sound the passing of the hour and announce visitors. In those days there were many servants and we had separate rooms for them to live in. Their rooms were arranged around another courtyard which directly led to the gateway and into the mardana. The mardana also housed the dewan, the manager who looked after the house and property. Beside this was a room for the maulvi who instructed the boys of the family. The staircase was outside. We spent a lot of time in the upper floor of the mardana which had airy rooms and pavilions. The zenana had rooms on three sides and the fourth side had the kitchen and the storerooms. There were no openings in the zenana and the parapet was higher. My grandfather used to tell me that the walls had to be so high that a man standing on the back of the elephant could not see within. When it was very hot my grandmother would hang reed mats on doors and arches. In the colder months the khus thatis would be replaced by the curtains, carpets taken out and spread on the floor and charcoal braziers lit. On one side of the mardana was the imambara and a small mosque for worship.'

'Imambara?' I queried.

'The Shias have a religious procession. In this, portable shrines representing the graves of Hussain and Hasan are housed in the imambaras before they are taken through the streets in palanquins called taziyas and ceremoniously buried. Because of this custom Asad-ud-daula built the great imambara which at one time had

the largest vaulted hall in the world. Some taziyas are not buried but kept in the imambara as they are made of beaten silver or finely carved ivory or wood. A few were kept in the imambara in the old house too. The big imambaras also became the place where the nawab and his relatives were buried. Asad-ud-daula was buried in the great imambara.'

'But they were not tombs?' I asked.

'Yes, that is the muqbara not the imambara,' Yusufbhai said. 'However, an imambara which has a tomb of some nawab is also called a muqbara. The imambara is also a different-looking building: it is a long low structure and the main hall is divided into three rooms. A muqbara is normally a square building with a semi-basement, a central dome over the main hall and a false tomb which is a raised structure in the middle. Although there are imambaras in the private houses, they never have a tomb.

'Once a year the taziyas are taken out from their imambaras and carried through the city. They are carried to the kerbala, a building which represents the battlefield and the burial place of Hasan and Hussain in Iraq. The kerbala in Lucknow is the Talkatora which has a large European gateway although everything within it is typically Islamic. It has a square surrounded by cells, and has a building in the centre,' he concluded.

Yusufbhai's wife brought us some pictures of Yusufbhai's father and grandfather. There were pictures of the old house: the mardana had cusped arches over round large round columns which looked somewhat European. Yusufbhai told me they used to be painted blue. Behind the columns in the dalan, the walls had several cusped arches sheltering alcoves, also coloured according to him. On the walls were framed photographs and mirrors. There were also some photographs of Englishmen. 'My grandfather had many English and some European friends. I remember going to some of their houses; they were very different. You can see many European houses in Lucknow,' he said.

'Built by them?'

'Yes. They wanted something that was European in style.'

'Why?' I asked him.

'Perhaps because they were homesick? They even used to wear woolen clothes! And they also built their houses all wrong. They lacked courtyards and were very hot. At first they lived on the first floor during the hot months, until they realised the ground floors used for storage were much cooler.'

'So they built European houses because they were homesick, and then sweated in them.'

'It was also meant to assert their superiority. Also they could build far grander houses here than in their own country. The houses became public property; people liked to look at them. The nawabs wanted to copy them as they provided prestige. Hazratganj was also made to look like a street in European capital.'

The European houses had no inner courtyards and they extended upwards and not inwards like the nawabi or the Hindu houses. The doors and windows became the essential decorative features. They had ornamental porticos with imposing steps and venetian blinds on the glazed windows; the towers in the corners contained circular staircases so you could climb to the top from within the house. These houses were built on broad streets and you could stand back and admire the houses. Unlike them, the Hindu or the Muslim houses were not made to be admired, but in conformity with the way the people lived. British houses in Lucknow were quite standardised: one storeyed, flat-roofed, with at least two verandas, thatched or tiled, and blinds at the windows. They were almost always painted yellow or off-white and if large they stood in a compound and had outhouses and servants quarters.

We went down to Yusufbhai's shop and I looked at some sarees and kurtas and eventually bought a beautiful white saree in chikan work. 'Don't forget to see the Panch Mahalla; it is a great building,' he told us as we were leaving.

We got into a taxi and headed for the Panch Mahalla not knowing what it was. The taxi driver told us it was the palace of the nawab on the river. It was an arcaded building which stood just inside the north wall of the fort. A pan-chewing guide, middle-aged, and extremely polite, came after us, trying to convince us into hiring him by the hour. Once in a while he turned away to spit the pan-juice on a hedge. Despite this obvious disregard for the city and the hedge and the fact that he looked unclean, I engaged him to explain the palace complexes. 'This gateway was built by Shuja-ud-daula in front of his palace. It later became the eastern gateway of the new square in front of the Great Imambara. The Rumi Darwaza is its western gateway.' He took us to an inner courtyard which he told me consisted of state apartments. He injected appropriate nostalgia to feed our tourist fantasies. 'You cannot imagine what it was like in the nawabi days. I have heard that in front of the rooms was a beautiful pavilion garden with a basin of water. The rooms were heated by flues under the floor and there were fountains with hot and cold water.'

He took us to the new palace complex: the Daulat Khana, the Chhattar Manzil and Qaisarbagh. What I gathered from the guide was that the palace complexes were built like small cities; they were self-contained and like the streets in a city, the palaces and other buildings were connected and separated by corridors, passages, courtyards, balconies, gateways, verandas, pavilions and garden paths.

'But the palaces were not self-sufficient, so they depended on the bazaars and gunjes around them,' the guide explained. 'Because of this bazaars and gunjes also developed around the places. Near Daulat Khana there still is a place called the milkman's quarter which used to provide milk and dairy products to the palace,' the guide said. He began to explain about Chhatri Manzil built by Claude Martin which I found interesting.

271

Saadat Ali Khan bought Claude Martin's town house and around it he built the third palace complex—the Chhattar Manzil, though the original Martin house is still called the Farhad Baksh. The main house had to be entered from a drawbridge as three sides of it were surrounded by a moat; on the fourth side was the river. Near the river was a great hall overlooking it. It was supported by piers in the water. The lowest room was level with the river at its lowest mark. This was used in the summer. When the water rose the second basement storey was used. When the water rose to this level, the ground floor was used. In the basement there were baths and fountains that sprayed water on the windows, which were covered with reed and bramble in summer and kept wet. When the river fell after the monsoon the mud in the rooms was removed and they were repainted and decorated.

I wondered how the guide managed to talk with his mouth full of pan juice. After a minute he looked around for a bush; having found one to his satisfaction he let out a deluge of red juice from his mouth on it. I wondered why it had always to be a hedge. All through the guide's discourse Prakash kept taking photographs of him instead of the buildings.

'What about the buildings?'

'You want me to shoot these four stucco mermaids and fish?'

'The fish was a symbol of the nawabs,' the guide said.

'Look at those wavy lines on the parapet.'

'They represent the ocean,' the guide said.

'Why don't you shoot this complex. Qaisarbagh.'

'It was considered to be an architectural failure,' the guide said.

'Why?'

'Because of the crazy blend of styles—Italian, Moorish, Hindu, Mughal, everything,' the guide said.

I thought about architectural decadence. 'What do all these palaces have to do with streets anyway,' Prakash muttered. He took a photograph of the guide against the Qaisarbagh gateway. A close-up shot. I was sure the gilt crowns, chhatris and statues would not be in the photograph. Instead we would see the guide's lean face framed by the gate.

Encouraged and pleased, the guide was willing to go on about the nawabs and the mansions that they had built. But we had to go to the tourism office to confirm our accommodation. I paid him generously but he seemed rather sad to see us go.

Mr Sharma whom we met at the tourism office was a typical government servant: he had two plastic trays on his desk, one blue and the other red, both of which were piled with papers. Stacked beside them were numerous files. His thick black hair was brushed back on either side of his head like neatly folded wings and the eyes were protuberant and solemn. His voice when he spoke was vibrant and harsh. I got the impression of a rather severe person.

He turned out to be rather helpful. He immediately arranged for us to stay in their guest house and ordered tea and biscuits for us. He called his secretary, dictated two letters and told him he was leaving early since he had to take us to La Martiniere which I had told him we had not seen. We left in his staff car, a white Ambassador with a uniformed chauffeur. Just as he got into it a peon rushed to his side and handed him two small packets. He also held out a pink plastic bin with a lid. He opened the lid and Mr Sharma chewed ferociously on his pan and spat into the bin. He then opened one of the packets and put another pan into his mouth he gave muffled instructions to the driver. As we drove through the older parts of Lucknow he explained about the buildings in the city. They were all built of brick and the stucco work was well known. There were very few stone buildings. 'A special brick was used,' he said animatedly, 'they called it lakhori. It was supposed to be from Lahore in Pakistan where the small brick was first developed. It was only three-quarters of an inch

273

thick and four by six inches in size. They also used larger bricks called pan patta or ilmasi. Claude Martin who built La Martiniere made his own bricks. He used the lakhori bricks as well as larger ones. He also used curved and triangular bricks. The bricks were also crushed to make surkhi; this powder was mixed with cement and used as mortar. Chunam, or lime, was used for stucco. There were many types of chunam: in Madras they used pulverised seashells but in Lucknow they made a very special stucco made of red lime, gum, urad ki dal, jaggery, shells and a sticky substance, seras. This stucco is so smooth, it feels like marble. You can see it in the Great Imambara,' Sharma told me.

La Martiniere was a mixture of architectural styles. It had minute stucco work, fretwork and enormous red lions with lamps in place of eyes, Chinese mandarins and perhaps all the mythical gods and goddesses displayed on its walls. It was built like a fortress and had subterranean rooms. 'Martin decided that it should eventually become a school for boys of all religions, so it is a school now,' Sharma said as innumerable children in school uniform poured out of its arched doorways. The sound of their voices penetrated the thick walls and the ponderous air of the building. We stopped on the way at a liquor shop. 'You will have rum, won't you?' Sharma asked Prakash.

'Yes, yes,' he responded immediately.

I hadn't heard him say a word until then.

Lucknow was a matter of scales, not large and small but lofty and lowly. The palaces, the gateways and the lonesome clock tower—all predicted a yawning emptiness. Then again, it wasn't necessarily the case because emptiness as in music is experienced when a movement is missed. Here there was tension caused by the intervals of historic time, intervals between scales, space. Streets appear empty in the absence of coordinates—of history, culture and economics. They form frameworks for determining distances, orientation, focus and landmarks; they give a sense of place, good or bad, old or new, rich or poor. There is a symbiotic exchange, even if it is contradictory, opposing; it is not an indifferent isolation. It is not empty.

It was the month of Ramadan and we went to spend our last day in Lucknow in Ameena's house. In her house and in the

neighbouring houses, perhaps the whole locality, people were well into Ramadan. I was the only one who was not fasting; even Prakash had made a solemn effort to stay without food and water throughout the day. 'Very early in the morning, long before sunrise, my son goes to our relatives and few friend's homes to wake them for the suhur, the early morning meal which we all eat assembled in this house,' Ameena's father explained to me. 'We try and finish all important work in the morning otherwise it gets a bit trying by the evening in this heat.' I noticed through the day, in the house and in the streets, that a certain lassitude had settled. By afternoon the streets were almost empty and soundless. In the evening Ameena, her mother and sister-in-law became busy in the kitchen, getting the meal ready for breaking the fast at sunset while the men sat in the dalans fanning themselves. Their mouths had acquired a thin white crust and their tempers were brittle.

As the sun sank the women laid out trays of food. The families

gathered around, hungry, with tall glasses of water in front of
them. They sat watching the shadows growing longer, tense and
listening, listening for the call of the muezzin from a nearby
mosque to announce the official moment of sunset. When the meal
was finished, the men in a joyous mood made their way to the
mosque. Prakash went with them.

I went up to the terrace alone and watched the winding lanes
fill up with people, laughing, talking, greeting each other, the
children running between them. I looked up at the sky studded
with stars, rimmed with the gentle luminescence of it all, and
wondered how it must feel to know that on that very day millions
of people had turned to face the same point, said the same prayer
and prostrated under the canopy of stars—all a part of a
communion that tied millions of Muslims together. A
phenomenon of that scale was beyond my imagination.

Chapter 18

BENARAS: THE PILGRIMS MOVE IN CIRCLES, FULFILLING VOWS IN the city of Shiva, a mandala that represents the entire universe, its powers, its interrelations and its grounding centre raised on three hills which represent the three points of Shiva's trident, secured from the all-destructive flood. The city ruled by King Kasa and called Kasi had five concentric sacred zones: Kasi, Varanasi, Avimukta, Antargribha, and in the centre, the sanctum of the Vishwanath temple. And in every alley, there is a linga, phallic symbol of Shiva, the column of light that blinded Vishnu and Brahma; or a bisexual representation of the womb and shakti, the receptacle for Shiva's piercing shaft among its many associations. There are idols of gods and goddesses so each worshipper can recognise them and address his prayers to the required one. And there is the Ganges, a hair plucked from Shiva's head, brought down to earth to bless the living and the dead.

*

We moved out of the bustle of the railway station into the street. Around us the town slumbered in tiers of buildings piled haphazardly, their shutters folded back from their windows like a thousand moths to receive the cool breeze.

Prakash kept a wary eye on the porter as he struggled with his long bag containing the tripod and another leather bag with all the other equipment, most of which I had rarely seen him use. My large suitcase swayed precariously on the porter's head. I trailed a few feet behind them, walking beside an elderly lady and her spaniel, both of whom had travelled in the same compartment as us. Her name was Lata and she had invited us for breakfast the next morning. Although talkative and jovial through most of the journey, she looked tired and a little lost now. We got into the rickshaw amidst piles of luggage and sped away towards the Ganges.

The dharmshala where we had a booking greeted us with closed shutters, not surprising as it was one in the morning. A man responded to Prakash's thumps on the rolling shutter and loud bellows. He appeared at the door looking dishevelled, and informed us that after waiting for us for two days he had given away our rooms. He eventually found me a spare room with a camp bed and an overused bedsheet but Prakash had to sleep on a string cot in the courtyard, listening to the chirps of birds that flew on taut wings hours before the tumble of dawn.

I found Prakash looking bright the next morning, a rare sight, sipping a cup of tea.

'I am hungry,' he said. 'Let's go and have breakfast with the lady with the dog. And,' he added, 'let's eat and not talk.'

Lata's house was close to the Benaras University, well removed from the activity around the ghats. Her husband Luxman was a scholar and had spent many years in England. I was at once struck by the contrast between them. Lata, though old, looked much younger; she was fatter in the cheeks and the colour of reddened caramel. Luxman was darker, his skin tight over his angular bones. I noticed the fine-quality brown suit he was wearing and the large opal ring on one middle finger.

278

He spoke English with great emphasis and a very British accent. It was presumably because of the years he had spent in England. He was a professor of sociology and the study of religion appeared to be his main line of interest. He had come a year ago with his wife and his spaniel, Alfie, to Benaras to research Hinduism. He hoped to write a book on the subject.

As soon as we sat down in the drawing room, the professor began to talk about his book on Hinduism.

'What about the breakfast?' Prakash whispered to me.

'It appears complex,' Luxman said, 'but it is a simple religion; it is an eternal religion,' he said clipping his words. 'It is the way of life which is put down in a set of books called sruti, which means "what has been heard".'

'What about eating?' Prakash whispered again, a little louder.

'The srutis are also known as Vedas,' Luxman continued, 'Vid means to know. You see, at first there were no gods.'

'Wonderful,' Prakash said.

'Ah, but they came much later.'

'What for?' Prakash said.

'When the gods were brought to earth, prayers were needed.

279

So the Vedas were made. The Rig Veda is about prayers and hymns; and the Upanishads which are the most important part of the Vedas give you knowledge. It is believed that the Upanishads do away with avidya, ignorance.'

'Are we having idlis? I can smell sambar,' Prakash said.

'Yes,' Lata said, 'come before it gets cold.'

Prakash leapt to the table and piled the idlis and sambar on his plate. Luxman placed a single idli on his plate and topped it with butter and waited for it to melt.

'This world was recreated using the Vedas,' he said. 'The gods recreate the universe at the end of each kalpa which is 4320 million earth years.'

'Nothing better to do,' Prakash muttered and cut the pile of idlis with a knife.

'Each kalpa has four yugas or ages. We are in the Kali Yuga; it is the time when everything will be finished; it will die. In the last kalpa, there was a big pralaya, a flood—the water flowed over everything, the whole world was finished.'

'Brahma prayed to the Great God to recreate the universe. Then God taught Brahma the Vedas and told him to recreate the universe with the knowledge he had given him.'

Lata came in with a plate of hot vadas.

'There are vadas also,' Prakash noted with appreciation.

'Have some south Indian doughnuts.' Luxman passed me the plate of vadas. 'It has a soul,' he went on. 'The universe—its soul is called Brahman. Brahman is the one God that the Hindus believe in. He is the Absolute. He is without shape and form, without beginning or end.'

Prakash smiled at Lata to inveigle more vadas.

'Man also has a soul—atman,' Luxman said nibbling his buttered idli, 'and atman is contained in the Brahman.'

'So two souls meet,' Prakash said and laughed. No one else did.

'But man's soul must get liberated—must find moksha, because man is tied to samsara and karma. Samsara is the cycle of birth, death and rebirth. Every soul must go through the cycles of death before moksha.'

'You believe this?'

'Why do we believe in samsara? How can we think that God could have created inequalities? He cannot. If they are there it is not because of him but because of us; it is our karma. We are born as a result of our deeds in our previous life. Karma is the law of cause and effect. And people come to Kashi to wash away their sins so that they are not reborn.'

'Are you going on a pilgrimage?' Lata asked.

'No.'

'You must. People take vows when they come to Kashi. It takes five days to go around the town. They walk on the Panchakroshi street. At its centre is the Shiva temple of Madhyameshvara.'

'There are five sheaths or layers in a person,' Luxman said. 'Kashi has five sheaths. Vishwanath is a new centre; Madhyameshvara was the old centre, the navel of Kashi. It was destroyed by the Muslims. Today the site of the Madhyameshvara is full of ruins of shrines and lingas.'

Kashi was called by many names, Luxman told us. It was also called Avimukta which meant not to let loose because it was a city never to be forsaken by Shiva. This was the place where the linga of Shiva was first established and worshipped. Even when there were floods Shiva never let go of Kashi and held it up on his trident.

'Where there are the streets of Varanasi was once a forest called the Anandavana—the forest of bliss,' he said. 'Chaukhamba and Thatheri bazaars, these are where the forest once was. The older people still remember Ban Kati—the cut down forest.'

Kashi was also called Rudravasa, the city of Shiva since Shiva is also called Rudra. Here the membrane between Shiva and the rest of the world is very thin, it is virtually transparent; and in Kashi one dwells with him.

Prakash took several pictures of him, talking, when his eyes were closed. He took pictures of Lata in her white saree with a string of rudraksha beads around her neck.

She said, 'Mishraji has very good beads and rudrakshas. He has a shop in Vishwanath Gali. He knows a lot of stories about Kashi.

He will tell you more about it.'

The Thatheri Bazaar was like any other bazaar—crowded. It did not feel like what Luxman had said about Kashi, Varanasi, Avimukta or Anandavana: there was no spiritual energy in it, only the perplexity of a rapidly growing town—streets full of people, shops where lights burned all day, dirty frontages slapped with hoardings and other devices, shouting out the wares that filled them; and houses like dustworn safes crammed with tarnished

valuables and the odd furniture of a people who are slowly being urbanised while they continue to live in the sacred carcass of the city.

Our rickshawallah stopped in front of a tiny lane and said, 'Vishwanath Gali.' We walked into it. The cool morning air was redolent with the scent of flowers and incense. The lane was narrow and full of people. It was also full of eager crows, sleeping cows, bulls, cats, and scurrying monkeys. I could hear dogs barking and the tinkling of cowbells as the indolent cows roamed through the lanes.

On either side were shops selling stone lingas and brass items for worship. There was a whole row of shops selling rudraksha malas. Mishra's shop was amidst them. A variety of malas, of rudraksha, tulsi and white, yellow and orange beads—hung in the glass cases attached to the folding doors. There were heaps more

inside the shop.

He became very friendly when we told him that Lata had sent us. He opened a cupboard and showed me some strings of rudraksha.

'I don't sell these, but you can have one,' he said. I bought one and conveyed to him our desire to see the city and hear the stories about it. He agreed readily and jumped down and bolted the shop. 'Let's go.'

'Which is the burning ghat?' Prakash asked.

'The Manikarna ghat,' Mishra told him.

'I want to shoot dead bodies,' Prakash said.

Mishra pulled at his ears and stuck his tongue out.

'Sometimes the bodies are thrown half-burnt into the Ganges. I want to photograph them for a foreign magazine. The light is just right in the morning,' Prakash persisted.

The sky was fresh and shining, not yet the fierce blue of noon but a milky opal.

'There are other ghats,' Mishra offered.

'I thought people came to Benaras to mainly see the burning ghat,' Prakash argued. Mishra marched us through the lanes to the Dasasvamedha ghat. The holy water of the Ganges was pallid, churned by people. They were there on the steps and in the water, bright like pollen—pink, red, yellow, blue. They bathed themselves several times and prayed, watched by men with bulging bellies who sat under voluminous bamboo umbrellas.

'They are pandas,' Mishra said. 'The pandas perform rituals for the pilgrims, particularly the Panchtirthi which involves walking down the river front and having ritual dips at the five holy ghats: Assi, Dasashvamedha, Manikarna, Panch Ganga and Raj Ghat.'

We sat on the steps and watched boys jump off the parapet into the river. He continued speaking: 'There were many deities in Anandvana before the great gods like Shiva and Vishnu. The deities lived in trees and stones, people worshipped them with flowers, incense, banners, milk, food offerings. This is what became the Hindu puja. Some were also given offerings of meat and liquor, or sometimes, blood.'

'Greedy,' Prakash said.

'Such worship was called bali. Then this was replaced by a smear of vermilion instead of blood. The Aryans worshipped in a simple way, by yagna—the ritual sacrifice. They had no temples or idols. Although gods were there in the vedic and Buddhist world, they were not important. The sages got knowledge through spiritual discipline and yoga. With theism all the gods came into the picture.'

A panda came towards us. Mishra whispered, 'You must be careful. Don't have anything to do with them. They cheat and rob people.'

Like pilgrims we walked from one ghat to another. Prakash ignored the architecture to photograph towelled men, and women whose wet sarees clung to their bodies like the skin of unripe soft peaches. Each of the ghats and the temples in its precinct had its own style of architecture. Some of the buildings along the ghats looked like tall fortresses, others like havelis, but none of the temples was architecturally remarkable. Even the temple to Pashupatinath at Lalita ghat built by the king of Nepal, though different in style, was small and not impressive like the temples of Nepal. It was made of wood and carved in a typical Nepalese style.

The sun was hot. It crimped the air and the clouds looked shaggy. The sweet flower-scent of the morning had evaporated. The ghats, the Ganges and the people, all sweltered in the heat. As we turned into a street we saw a small procession of people. They carried a body wrapped in white, covered with withered

flowers. Prakash followed them as they entered into a small lane selling flowers and other items necessary for the last rites. Mishra pulled Prakash back.

'Where are you going?'

'I want to shoot the dead bodies.'

'They will beat you up. I will bring you back in the night. You can shoot then.'

'In the dark?'

'Don't you have a flash!' I countered.

We walked back into the inner lanes wreathed between the ghats like whorls of an exotic and immense flower, rustling with life and wrinkled with the intensity of it. The cows made the passage difficult and I was forced to look down rather than up at the buildings to avoid stepping into their dung.

I smiled at a foreigner, his pale skin flushed and covered with sweat, a red spot of vermilion on his forehead. He wore a white vest and a dhoti. This was the fourth time I had bumped into him in these lanes, and he smiled back. Very often we met the same people. What seemed to be a chaos of winding lanes at first now appeared to be a coded network which appeared complex to the mind, but became instinctive for the feet. There were temples, shrines and lingas in the lanes, each with a name, and these helped identify our location.

The houses in the lanes were tall, more than three storeys, with narrow frontages. Some of the houses had arched recesses which contained shops in a row, making the activity on the street swift and similar to that at a fun-fair. The buildings had a strong connection to the ground and therefore the street. The kind of connections differed: some were rooted to the ground, others were raised on arches and verandas, some had steps; with every type of connection, there was a different aspect of street space. No building was monumental because, as I saw it, there was no strong dividing line between the building and the ground. They belonged to the ground. And because of this there was a linear movement of space: it penetrated into the form of buildings just as the form penetrated into space, intermingling. The motion of space was accelerated by the narrow width of the lane, the people walking in it in a steady flow, and the destination of the lane which was either a ghat or another winding lane.

'I want to see a typical house,' I said.

We passed a house painted in ochre, the colour of faded marigolds. In the centre of the wall was the main door framed by two elaborate stone columns supporting an arched stone panel. The columns were painted strawberry pink. Opposite this house was a large house with a veranda along its facade. On one end of the veranda was a small shrine with a red mandap (dome).

'This is Punditji's house.' So saying Mishra climbed the steps to the veranda and walked into the house. We followed. The door opened onto a large passage which led to rooms beyond. A staircase led to a landing with a stone balustrade. On the wall opposite the main door was a window under an arch. Its brass hinges shone like gold. Mishra went up the stairs to a room above and reappeared accompanied by an old man. He signalled us to come up.

The wall along the stairs was crumbling. It was an ancient brick wall that had been plastered over, but now the plaster was bulging and sagging. Here and there large pieces of it had fallen off revealing rows of bricks. The room which we entered had an atmosphere of ancient melancholy: cracked and peeling walls, echoing spaces, tables piled high with dusty books and a perpetual grey twilight. There was a decrepit sofa, used and worn like the galis, and a few chairs with effete cushions that could take no more. The polish on them had cracked and bubbled in places. The cracks had been ingeniously cellotaped to keep them in place. The walls were painted a daffodil-yellow and were full of pictures of gods. The shelves in the walls were full of books, covered with fibrous dust and mosquitoes ensnared in cobwebs.

He took us back to the ground floor and deeper into the house. We went up and down staircases as we moved inwards. In the last

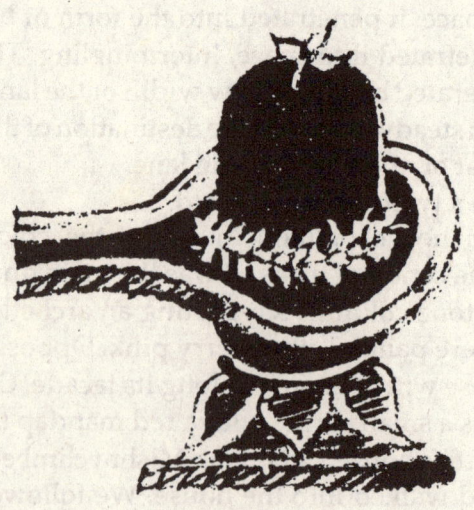

room there was another flight of steps down. We entered a small room and over the balustrade in its centre looked into the chamber below. Light came in through an opening on the river side. In the middle was a large Shiva linga made of black stone. It was marked with red vermilion and covered with flowers. 'Many houses have their own Shiva linga,' Mishra said. 'When the Ganges rises the water flows in and washes the linga. So the house has both the linga and the Ganga.'

We exited through a rear door into another lane. We walked towards the temple. The few trees undulated gently in the breeze as if they were painting the sky a brighter blue for our visit to the temple. Flower merchants stood outside the shops with baskets heaped with marigold and jasmine.

'Be careful of the pandas,' Mishra warned us as he hurried back to his shop.

'Are you going into the temple ?' Prakash asked me.

'Why not,' I said.

As we walked through the lane one panda approached me with flowers and a leaf-bowl filled with some sweets. 'Eighteen rupees for one,' he said. He looked harmless and in need. I looked for Prakash but he had gone on ahead. I bought the flowers and sweets. The panda said I could pay for them after I came out of the temple. He was very considerate and quite unlike what Mishra had said the pandas were like. I thanked him profusely. He also told me that it would be a better idea to remove our shoes and leave them in a shop. He pointed to a particular shop. 'I know the owner. He will look after your shoes. They are Nike, aren't they? Anyone would want to steal them.' I was very pleased with him. I called out to Prakash, who had already discarded his shoes on the street. We left our shoes with the kind shopowner.

The temple was unlike the marvellous temples I had seen. It was set in such a crowded place that one could hardly see it at all but for the doorway. It was odd that Benaras which was the most religious place should have no temples that were architecturally splendid.

'It is not such an old temple,' Mishra had explained. 'It was built

289

by the queen Ahalyabai of Indore in the eighteenth century. There were many temples that were built on this spot; they were destroyed and looted one after another. The history of these previous temples that housed the linga is a thousand years old. There is a mosque behind the temple. The temple must have been larger before. Part of it is in ruins now because Aurangzeb destroyed the old temple and built the mosque.'

We entered into a courtyard in the centre of which was the temple. There were many shrines around it. The courtyard was dim, the air cooler and richly scented. 'Om namo shivaya, Om namo shivaya,' the people chanted as they offered flowers, sweets and Ganga water to the linga and the shrines around. The linga was set on a recessed altar of silver. The seat of the linga was also of silver and the shaft was of a smooth black stone. The atmosphere was one of utter devotion. People drenched the linga with water, covered it with flowers and bilva leaves and bent down to touch it with their hands. The water flowed over the temple floor which was littered with flowers.

It was noisy but the jostling crowds and their chanting and the clanging of bells contributed an aura of sanctity. I found the ritual

far more potent and consuming than the architecture and aesthetics of the place.

Preoccupied with all the ritual, I had lost Prakash. As I was looking for him a panda boy with remarkably innocent eyes came to me. He guided me to the shrine of Annapurna and chanted a shloka. Then he asked me to give a hundred rupees to the Brahmin attending to the shrine. I did. He took me to the shrines of Avimukta Vinayaka, Nikhumbha, Mahakala and others and at each he made me pay a hundred, sometimes two hundred rupees. He told me he was saying special prayers for me and the money was part of the ritual; it was a daan, sacred donation. Then he took me to the court of Shiva lingas. He told me that it was a very sacred place and asked me to pray for my parents and pay five hundred rupees. I resisted but he convinced me that it was required. I paid the money and desperately looked for Prakash, afraid of the gods and the pandas.

I came out of the temple and into the quadrangle where the mosque was. It was a large mosque but not architecturally beautiful. There were elements of Hindu, Jaina and Buddhist architecture. On three sides of the mosque there were old Buddhist pillars of the early style. Between the mosque and the temple was the well of knowledge, the Gyan Vapi. People prayed at the well, throwing offerings of water and flowers into it. Not finding Prakash I proceeded to the shop where our shoes were kept. The 'kind' shopkeeper charged me four hundred for two pairs of shoes; he refused to return the shoes without payment. 'It is all because of inflation,' he muttered. He said that the shoes were imported and must cost a lot of money. The flower-seller who had introduced me to the shopkeeper appeared and I looked anxiously at him. He demanded that I pay two hundred rupees for the flowers and the sweets. I argued that they were only for eighteen but he insisted that I had not heard right and it would be a sin not to pay for the flowers that were offered to Shiva. I paid both of them and retrieved the shoes. Fifteen minutes later I spotted Prakash coming out of the temple.

'These pandas are terrible, I paid fifty rupees,' he said, 'Imagine,

fifty rupees. He was trying to cheat me of much more. But I was too smart for him. Mishra was right. They rob gullible people.'

This once I felt it was judicious to remain quiet.

After a rushed dinner at the hotel we went back to Vishwanath Gali and to Mishra's shop. He was waiting as promised to take us to Manikarna Ghat which he insisted that we see in the night. It was close to nine and the cows dozed under the streetlights.

Mishra swiftly trotted through the lanes, a yard ahead of me. I walked gingerly, worried about stepping into cowdung or sleeping dogs. Prakash followed, one camera hung around his neck, another in his hand.

'Shiva,' Mishra said, was a mountain ascetic. He wanted to marry Parvati, the lovely daughter of the Himalayas. He needed a suitable home where they could live. Shiva looked and looked and found Varanasi. But he could not bring his bride to Varanasi.'

'Why not?' I asked.

'Because the city was occupied by King Divodasa. Empty the city, Shiva told his attendant Nikhumbha. Nikhumbha appeared in a dream to a barber who made an idol of him and worshipped him. The others did too. The king's wife who was childless worshipped Nikhumbha but he did not answer her prayers. The king was angry and he destroyed the shrine. In return, Nikhumbha cursed the king and the city and the people left the city. When the city was empty, Shiva established his residence and became the lord of the city.'

'Clever,' Prakash muttered.

'Shiva is the great God, the Maheshvara,' Mishra said, looking fiercely at Prakash. 'Shiva liked the number five. It represented wholeness; a round wholeness with four directions and the centre. Like the material wholeness of the five elements and the bodily wholeness of the five senses. Everything is five. A person is supposed to be made of five koshas or sheaths, the outermost is the body and the innermost is the spirit. The om is the five-fold symbol of wholeness—o-o-o-o-m.'

A number of people passed us in the dark. Mishra held me back and let them pass; they carried a dead body. We walked behind them. We walked up to a small platform that overlooked the burning ghat. There were three bodies already burning. The flames that nipped the air made it hotter, yet there was a certain coolness like that one experiences in vacancy or silence. I felt this coolness as I watched the bodies burning. The body that had just arrived was set down and had to wait till the ashes of the others were emptied into the Ganga.

Prakash began to shoot.

'When Kapila, a muni, was meditating,' Mishra said, 'King Bhagiratha's ancestors disturbed him so he burnt them with his angry glance. Their souls were trapped and they could not cross over to heaven. So Bhagiratha prayed to Brahma who said to go and immerse their ashes in the cleansing waters of the Ganga. Bhagiratha then prayed to the Goddess Ganga to come down to earth from heaven. She could not because her force would destroy the earth. So Bhagiratha prayed to Shiva who took the force of the river on his head and it flowed down from his locks onto the Himalayas towards Ganga Sagar in the Bay of Bengal. On the way she passed through Varanasi. Seeing the beautiful city she did not wish to flow on and so she turned back. Bhagiratha persuaded the river to flow on.'

Prakash loaded another film.

The sky above the fire that crisped the dead bodies was blistered and there was the acrid smell of woodsmoke and burning flesh. The Ganges crept by, a dusky, solid mass slashed by silver where the moonlight touched her. Benaras was

293

moistened by the night; it would be radiant with the early morning sun, full of stirring life. For now we watched the dead.

Chapter 19

DELHI: RITA FIXED A RED BINDI, SPRAYED A MIST OF PERFUME on her arms and neck and said, 'Let's go, we will be late, Bibiji will be expecting us.' She wore a pink chiffon saree embossed with gold dots; her raven black hair was cut in a fashionable blunt style and her nails were polished a frosty pink. Her face was carefully made up with ample quantities of rouge and mascara. Numerous strings of pearls and gold beads hid her neck.

She used to be a careless and carefree person, dressing casually and only in cotton. I had known her for a long time: we were neighbours in Baroda and went to the same school. She belonged to a middle-class Bengali family and met her husband, who was a Punjabi, during a visit to Delhi. When she shifted to Delhi after they were married, the transformation began. She had also become fat.

She lived in a modern, split-level house in Panchsheel Enclave.

It was made of exposed bricks and patterned concrete, a style that had become popular after Corbusier initiated the modern style in India. But the sparse effect was limited to the outside: within it was like a typical nouveau riche Punjabi's house. The living room had suede covered sofas and gilded Tanjore paintings on its walls. Large imported chandeliers hung from the ceiling; they were fixed with pink and yellow porcelain flowers. Crystal and porcelain pieces crowded the tables and shelves. Quilted silk curtains hung from polished brass rods. The curtains were specially made in her husband's factory in Ludhiana, she had told me with pride. He was in the textile business; they had cloth shops in Connaught Place and Chandni Chowk. Like Rita herself, her house also displayed a degree of superficiality, a duality: of an innate core and an acquired veneer, an aspect evident in the way old houses were changing, as also the entire city. There was less of the innateness, more that was appropriated.

We parked at the Red Fort, as it was impossible to drive in Chandni Chowk. The street was dense with people on foot; and the constant traffic ejaculated thick clouds of smoke on the merchandise laid out on the pavements—handkerchiefs, shirts and vests, toys, chappals and a hundred other things spread out in profusion. Behind them like a backdrop were the lacerated images of the past.

I trailed Rita's perfume as she swiftly walked through the lanes. The heat and the people were stifling, and I looked longingly at the stalls selling sherbets and fruit juices. We walked into a lane full of bright nylon sarees and sarees fixed with beads, pearls and sequins. There were georgette duppatas of different shades folded and stacked in slippery bales. Gaudy nets of gold and silver shimmered on top of them. We crossed Parathewale Gali where men with bulbous stomachs sat in the lane frying parathas. The heat of the day, the heat from the stoves and the smell of the leavened wheat frying in clarified butter made my stomach turn. Flies swarmed as if possessed around heaps of sweetmeats on shelves and counters and milk simmered in large iron kadais in front of shops selling toffee straws made of flour, sugar and ghee. Rita bought a large box of the straws. 'Bibiji loves them,' she said.

We turned into another lane, this one full of silversmiths and jewellery shops. There were small open shops that sold silver ornaments and larger shops with glass doors and show windows selling gold and diamond pieces. Rita walked into one of the large shops which had powerful spotlights and an oversized chandelier whose light made the diamonds sparkle. There were many women in the shop. They were already laden with gold; they were looking for some more. Rita enquired about her order, inspected the gold bangles when they were brought to her and smiling contentedly, slid them on her wrists.

We turned into a lane full of wholesalers selling silver and gold braids, garlands, rosettes and turbans. Mothers of enlarged girth accompanied by young nubile girls bargained rapaciously. The shopkeepers, fearless, held their own. We walked past astrologers and palmists, past their strange contrivances and herbs spread on the pavement, past parrots in cages, birthstones and gems in boxes. We walked towards the Jama Masjid. Its bulbous dome of white marble with black marble stripes rose majestically above the

crumbling lanes.

We passed a poultry market. Hens were squashed in cages piled high, and every time they squawked a few more feathers were released into the air. A sweet scent fused with the organic smell. It came from shops heaped with garlands of roses, marigold and jasmine.

The character of the street changed. The women were mostly in burkhas and the men wore skull caps. The shops had rich varieties of velvet and brocade. There were many mosques in the street, and at the restaurants the heaps of thick rotis on the counters were surrounded by the poor and disabled, waiting in irascible queues for their free daily meal. It was a Muslim area.

Contrasting with this was another lane with large mansions which looked as if they had been inhabited by nobles or wealthy merchants. Now the houses were let, sublet, partitioned, baricaded. Clusters of bawdy women stared from the balconies. They looked like prostitutes; they were. Below them were shops selling copper and brass vessels and in front of them gutters overflowed with viscous wastes. Lingering here and there were the ubiquitous cows and dogs. Like bindweed, commerce had grown parasitically on its host streets, strangling them. Old Delhi had become a corpse.

I don't know how far we walked; it seemed a long time but we had been walking for less than half an hour. We came to a brightly painted arched doorway. 'This is my father-in-law's haveli,' Rita said as we walked into a passage. We walked through another doorway above which there was a room with a balcony. In it brightly coloured sarees and other clothes were hung to dry. At the end of the passage, there was a carved wooden door which led to the main part of the haveli. What surprised me was that the door immediately opened onto a wall. It was silly to have a wall just after the door. Behind it was an open court faced by two tiers of verandas. An old man sat in a cane chair in the upper veranda. Bulging fluted columns held cusped arches which supported the ceiling.

Rita bent and touched his feet. 'Papaji, my father-in-law,' she said, turning to me. He led us into the diwan khana. It was furnished with sofas and chairs covered in red velvet. Dusty high

chandeliers with parts missing or broken hung from the ceiling.
There was a veil of dust everywhere, in the crevices of the velvet,
on tables and picture frames on the walls; dust that could not be
dislodged, dust that settled with age. The dust covered the past.

Rita went in to meet her mother-in-law. I talked to Papaji. He
spoke in Hindi mixed with English and Punjabi words. His voice
trembled and his eyes looked shrivelled. He was eighty. 'We lived
in Sargoda near Lahore in Pakistan,' he said. 'My father was a
zamindar. We came to Delhi after the partition. We had to leave
behind everything that we had, our fields, our shops and our
havelis. We were very poor. At first, we lived in two tiny rooms
in Chandni Chowk. We had a small cloth shop there. I couldn't
find any work as an engineer so I looked after the shop. Then when
we had made enough money we bought this haveli. It used to
belong to a Muslim merchant. Now both my sons are rich. My
older son has a large cloth factory in Ludhiana. He sends all the
cloth to Delhi and we sell it at our two shops.'

I asked him about the wall at the entrance. 'Oh that. The
merchant had obviously built the haveli for his use. It is the
purdah divar. And the long passage is the chhatta. That is where
the visitors are made to wait and while they are waiting the

purdah divar blocks their view so that they can't look inside the house. You must have noticed the room above the archway too. That is the naqqar khana, where the drums used to be sounded.'

Bibiji and Rita joined us. Bibiji's gold bangles clinked as she gave me a glass of jal jeera, and she listened politely as Papaji talked about the price of gold and property, about their son's business and the crumbling haveli. Soon it was time for lunch.

We walked into the mahalsarai. It had a beautiful courtyard, though broken down and neglected. There was a dalan and, six inches above it, a dar dalan surrounding the court, in the middle of which was a baradari. But what really interested me were the du chatti, two mezzanine floors on either side of the veranda. They

were covered with carved stone jaafris and looked into the courtyard. Papaji told me that in the past the courtyard was used for gatherings and performances and the women could watch unseen from the du chatti. I also learnt that the mahalsarai was like an intermediate space and the baradari was built to reduce the heat in the courtyard. There used to be fountains around it but these were no longer in use. The zenana adjoined the mahalsarai. It contained a few rooms, windowless, and a large kitchen.

Lunch was served in an airy room in the mahalsarai. The table was crowded with silver dishes filled with rather rich preparations of vegetables and meat, served with hot puffed puris. I was compelled to eat a large quantity of the puris. Papaji ate very little. He finished quickly and began to peel an apple with care. He started talking about the haveli again.

'There are so many rooms that we don't use. There is a large basement and several terraces. We don't use either of them.' He took me to both later. The tehkhana was dark and dingy. It was fairly deep and large and had skylights that let the light in.

'In the earlier days the family used the tehkhana during the summer months,' Papaji told me. 'We don't use it at all, except for sto: ing old furniture. We don't use the terrace also. In the summer they used to sleep on the terrace. There is a small room where they would store mattresses.' There were many terraces at different levels and small flights of steps led from one terrace to another,

each with its parapet walls. I realised this was necessary so that many families could use the terrace as in those days many families lived together. I walked to the edge of the terrace. I noticed that there were double walls at the periphery of the building. I asked Papaji about it. He said, 'It is to catch the wind. In Lahore all the havelis had it. When the purvaiya (cool wind from the east) blows it is channelled into the haveli. These were the old systems,' he said.

He took me to see his shop. We walked through streets crowded with people, cycle-rickshaws and hand-carts pulled by sinewy, sweating men. The road had cracks and fissures and the electrical wires formed complex networks overhead through which patches of sky could be seen. The sky was further broken by jharokhas, banners and little flags that conveyed some message or the other.

We passed a small garden. Papaji stopped and said, 'They love changing names. This is now called the Mahatma Gandhi park but before that it was Queen Victoria's garden. And before that, Begum Bagh. For that matter, do you know this street was not called Chandni Chowk? That was the name of an octagonal open space in front of Begum Bagh. It had a pool of water in which on certain nights the moon could be seen reflected and so they called it Chandni. Jahanara built it, Shah Jahan's favourite daughter.' Papaji continued his description of the street as we walked on. 'She also built the entire street. A canal flowed through the centre. She called it the Nahr-i-Bihisht, the canal of paradise, and there were trees on either side.'

We came to his shop. It was air-conditioned and brightly lit, with plenty of glass on the outside. The adjoining shops were similar. 'The shops have all been redone. There used to be a long arcade and the shops were pretty much alike. A little door led from the back of the shop to a small warehouse where goods were stored. The merchant, his family and servants lived above the warehouse in a small house. The terrace over the shops was used to sleep in the night.' He offered to take me to meet his friend Karim. 'He can tell you a lot about this place.'

*

Papaji's friend Karim was a cloth merchant. He often came to Papaji's shop with samples of cloth and they had known one another for several years.

In fact it was from him that Papaji had learnt a lot about the cloth trade, as Papaji who was an engineer knew nothing of it. In a sense he was indebted to him. Karim lived in a small portion of a haveli near the Fatehpuri mosque.

The haveli was called Namak Haram ki Haveli. I was surprised by its name. We passed through an archway into passage and thence through another gateway into an open courtyard. There were a number of people in it. The paved floor was rutted and the air was full of cement dust. The walls around the court stood

decrepit but spoke of elegant times. In the centre of the court a stone fountain looked like some exquisite leftover of better times.

An old man who had been talking to two other men approached us on seeing Papaji. He was Karim. He led us up a dark and musty stairway to his room. It was small and contained within its aged and unkempt walls a bed, a small table and chair and a cupboard. There were some old photographs on the wall and a calendar with the dates in large blue and red numerals. We sat on the bed while Karim told us the story of the haveli:

'My uncle used to live here before. I came to live with him when I was a small boy. My mother and my sisters lived in a village. We are tenants. There are many other tenants—the haveli has been divided into small rooms. My uncle told me that the haveli belonged to Bhowani Shanker. He had left Delhi to join the Maratha rebel Jaswant Rao Holkar. Later he left Holkar and joined the British who rewarded him by giving him a good position. He became a rich man and built this haveli, but because he had defected to the British the haveli came to be called Namak Haram ki Haveli.

'That was Shankar's baradari, at least part of it,' Karim said pointing to the court outside the window. 'You remember seeing the fountain in the centre? There used to be a garden there with several fountains and waterways; only this remains now,' he said. There were ninety tenants and one part of the haveli was a wholesale flower market, Phool Walan ki Mandi. As we walked out of his room I could detect the smell of flowers mixed with the smell of cement dust and decay.

Papaji then took me to the Hakim Ahsanullah Khan's haveli. 'He was the personal doctor to the last emperor, Bahadur Shah Zafar. The haveli was more like a palace: it covered an entire mohalla. Its entrance was next to Excelsior cinema.' He waved towards the cinema. 'This area used to be the mardana. At the back of the theatre were turkish baths, gardens and guest houses and behind it the zenana with sculpted doorways and stained glass windows. The haveli used to have thick silk curtains and Persian carpets on the floor. Hakim Ahsanullah Khan was suspected to have had clandestine negotiations with the British and an angry mob looted the haveli. Mirza Ghalib was a friend of the Hakim. In fact he lived close by.'

Papaji rang the doorbell. A young man opened the door. 'This is Nawab Saheb, the new occupant of the haveli,' Papaji said to me.

I learnt a lot more about old Delhi listening to them talk. They talked about Shahjanabad and how it used to be. They talked about the bazaars: the Faiz Bazaar, the bazaar of plenty where everything was available, and through which a branch of the Nahr-i-Bihist flowed. The Khas Bazaar where there were dancing girls, the Dure be Baha—the pearl without compare—now called Dariba Kalan, where there were splendid jewellery shops, and the Chawri Bazaar where noblemen sat in the chowk and settled disputes.

'Shahjahanabad was built according to the Vastu Shastras,' Papaji told me.

'No, I think it has Islamic influence,' the Nawab interrupted him but Papaji continued expounding his view.

'The mansâra listed a semi-elliptical design called karmuka (bow) which it said was good for a site near a river or sea. I am telling you that it is the karmuka plan that was used for

Shahjahanabad. Look at the roads and you will see. There was one road that connected the two gates of the wall which formed the bow string and another curved road connected several gates which formed the curve of the bow. Chandni Chowk, which ran from the Lahori Gate of the Fort to the Lahori Gate of the city became the arm of the archer. A Vishnu or Shiva temple was built at the crossing of the roads according to the karmuka plan. They don't have a temple but they built the Red Fort,' Papaji told me.

'All this is not very certain—it may be true—I am not sure,' Nawab Saheb contradicted him. 'I think Shahjahanabad was influenced by Islamic concepts, not the Vastu Shastras. Its plan was based on the Rasail, a collection of writings by a group of Shia scholars. According to it, the cosmos was made of the microcosm (man), and the macrocosm (universe) and the great chain of being. Both have three divisions: body (jism), soul (nafs), and spirit (ruh). The macrocosmic energy moves from the body outwards towards the heavenly spirit and the microcosmic force moves inward into the body towards its spiritual centre. Traditional Islamic architecture and cities were built according to the images of both the man and the universe. Because the man contained the universe within him the plan of the Islamic city was based on the anatomy of man. In Shahajanabad, Chandni Chowk was the backbone, Red Fort the head and Jama Masjid the heart. The walled city represented the cosmos with its eight gates, the four cardinal points and the four gates of heaven.' Whether Shahjahanabad was based on the Vastu Shastras or the Islamic ideology, I could see not much of either had remained.

'There are no canals and gardens now, of course. The mohallas and havelis are long gone,' Nawab Saheb summed up. 'The Nahr-i-Bihisht is covered by cement and concrete. A branch of Nahr-i-Bihisht used to flow into this haveli. The tehkhanas have been sealed because there was a rise in the water table. The galis are full of shops selling iron pipes, paints, chemicals, other building materials and automobile parts and there are factories in 'the smallest of lanes.'

*

For the next few days I wandered about the streets of Delhi, particularly the older streets of which there were many. They were changing rapidly, haphazardly. Through it all I noticed the disrupted inner order. It was a cultural change and it affected everything: the city, its architecture, people and how they behaved; it was cancerous. It was the poorer areas, particularly the villages within the city limit, that were the most affected. I noticed this in Mehrauli to which I had gone when I heard that it contained the palace of the last Mughal emperor. It was a dusty overgrown village like any other when I first saw it.

Mehrauli was a town in the kingdom of two Rajput dynasties. It was the capital of the Tomar king Anang Pal of the Rajput dynasty. It was called Lalkot because of the red brick with which it was built. Later Prithviraj Chauhan extended the capital calling it Qila Rai Pithora. This was the first of the seven cities of Delhi.

The Muslims then built their capital around it and thus the other cities succeeded the first: Siri, Tughlakabad, Jahanpanah, Ferozabad and Kotla, Dinpanah, Sher Shahabad and Purana Qila and Shahjahanabad and Lal Qila. The Britisl. brought to Mehrauli a colonial flavour. It was now one of the three hundred villages within Delhi and was fast being transformed from a village to an urban settlement.

I also went to the Hauz Khas village I had heard Rita talk so much about. She was a frequent visitor to the village and bought all her expensive clothes from the boutiques there. I went there not really to look at the fashionable clothes but to visit a gallery which was showing drawings by Satyajit Ray. I had tried to get some information about the village before I went to see it. It was Alaudin Khilji who had excavated a large tank (hauz) six hundred years ago for the people who lived there. Later Feroz Shah Tughlaq re-excavated the tank and built several buildings around it. It was then named Hauz Khas, royal tank. It had also served as a war camp during the time of Taimur. A dusty mud track led to the village but in the narrow space where it began six or seven imported cars were parked so close together that it was difficult to walk through to the main street. There were shops with glass fronts and artistic hoardings and restaurants and more shops in the upper floors, access to which was provided by small whitewashed staircases. For all this sophistication the smell of mud and cowdung filled the space, and the atmosphere remained that of a village.

I walked into one of the fashion stores and talked to the owner, a tall, delicate, perfectly made-up lady. Her delicateness was not about her personality which appeared to be one of a tough businesswoman, rather it was of her person; she was dressed in a delicate chiffon blouse and a grey textured skirt, both of which

she must have bought at a boutique in Europe. 'It all happened overnight,' she said exuberantly about the transformation of a quiet village into a chic shopping area. 'Because of the low rent a fashion designer rented a residence to manufacture her goods. Then she started a shop in the village. Her rich clients liked the village atmosphere and she selected a few of her friends to set up boutiques here. They rented rooms from the villagers and without dismantling the mud walls or making modifications, they decorated them and set up their shops.'

I met one of the long-time residents of the area. He took me to his house which was in a lane behind the main street. 'In the beginning it was all right,' he said. 'Some of us rented out our front two rooms. They paid a good price and we needed money. We used to store fodder for the cattle in these rooms. They cleaned and repaired the rooms and made them into shops. But then more people came. The open courts in the house were covered and given on rent and we started living in the rear rooms of the house.

'The prices increased rapidly as more shops opened and eventually all the houses were rented out. Now the main street is purely commercial. Multi-storey buildings have come up, even on plots which are just enough to accommodate a hut. Everyone is after money. And we have become secondary citizens. We have been sold out.'

*

Rita drove me to Connaught Circus where Kanvinde had his office. He was an old and famous architect and a friend of her father's; he had designed their house in Baroda. It was a lovely house, understated, full of space, with an absence of form. I had liked the way in which Kanvinde had brought in the landscape into the house and around it as though it embraced the house and then penetrated within. There was a central courtyard filled with large pebbles. In the centre was the root of an old and enormous tree placed upside down so that it looked like a piece of sculpture. A grille separated the garden from the courtyard so that visually the two mingled.

This aspect of the house was ingrained in my mind since the days I was at school and it influenced me so much that I used versions of it later in the houses I designed at college and for other people. I had never met Kanvinde and was very eager to do so. He was one of the first few architects of the country to build in the international style, although later, like everyone else, he was influenced by the modernity of Corbusier and his tempestuous aesthetics of brick and concrete.

We drove past the curved buildings of Connaught Circus, white, commanding. They were arranged in two circles: the inner circle and the outer circle. In the centre was a park. Radial roads connected the two circles. The whole complex was unified architecturally by a double colonnade mounted with Palladian motifs. Kanvinde's office was on one of the radial roads in the outer circle. A creaky lift took us to his office which was full of models, drawings and young architects. He was a small, mild-mannered man. As one would expect, after enquiring about Rita's father Kanvinde started talking to me about architecture.

'Look,' he said pointing out of his window. 'A few years ago there were no tall buildings here. Now there are very many and they spoil the classical look of the place. Everyone thinks Connaught Circus was designed by Lutyens. It wasn't. It was designed by W.H. Nicholls.

'As you know, Delhi is full of British architecture along with the older Mughal architecture. When the British reconquered Delhi, they wanted it to symbolise their power. They wanted to demolish the Jama Masjid and replace the Red Fort with one of their own, to be called the Victoria Fort. In the end they decided to retain them as historic monuments. But they destroyed all the fine houses of the Delhi aristocracy close to the fort.

'The new government buildings were built after considerable thought, which was a good thing,' Kanvinde confessed. 'The viceroy, Lord Hardinge, wanted an indigenous style of architecture for New Delhi. He did not think a European style would fit. But Lutyens wanted only European classicism and was averse to Indian architecture. He said that a truly Indian architecture did not exist and that there was no great tradition of building in India. He thought that the only way India could ever have an architectural tradition was if Western architecture were introduced. Indian architecture, he felt, was all about scenery and picturesqueness; it wasn't intelligent at all. Do you know what he said of the Taj Mahal? He said that it was wonderful, but it was not architecture, and that its beauty began where architecture ended.'

Rita at this point told me to meet her near a restaurant in the inner circle and left. Kanvinde continued with his analysis of Lutyens. 'The government complex which Lutyens designed is on an extraordinary scale. It is ceremonial. He built it in the baroque classical style. It has a long ceremonial axis at the end of which is the palace of the viceroy. On either side of the axis is the secretariat; they are two symmetrical buildings. It was a good thing that Herbert Baker collaborated with Lutyens in the design of these buildings. He wanted them to be imperial rather than purely European architecture. He found many similarities in Indian architecture: in its colonnades, arcades, open courts and domes which he thought were similar to Western classical architecture. He used jalis (carved screens), chhattris (small canopies), and chhajjas (sunshades). He also used Buddhist railings like the ones in Sanchi. Because of this, the complex appears Indian. I think the British architecture in Delhi looks most Indian. But this is true only of the main government complex. In all other buildings they used a purely classical style, as in Connaught Place.'

He then talked to me about the modern movement of architecture in India: 'Corbusier is criticised today, but both he and Louis Kahn influenced a whole generation of Indian architects,' he told me. 'When Corbusier began to build in India, his style revolted against the monumentality of colonial architecture and the few Indian styles. However this did not last long and architects began to look for a new ideology. Something that was based on social values, culture and modern technology.

'But these days they use traditional concepts with modern values,' I said.

'In the past cities were planned to give security. So they were built like fortresses. The people were huddled together within these walls,' he replied.

'If you compare the cities of the north and south, they are different. In the south they are built with more freedom because they were never worried about invasions. So tradition always had solutions based on the need at that time. The courtyard house was built in the past keeping in mind the climate and the way people lived, but it's relevance today must be questioned carefully. And whether people want to live in courtyard houses. Maybe many still do. I have seen that people understand and use tradition differently at different times. Before the war, architects believed tradition was building an external envelope in Buddhist, Muslim, Hindu or classical style. This was because of the influence of the beaux arts school. Then there was a post-war revolt and this attitude changed.

'Architects started building in the international style. But this did not last either, because architects felt a universal style was too regimented. So they began to search for their roots; they returned to their heritage. But I believe tradition must not be merely re-used. With modern technology and new cultural values everything is going to be different, and we have to build according to that.'

Twenty minutes later, with my extended knowledge of Lutyens's architecture and modernism, I left Kanvinde's office. One thought remained in my mind, and that was that every successive architecture was not necessarily original; it took considerably from what preceded it. I did not know whether to call it imitation or continuity; whatever it was, the line of descent in architecture was straight and clear: the Greeks had handed over the torch to the Romans, they to the great Italians and on to the French and the English who then passed on a bastardised version of it to their colonies.

Preoccupied with this line of thought, I decided to wander about the streets before meeting Rita. I walked through the circular arcade formed by the buildings in the inner circle. Outside the arcade was row upon row of parked cars. It was because of the monumental presence and the geometry of the structure of this complex that the entire place did not seem a large municipal parking lot. The scale of the complex was intimidating and was meant for large numbers rather than a single person. I presumed it to be an expression of colonial power and superiority.

It was the people and what they did which broke down the scale making it more intimate. They stood by the shops and talked, vibrating like iridescent specks of colour against the white of the colonnades. Helping in this process were the vendors selling books, toys, leather goods and various other items spread out on the pavement. I walked into Palika Bazaar, an underground shopping complex. People crowded the corridors, people who should have been in the sunshine and air. If anything, it was the cars which should have been in the dingy, artificially lighted and poorly ventilated basement.

*

Later in the evening I went to have tea with an old English acquaintance, Bob Thompson, whom I had met in Tokyo. He was at the time the first secretary at the British consulate in Tokyo. He had lived in India for many years with his father and always said he wanted to return to it, and he did eventually. Seated in the front lawn of his house drinking tea from handcrafted pottery, perhaps from Pondicherry, I talked to him about Delhi, British architecture and the uses of imitation. 'What's new about it? People have been imitating for a long time.

'The Renaissance architects, particularly of the later period, copied the classical art of ancient Rome which had been ignored in the Middle Ages. Then there was the Palladian imitation: the great Italian architect Andrea Palladio designed Roman-inspired villas and palaces. Baroque architecture began in Rome and spread to other parts of Europe and culminated in rococo architecture, which was light and delicate and even more elaborate than the baroque style. There was a Palladian revival and country houses began to be built in that style.

'Neoclassical architects arrived with a new interest in Greek and Roman styles. They designed colonnades and large structures, using simpler geometric forms rather than the baroque's swirls and curves. On the heels of the Industrial Revolution came another Greek revival. Museums, banks and large offices were constructed as re-creations of Greek designs. It was followed by the Gothic revival and churches, hotels and government buildings were built in the Gothic revival style—great domes, expansive arches, buttresses. Whatever the style and period, the urge was the same: look back and copy. Today we are still suffering from it: imitation. Don't you think so?'

He sat back and looked at me quizzically.

'But they all did well, didn't they?' he continued. 'They built well and beautifully, because they were artistic and had a good sense of form, and because people were conscious of beauty and appreciated art, even if it was borrowed art. They could relate to it.

'It was after the Industrial Revolution that the whole idea of a building changed. Buildings became machines and machine aesthetics ruled. Cars, planes, printing presses, typewriters and even home appliances, the refrigerator and mixies—all had this new aesthetic, and buildings began to resemble them. They became plain, antiseptic, functional.

'Then came mass production, standardisation. There was imitation, duplication on a large scale. Machines were made in factories; buildings followed suit. Building materials were manufactured somewhere and used elsewhere. Also the sense of the local changed; everything was local because of advanced transportation, communications and trade. For every design there were a million xeroxes. Buildings were copied, copies were imitated, imitations were duplicated, duplications were marketed. You could get anything. There were imitations with varying price tags; high-priced for the rich and famous, cheap ones for the middle class. Everyone could have the Taj Mahal, or at least versions of it. That's what it is now—it is the age of acquisition. And it has suffocated art forms, and style has become superficial decoration: paints, textures and motifs, collages. Imitation has become an epidemic, it has strangled creativity.

'Have you seen this?' he asked, showing me a book. It was a book on Vijaynagara and Hampi by George Michell. We both knew him. I told him that I had met George when he was in India researching for the book. Bob began to talk about the contents of the book and temples. 'When the Aryans came, they were literary and intelligent, but they didn't bring their art or architecture with them. They ultimately mixed with the local people and adopted the absurd fables and monstrous superstitions of the Turanians. This brought God to earth, to mix and interfere in mundane matters, and degraded their purer religion into a system of idolatry. In the south the Dravidians, an indigenous Turanian

313

people, though of lower intellectual level than the Aryans, were enthusiastic builders. They created architecture of their own with mediocre intelligence, inspired by a religion of degrading fetishism and so they built nothing grand or imposing. All they offered to God was the labour of ornamentation: every part of the building was carved with the most difficult designs. It was very elegant but not true architectural art.

'The Aryans looked at the specimens built by the natives, they adopted them, copied them. It wasn't great architecture. The temples were primitive in construction. After all, what were they: horizontal heaps piled one on top of other like a pyramid, held with brackets and ornamented profusely. Hindu architecture had never reached the intellectual supremacy of Greece. What it displayed was an exuberance of fancy, a lavishness of labour, and an elaboration of detail. There was visibly nothing in comparison or as sublime as the hall at Karnak, nothing so intelligent as the Parthenon, nor so constructively grand as the medieval cathedral.

'I think the high water mark of Indian architecture was, if at all, the Buddhist monuments at Sanchi,' Bob said. 'They were inspired by Greek art. Buddhist art didn't spread far but the Hindu temple building continued, fanned by Aryan enthusiasm and Brahministic domination. The basic form was copied, imitated, multiplied until its art declined. The decline was not just a matter of precision in sculpting but also to do with the delicacy of morals. The decline was arrested temporarily by the classically influenced Gandhar art, it was a product of Indo-Greek colonies combining classical with Buddhist forms. It brought new vitality. But with the waning of Greek influence after the fall of Bactria, together with the subsequent decline of Buddhism under the impact of the revived Hindusim, the Gandhar art collapsed.'

'Then?' I asked entranced by all that he had been saying.

'Then the Muslims arrived,' he said in a matter-of-fact way. 'Unlike the Aryans they brought with them the art and architecture of the Middle East. Islamic art was essentially a result of the confrontation between Islam and the West. It derived its style from Rome and it was transformed by the Christian builders, particularly in its central features, the arch and dome. They added the minaret to it and produced a group of architectural forms which had dignity, elegance and picturesqueness combined with perfect constructive science. They were unlike the horizontal styles of Hindu temples loaded with ornamentation; they had constructive and aesthetic thoughtfulness.

'They not only used Hindu artisans but also used the material of the temples they demolished. The true Saracenic art changed; it transformed into Indo-Saracenic architecture. The large and grand Islamic arches were plugged with the delicacy of Hindu ornamental screens. Also plugged was the continuation of the purer Saracenic style of which only a few were built: Muhammad bin Tughlaq's tomb which is undoubtedly the best of Islamic architecture. It showed no influence of the Hindu decorative style and its sloping walls and massive towers are impressive. Mandu's architecture, its large structures, simple grandeur and expression of power showed how wonderfully the builders had grasped the true elements of architectural design. Or the Gol Gumbaz in Bijapur: it was bold in construction and had the largest domed space in the world.

'The corruption of styles continued: in Lucknow the buildings of brick and stucco were draped in Indo-Saracenic styles to which were added European motifs and classical orders; architecture declined. Then the British arrived. They were in a dilemma, they didn't know what style to choose: native, Islamic, Indo-Saracenic, or European. They wanted to show off their power, their superiority. They also felt that they should not introduce a new style of architecture into India because the architecture of the West could never suit the natives of the East. Like the Muslims, they wanted to use the art of the land they had conquered and adapt it to suit their ideas and needs. At that time even in Britain there was an ongoing debate between classical and Gothic styles, so it wasn't surprising that they were in such a dilemma.

'It was not just the style but also the climate of India and ways in which a building could be built to suit the heat and the rains and the humidity that baffled the British. The local people had developed simple ways to beat the severe climatic problems. They had built enclosed courtyards, small shuttered windows, basements, etc. So the British adapted formal classical forms toned down by Indian elements like the jali, chhattri and the chhajja for

the government buildings. But for their domestic architecture the British looked to Bengal—a thatched roof hut with a broad veranda on all sides. They preferred the bangla, which eventually came to be called the bungalow because it combined a climatic purpose with a social one—that of social distance and of superiority, particularly when the bungalow was placed in a compound.

'They learnt to build suitable houses which had walls of ample thickness, an absence of vertical forms such as buttresses which would stop air flow and showed a preference for horizontal bands, cornices to cast shade, ample openings, piers, columns, balconies and corbelled projections. This was the beginning of colonial architecture in India and it was neither Indian or English; it was a bit of both. In a way it was a dilution of styles. Another phase of the decline began. Corbusier arrived. Chandigarh was built for the Punjabis who had lost Lahore in the partition. With Corbusier came reinforced concrete, plastic forms, modular windows, doors, openings, modular everything, even modular culture. Buildings became cubes, cylinders and pyramids. Everything had concrete sunshades, even PWD public toilets. Modern architecture was bastardised. So you see, it all began with imitation and ended with it,' Bob said fretfully.

'But what about Lutyens's architecture? Everyone is talking about it now,' I argued.

'Oh Lutyens,' Bob said amused and added, 'Have you read the book about him written by his daughter Mary?'

He went in and came back with the book. He scanned through the pages and finding the one he wanted, began to read:

'Lutyens sent Baker two recipies for Indian styles: Hindu: Set square stones and build childwise, but before you erect, carve every stone differently and independently, with lace patterns and terrifying shapes. On top, over trabeated pendentives, set an onion.

'Mogul: Build a vasty mass of rough concrete, elephant-wise, on a very simple rectangular-cum-octagon plan, dome in anyhow, cutting off square. Overlay with a veneer of stone patterns, like laying a vertical tile floor, and get Italians to help you. Inlay jewels and cornelians if you can afford it and rob someone if you can't. Then on top of the mass put three turnips in concrete and overlay with stone or marble as before. Be careful not to bond anything in, and don't care a damn if it does all come to pieces.'

Bob laughed, amused by the description. It did sound funny; I had never heard or read Indian architecture described like that.

'Lutyens had nothing but contempt for Indian architecture,' Bob said. 'In his youth he had built many romantic English country homes and then later had turned to classical models. He was captivated by Palladio's architecture. In a letter to Baker, he wrote, "Would Wren, had he gone to Australia, have burnt his knowledge and experience to produce a marsupial style?"

'Lutyens did what Wren did: Wren tried to make classicism sane for England, Lutyens tried to make it sane for India and he succeeded, I would think, because his architecture is at least more Indian than Corbusier's. I think it was primarily because of Herbert Baker. He took charge of the design of the secretariat blocks. Before coming to India, Baker had built in South Africa so he knew about the tropical climate. He understood the necessity of spacious colonnades, open verandas, overhanging eaves, cornices and small high windows. All these increased the

317

circulation of air while keeping the sun out. These elements were also part of Mughal architecture. So in the end there was a grafting of Indian motifs on a classical surface,' Bob explained.

Lutyens did the Viceroy's House and the overall layout of New Delhi. In the latter he was helped by many others, planners, engineers and architects. The Parliament building was designed by Baker, the churches were put up by Medd. Connaught Place was designed by Nicholls, Bob said.

'Then why do they call it Lutyens's Delhi?' I asked.
'God alone knows!' I heard him say.

*

Later that evening, after a rich Punjabi dinner at which Rita also served Bengali fried fish, I thought of the pretentious buildings built by the British in Delhi. I also thought of Calcutta where the British had built large mansions, different from the ones in Delhi. The last time I was in Calcutta was with Rita; I thought of her father's house and her grandfather's haveli.

Rita's father, Abhijit Dasgupta, had worked for an Indian drug company in Baroda, which he left to work for a another drug company, a multinational, in Calcutta. Within the first year his accent had become free of the rounded vowels the Bengalis can shed only with great difficulty. He also came to possess a smug and condescending demeanour becoming of a high-salaried cosmopolitan executive, besides possessing, as long as he served the company, a furnished bungalow and other trappings of his status.

Dasgupta was, like many Bengalis, very artistic. He was interested in music, painting and even architecture. It was because of his interest in architecture that he had been very keen that Kanvinde should design his house.

Dasgupta's company accommodation was an old English mansion. Perched on a large hump, pearly white as polished rice, except for the green louvres, it had a broad veranda on the first floor, which was hung with thick latticework screens reaching halfway down the alpine columns. In front of the house was a handkerchief-sized parlour rounded and walled by four classical columns which propped drunken creepers that clambered over them. The parlour opened into a small hall with a large wooden staircase. There were two doors in it: one led to the formal drawing room which had large windows set in arches with a keystone in the centre, although all the British buildings in Calcutta were built in brick. Perhaps it was brick that was shaped like a keystone.

The other door in the hall in Dasgupta's house led to the dining room. Next to it was the pantry. The kitchen was a separate building connected by a covered corridor. 'Most British mansions had a detached kitchen. They never liked to see the mess the Indian cooks made in them,' Dasgupta had said to me when I had questioned him about it. 'All houses also had terraces and in the evenings the English family would go up to escape the hot interior of the house. Within the house, to cool it, they installed punkhas. These fans had a light wooden frame fifteen feet long and four feet wide. After a lot of study the British derived optimum dimensions for it: the frame was to be 8 to 12 inches wide with a heavy fringe 18 to 24 inches deep and they had to move it in an arc of five feet with a velocity of two-and-one-half feet per second.'

There were many other mansions like Dasgupta's. They were like Greek buildings with porticos and tall classical columns and huge windows. There were louvres over the windows and latticework screens spanned the columns. They were invariably painted a leafy green. When I had asked Dasgupta about this he had said, 'The English did not know how to build in a climate that was hot and humid. The natives built their houses to avoid light and remain cool. But the British built their mansions to show off their wealth and power. Their houses were built in the Renaissance classical style. They felt that since the classical style was okay in the sunny Mediterranean areas, it was okay here. Besides it was used all over Europe. To counter the heat and the glare, they had to put up all those louvres and screens. Just because Palladio's work became popular in England they began to copy the Palladian country house, and it became the model for their mansions in Calcutta.'

'There were other problems that the British faced,' Dasgupta had told me. 'They couldn't find stone for their buildings which troubled them because they were afraid that the buildings would become discoloured with time. Because of this they used a lime plaster made of seashells which was used in Madras. It gave the brick a surface comparable to stone. When the chunam mix was rich, it gave a surface that was as good as marble. The British were also afraid of Calcutta's night fog, a saline nitrogenous miasma which stayed close to the ground. Because of this the ground floor was kept at an elevation.'

We had often gone to Dasgupta's father's house. We had to pass a narrow lane through a congested area crowded with hutments. At the end of the lane was the house, but it was not like the ostentatious mansions of the English with showy facades and formal gardens; it was large but simple with private courtyards within. The house had two storeys and the lower one had a number rooms used as storerooms or just left vacant. On the northern side was the Thakoor Ghar, the gods' room. The family rooms were upstairs connected by verandas. Dasgupta's father, I called him Dada, was an old man who laughed a lot. He used to sit on a white mattress on the floor in the veranda.

He loved to talk and he would address people as they walked

in and out of the rooms engrossed in their work. It was not necessary that they heard him. I liked sitting beside him, talking to him. He would talk of the days when he was young. 'We were very rich,' he had told me with a smug grin, ' but we never liked to show our wealth. So we built our houses with rooms in the front made of mud and thatch. We did not want people to know we were rich, or the robbers. We rented these rooms to poor artists. Then when land became more expensive, a lot of us sold our excess land to men who built many huts and leased them to poor families. These became the bustees.'

He talked to me about the British: 'They liked to fill their houses with furniture,' he said with disapproval. 'Sofas, chairs, tables, beds, pictures on the walls. Our walls are almost bare and so are our rooms. We use mats and charpoys, or a divan.' The lack of furniture, he explained, gave flexibility to the interior. People could sleep anywhere, sit anywhere; they could take advantage of the cool breeze, move away when it rained.

During the time I was a visitor there, Dada's granddaughter had given birth to a baby boy and had been staying in his house for a month. She would bring the baby to the veranda find a sunny spot and rub its body with mustard oil till it shone. The smell of the mustard oil would mingle with the smell of the fish being cooked, also in mustard oil, in the kitchen. Her three-year-old son would now and then rush to her with his mouth wide open, and she would pop a small ball of boiled rice with a piece of hot fried fish into it. I used to like sitting in the courtyard with Dada and watch people moving about. His two sons and their families lived with him, and there was always some activity going on in the courtyard.

In the evenings there would be a breeze blowing through the courtyard. When it rained there was the smell of earth-musk. I was there when the first kal-baisakhi rain broke. The light greyed suddenly and rapidly. Bits of paper and leaves lying in the courtyard swirled up into the air. Someone gave a cry of warning and we rushed to the terrace to collect the clothes hung to dry.

Then the rain came down in large drops like a procession of fervid disciples; the earth-musk evaporated. In its place was the smell of damp lime walls. We rushed to shut the windows after

Ahuja

Sarayu Ahuja

which we sat in the veranda watching the rain. Dasgupta's British mansion would get stuffy in the rain as soon as the windows were shut, but here, in Dada's courtyard, the cool breeze fanned our sweltering skins.

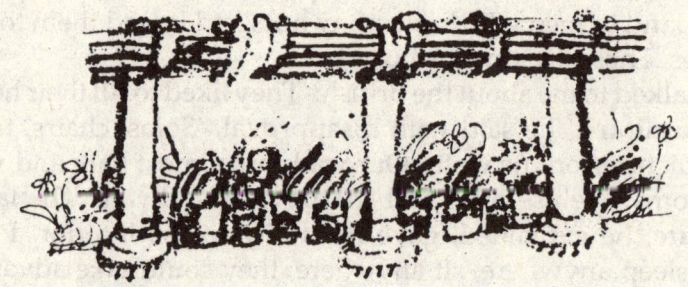

322

Chapter 20

CHANDIGARH: I HAD NEVER MET SATISH GUJRAL BEFORE. HE was a painter and sculptor; he had also turned into a self-taught architect. While in Delhi I had gone to see the Belgian Embassy designed by him. It had received considerable review. I was amazed by its hedonistic fusion of form and space: its sculptural phallic and womblike forms. I was curious to meet the artist who had conceived them, particularly because I like meeting people who are different. I did not know until I met him that evening that he was deaf and therefore spoke in an amplified and elongated voice; it was difficult to understand him. His words at first seemed to me more like sounds; then, as he talked to me, I began to decipher one word from another. His wife Kiran was always close to him and communicated for him patiently, which I thought was very commendable. He looked anxious that evening when I met him because he had made some caustic remarks about Corbusier and all the newspapers had published the remarks.

They had not met with positive sentiment.

'I think I have overstated myself perhaps,' Gujral said to me. 'Many architects are angry with me because I said many things against Corbusier. How can he say such a thing about Corbusier, they are saying. They think it is unpardonable. Even the French Embassy people are upset and their delegates are coming to see me tomorrow. They want an explanation. What I said is perfectly true. I am not afraid, I will tell them. I have even got letters from American and Indian writers saying I must be mad.' He chuckled.

Out of curiosity, I asked him to explain to me exactly what had happened. 'I was working for the Punjab government, at its base in Shimla. I was also a close friend of Nehru. I know Nehru never wanted a foreign architect for Chandigarh! People believe that Nehru and Corbusier were friends. That is false. Nehru had asked the American town planner Mayer to design Chandigarh. Nehru wanted someone who would be conscious of Indian culture. Not Corbusier! He did not know anything about India; he did not even take India seriously. Do you know what Corbusier actually said? He said: "You wear trousers, follow the British parliamentary system, drive a car . . . What's so Indian about it?" That's what he said.

'Look at Chandigarh. Is it India? Tell me?' he asked, holding my arm and shaking it vigorously. 'Does it have any local character? No. It has an imperialist attitude, like the West. He did not design buildings for the local people. They are just calculative and repetitive—so shoddy. And people call it creative!'

'You mean to say Corbusier did not travel all over India?' I asked him, shocked. 'How can that be possible? I have heard that he travelled, he looked at the people, the landscape, even animals, and that he was inspired by all their forms and he has used these forms in his design,' I said. I had idolised Corbusier when I was in college and wanted to retain my admiration for him.

'Oh, Corbusier was a pompous talker,' Gujral retorted. 'He boasted about loving India and then built a building that looks like a chimney in an Ahmedabad factory. Lutyens was different. He always said he hated India. He refused to travel within India. He hated the natives. Yet, his work is more Indian. And, anyway, what Corbusier built in Chandigarh was not even designed for it.

He had designed the "City of the Future". He peddled this idea which he had conceived in the thirties. He showed it to Hitler when he was planning the rebuilding of Berlin, but the Fuhrer's architect, Albert Speer, rejected it. Then he heard that Mussolini was thinking of rebuilding the Roman Empire. Also about Stalin's ideas for Moscow and Roosevelt's dream for America. They all rejected his ideas. Corbusier was nothing but a fascist, let's face it. His architecture reflects this.'

When I went back that evening I felt confused. I had been to Chandigarh when I was in the second year of college. I believed then that Chandigarh, aesthetically and technically, was a stepping stone to a new future, a modern future. I remember standing in front of the tall concrete pillars of the high court absorbing it all in reverence: the raw concrete, the parasol roof, the tall ascending pillars, the colossal scale.

It was like the feeling I experienced when I would go with my grandmother to the temple and stand in front of the idol. I would hear the singing of the devotees and the ringing of bells. I would sway with them and imagine God had actually come down from heaven. I had, over the years, grown out of that feeling. I wondered what I would feel about Chandigarh now. Would I have grown out of it too? I decided to go to Chandigarh and see for myself.

I knew only two people in Chandigarh. One was Harpreet Singh, a retired IAS officer. He was with my father in Shimla where they were trained. He was a Sikh. I was only six years old then and would watch in amazement as he rolled up the yards and yards of his turban.

The other person I knew in Chandigarh was Sangeet Sharma and his father, both of whom were architects. I had met Sangeet at a national seminar of architects in Delhi and he had invited me to come to Chandigarh. 'Whenever you come to Delhi, you must come to Chandigarh. You must come and meet my father. He worked with Corbusier,' he had told me.

It took some time to find a suitable hotel. As the taxi driver took me from one to the next I noticed the city. The streets appeared deserted, there were few cars and not many people moving about.

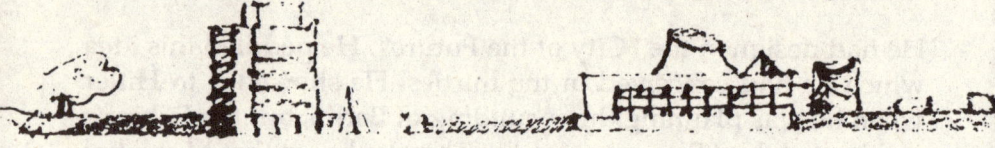

It was unlike the normal Indian streets full of everything: cars, buses, carts, people, animals, noise, dust, chaos.

The streets and the buildings on them had a relationship alien to Indian cities. They were more European: straight and regimented. There was a grid of fast traffic roads, like the ones that Corbusier had used in Marseilles. I remembered Corbusier's plan for the streets: he had wanted to segregate traffic and so he had devised a plan where there were a variety of roads from arterial roads to lanes leading to the apartment blocks. He called it the seven Vs. The V-1 were the regional roads leading into the city, the V-2 were two major cross roads, one of which led to the capitol complex. The other served the cultural-commercial complex. The V-3 were the fast moving traffic roads that formed a grid pattern and enclosed the sectors within them. V-4 were the bazaar streets; they were slightly irregular and they ran through the sector connecting to other sectors. The traffic in these streets was slow. They had shops on the south side so that the people could walk in the shade. V-5 was the loop road within the sector; V-6 were the lanes leading up to the houses; and V-7 was a strip

326

of parkland which contained schools and pedestrian pathways which connected the sectors. Corbusier had later added the V-8 which were bicycle paths.

He compared the seven Vs to the bloodstream and believed that they created order in the city. Corbusier was obsessed with the idea of the city as an organism. Therefore he designed Chandigarh like one: the head was the capital complex, the heart, the city centre, its hand the industrial area, its brain was the parkland with the museums, university and library. Its stomach was the service centre, its veins and nerves were the roads and the green areas formed its lungs.

We drove past a shopping street. The shops were of the same size and so were the hoardings that were fixed to large concrete facia slabs, all of the same size. There were rows and rows of

blocks containing rows and rows of shops behind corridors with tall concrete columns. There were rows and rows of columns. We sped past the industrialised, standardised, mass-produced blocks. After all these years, they still looked lifeless. They were different from any other Indian shopping streets I had seen. Only the people were alike and what they did on the street seemed to bring some life into an otherwise over-designed, sterile environment. I was startled by my observations and my thoughts, which were quite different from those when I had seen Chandigarh the first time. Then, perhaps, I had seen Chandigarh as a trained architect would see: as a three-dimensional version of a plan, like a gigantic model. Now I saw it as a city in which people lived and not as an enlarged model. But the problem was that it felt as unreal as a model and as though the people had been thrown into it.

The taxi driver took me to four different hotels which looked more like oversized houses. None appeared reputable. He would disappear inside and then emerge to coax me to check into the hotel each time. He would praise the hotel, the comfort of its

rooms, the service and the food in the restaurant. His enthusiasm made me suspicious. I asked him to drive back to the main street where I had spotted a place called Piccadily Hotel. 'That is not so good. And it is on the main road,' he argued. He drove back reluctantly, a frown on his face. We drove past residential apartments. Like the shops, they looked stereotyped, made out of machine parts, assembled together. They lacked the spontaneity of the mohallas which were built by people, and which grew organically.

As we drove I tried to recollect what I had seen of Chandigarh when I had come the first time. Surprisingly, I couldn't remember much. Every city has something about it that makes it memorable: its people, its culture, its history. Undoubtedly Chandigarh did not have any of this. All that I remembered was the capitol complex: the secretariat which looked like the Marseilles block. I remembered the ramp that curved its way to the top. That was the only feature that broke the monotony of the entire stretch of the building, which had fenestration fashioned like the radiator grille of a car: a lot of holes of the same size. I remembered the assembly building which was crowned by a phallic form which to Gujral had resembled a factory chimney. I remembered the brise-soleil and the parasol roofs of the high court, both of which were designed for climatic purposes, the brise-soleil to protect from the harsh sun and the parasol to protect from rain and sun.

I remembered the sheet of still water around the buildings which reflected their monastic bleakness. I realised then that the idea of having a bit of the past in the present was not so much a matter of copying the past but providing a continuity, something one could relate to easily. Change was essential for progress but so was continuity. History provided the continuity. In Chandigarh the people had not changed, they were the same. How could they have changed just because they were ushered into mechanised dwellings for living and working? So the skeleton remained modern but everything in it was as traditional as ever.

Soon after cheeking in at the Piccadily I called Harpreet. He arrived within half an hour to fetch me, looking much older but still as warm as ever. We drove down V-2, the most important street of the new town, then turned into a narrower street which I remembered was the V-3. This was meant only for fast-moving traffic and no doors opened directly onto these roads. And no car could stop, if I remembered correctly, for 400 metres, after which you could drive into the sectors. It was a city planned for cars, not for people without them. I acknowledged this fact with growing displeasure. The idea of broad and straight avenues had thrilled me before but not any more. It looked desolate and monotonous, impersonal. I remembered all the streets I had walked through: the pols of Ahmedabad, the mohallas of Lucknow, the bustees of Calcutta or the lanes of old Delhi; they were so spontaneous. They had a hierarchy of streets, Chandigarh had it also. At the same time they were very different: the older streets were organic, full of surprises. They were the result of people's interaction with space and had evolved over a period of time corresponding to the needs of the people; hence they were more intimate and teemed with personal life. The streets of Chandigarh were straight and cheerless, anonymous: they belonged to everyone and no one; the scale was meant for automobiles, not few but many of them, not for people. The main streets were never meant for walking. They were channels of mechanical transport.

We drove past many sectors, all alike and tediously prescribed, before we came to Harpreet's flat. It was a small two-bedroom flat. His wife Sumeet was waiting for us when we arrived. Both their sons had settled in the United States and they lived alone. 'Chandigarh is good for a retired life,' Harpreet said as he led me into the living room. It was simply decorated: it had a rexine covered sofa-cum-bed on which were phulkhari cushions in violent colours. There were two chairs on either side of it and a centre table. Against the wall was a glass cabinet with crockery and on top of it a Sony TV; beside it was a National tape recorder with two large speakers.

We talked about Chandigarh and how it came about. 'Punjab did not have any capital because it had lost Lahore. It was decided to build a new capital as none of the existing cities, it was felt, were good enough. They did not have sufficient infrastructure and they could not take on the role of a capital without huge investment. It would be as expensive as building a new city.

'They wanted to build a magnificent city to make up for the psychological loss of Lahore and to appease the Punjabis who had lost everything when they left Pakistan. They also decided that the new capital must have a large industrial complex. This, they felt, would give jobs to the uprooted people.

'They had to decide first how big the city had to be and invited applications from people who were interested in setting up industries, business and also people who would like to live there. At that time P.L. Varma was the chief engineer. He was with the Punjab state government and in charge of development. He said that the new capital should be built for 500,000 people.

'But Fletcher rejected this. He was the officer on special duty and he said it was not possible that the capital would grow to such a large size even at the end of twenty years. He said the capital should be only for a hundred thousand people. He said that Lahore had grown over centuries and it was totally unrealistic to replace Lahore in twenty years.'

'There was another problem. Where should the new capital be built? The central government and the state government started looking for sites. They wanted it to be away and safe from Pakistan. They also wanted it to have proper road and rail connections to other cities. At that time the governor of East Punjab wrote to Nehru about the selection of the site. He was very worried because he felt that it would create discord among the leaders of the constituencies. Each political leader would want the capital in his constituency. Whatever was decided had also to be a political solution. He was right.

'They made a terrible mistake, I think,' he said, pressing his lips together. 'What they did not do was link physical planning with economic planning and also how the capital would relate to the other towns. This was very bad for its future. Actually the debate about the new capital would have gone on and on but Nehru

stepped in and said, let's look for the site. They decided on three—Ambala, Chandigarh and Ludhiana. They selected Chandigarh because it was at a safe distance from Pakistan and the cost of buying land was cheaper. Its name was derived from a temple of the goddess Chandi, the goddess of power, in one of the acquired villages.

'Nehru wanted the capital to be an expression of creative genius, of a modern world. He wanted a new city which symbolised India's new found freedom and which was unfettered by the traditions of the past. At that time there were not many trained Indian town planners to build a new city so Nehru thought about hiring a foreign consultant. He decided on Albert Mayer.

'Mayer wasn't new to India,' he said, offering me a spicy papad that his wife had placed on the table. 'During the Second World War, he had served in the country as a lieutenant colonel in the U.S. Army, building airfields in Bengal. He was so drawn to Indian life that he had proposed a programme for model villages to Nehru. So Nehru asked the Punjab government to appoint Mayer. When the Punjab government approached him for the design of Chandigarh, Mayer was already associated with the Etawah rural development scheme in Uttar Pradesh. He was also involved with several other post-war town planning projects in India which included the master plans for Greater Bombay and Kanpur. Mayer agreed to design the new capital which was to accommodate a population of 500,000 in two phases of 150,000 and later 350,000.

'Albert Mayer could not handle such a large project himself and asked Matthew Nowicki, who was then the head of the school of architecture in Raleigh, to assist him. They prepared the first conceptual blueprint for the city. It was fan shaped, and as the architects did not want a sterile geometric grid, they had designed curving roads and sectors. that were not so regimented. They also made a detailed architectural scheme for one super block. But then Nowicki died in a plane crash and Mayer withdrew from the project.

'It was then that P.N. Thapar, the administrator of the capital project, and Varma were sent to Europe to select other architects. They did not want American architects because the cost of paying them in dollars was becoming too high. So they went to Europe instead. There were to be two conditions: that the architect move to India for three years and that he accept a yearly salary of three thousand pounds. That is how they landed at the door of Swiss-born French architect Charles-Edouard Jeanneret, better known as Le Corbusier, in Paris. He was then sixty-three years old and tired of disappointments. You know what Corbusier had declared at that time? He had said in utter despair: "I am so glad I am going to die soon, people are so stupid. They have tried to crush me so often. First they called me a dirty engineer, then a painter who struggled to be an architect, then a communist and then a fascist. I don't care. I have an iron will." He was very bitter then.'

We sipped our lemonades for a while then Harpreet continued. 'Many of his schemes had either been rejected or had not materialised. He did not think anything about the Indian project. He also felt three years in India was too much and the salary too little. "We can build your capital right here in the office. We are capable of finding a solution to your problems," he said. He had been working on a revolutionary philosophy of sun-space-quiet and both Thapar and Varma were impressed. But later when they went to see Corbusier's housing development in Marseilles, they were not very sure that his ideas would fit into India.

'Thapar and Varma then went to London and met the architect

couple Edwin Maxwell Fry and Jane Beverly Drew. They had already worked in areas with heavy rain, high humidity and mosquitoes. Jane was excited when told about Corbusier and said that it would be glorious if he did the project and that she would convince him. Corbusier agreed but also wanted his cousin Pierre Jeanneret to work with them. Corbusier was appointed the architectural adviser and a three-year contract was signed with Maxwell Fry, Jane Drew and Pierre Jeanneret.

'No one knows the real story and all the problems that went into building Chandigarh. Now people think it was Corbusier who designed Chandigarh. Only Corbusier is known for its design,' he said regretfully. 'Corbusier radically changed Mayer's plan. He straightened all the roads, formed grids and made it more rigid. Mayer had planned for smaller sectors so that it would be cohesive and more people-oriented. But Corbusier designed large sectors. Actually they are too overscaled and people feel lost in them. Mayer had also planned central shopping areas which were introverted. But Corbusier wanted a large shopping street. Corbusier liked large plans that were classical and formal.' Then he added more mournfully, 'Look what has happened to it now. There are slums in it. The inner streets are dirty and the service streets are full of garbage. Chandigarh was designed for neither India nor Indians.' He smiled, his blue eyes twinkling, 'Let's have lunch. Sunita has made parathas which you like so much.'

*

It was a lovely evening, I remember, with a wisp or two of cloud in a pale blue sky, and the air had that perfect clarity you only get on an early winter evening. I drove in a taxi to Sangeet and his father's office. It was a small flat converted into an office. Sangeet introduced me to his wife, a fair and very slim woman, and then took me to meet his father, S. D. Sharma. He was sitting in a darkened room at a desk strewn with drawings.

Behind him on a table were several rolls of tracing paper and also a model of a large complex. Above it on the wall was a board pinned with many photographs of buildings. They were masculine buildings made of brick and raw concrete. I could see how much Corbusier's and Jeanneret's buildings had influenced him. He showed me more photographs of his projects that he had built over the years. He was particularly close to Jeanneret or so I assumed from the way he talked about him. I asked him what it had meant to him, particularly at such an impressionable age, to work with Le Corbusier and Pierre Jeanneret.

'It was a wonderful experience,' Sharma said. 'It was a search for a new order. That was what modernism was all about. It was a feeling of internationalism, a post-war expression of a world which had run out of resources. No one really understood what Corbusier was all about. His work had a very special style and content, they died with him.

'His style is very difficult to imitate. Some may say it is inhuman and not practical but he was a great source of inspiration. I was young then, without any preconceived notions. I was therefore influenced in a big way by the purity of his forms, the honesty of his structures and the simplicity of expression. I didn't work much with Corbusier, more with Jeanneret. It is not true that Corbusier did not care for things Indian. He did care although it may not have emerged in his work. To him the spirit of the world was more important than the local culture.

'He liked the mountains and rivers and the misty sea. You can't believe that, can you? Yes, he liked the trees and flowers. He liked nature. People are saying all kinds of things about Corbusier now; they criticise him. But one has to know his mind thoroughly to understand his revolutionary architecture. Because that is what it is. Revolutionary. We must admit this. Don't you think so?' He waited for me to reply.

At this point Sangeet's wife, who had left the room, came back smelling of freshly sprayed perfume and said that she had booked the table at the restaurant for eight-thirty. 'We have half an hour. Let me drive you to the capitol complex,' Sharma said to me. He continued talking about Corbusier on the way. 'I learnt many things from his architecture. He had many theories. Yes, people said he was theoretical and not practical, but then his theories had some truth. Architecture to him was a plastic art; without the connotation of style. He didn't believe in style. He believed that architecture was stifled by custom and style was a lie. What is style, after all, it is only what a number of people are thinking at a time. We don't have to depend on old styles. We have to create our own style. This is what Corbusier felt. So he created his own style and philosophy. He felt that the house was a machine for living and therefore had to be mass produced. And like all industrial products houses had to be built in an assembly-line way. Just as planes are for flying and their design is a product of careful study and selection, based on logic and economy, he was convinced that the house must be a product of logic and economy.'

I recollected what Corbusier had written in his book on architecture. I remembered the way in which he had defined architecture into four elements: mass, surface, plan and regulating lines. Architecture to him was much more than just building. To him mass was very important. The object could be perceived because of its mass. It made it plastic and when the masses were brought together in light, then the light revealed the forms: cubes, cones, spheres—their images stood out, distinct and tangible, not ambiguous. Corbusier never considered the cathedrals to be beautiful and plastic, they were merely dramatic. I never understood this then but now I could understand what he meant. He was referring to primary forms like the pyramids which made architecture plastic. He liked primary forms and was particular about the arrangement of forms. He loved geometric forms. According to him, forms and shapes affected our senses, they gave a measure of order. Surface was also important to him because it clothed the mass. Surfaces, according to him, had directing and generating lines which reduced or enlarged the sensation and plasticity. The plan was the generator of mass and surface and it fixed the object to a place. It brought order. The regulating lines induced a perception of order and measurement. It made the object have a definite proportion, it was a basis of orderly construction. He believed that contour and profile were the important aspects of architecture and it was this that differentiated an artist from a mere engineer. Contour was free of constraint of custom, tradition, of construction or adaptation of utilitarian needs.

Sharma broke into my thoughts. 'He tried to achieve perfection. How does one achieve perfection? It comes only through fixed standards and logical selection. This is what he believed. Selection was a very important tool of design to him and standards were a matter of logic and experiment. They were based on a problem that was well stated, so he felt. So the problem of modern housing had to be well stated. He was particular about this. The problem of housing was not one of construction but its architecture. He looked at architecture differently from construction. Architecture, of course, was different, as it also had to deal with emotions. I agree with this entirely. It does this through the use of raw materials and other elements like light, shade, walls and space. Architecture goes beyond utilitarian needs. It is not all about function. It is plastic and full of order.'

We walked around the complex for a few minutes and then drove to the restaurant which was much like any Punjabi

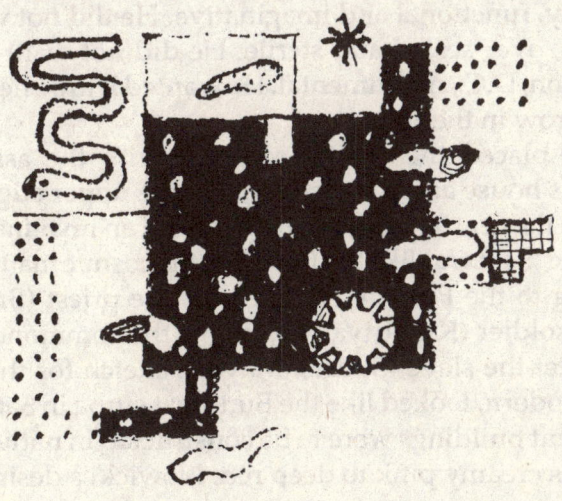

restaurant. As we sat down at the table after ordering the drinks Sharma ordered buttered chicken, black dal, creamed cottage cheese and vegetable, also in rich gravy, and tandoori rotis. It was the same kind of food available in any Mughlai restaurant. Nothing had changed, nothing was different. Culturally and socially the people who lived here were the same as before, the same as people anywhere else. Sharma bit into a pickled onion and went on.

'Mayer's ideas for Chandigarh were different from those of Corbusier,' Sharma said. 'Mayer wanted to create a thoroughly Indian modern city. He felt that in India people were essentially villagers at heart. And also that they preferred to live in very intimate places. He had felt this intimacy in the bazaars. So he planned a super block like a large urban village with a village centre much like the market square of medieval towns. He believed that the functions were the same: meeting, gossiping, shopping and listening to speeches. Because of the strong sunlight he planned a variety of streets, large and narrow, offsetting and breaking at places. At the narrow points he designed houses with inner courts and with small openings on the street side. He also placed a cluster of houses round a court with narrow ends. These aspects were like our chowks. There was a casualness to his plan and it was done to avoid monotony which is often there in planned cities. It was not to be a city of high technology but a simple city, functional and imaginative. He did not want it to be like Delhi, over-scaled and sterile. He did not want it to be like Washington, D.C., monumental. He wanted it to be flexible so that it could grow in the future.

'Mayer placed the capitol complex with the assembly, the governor's house and the secretariat at the upper edge of the city and not in the centre,' he said, drawing out an imaginary diagram with a fork. 'So it was like the Purusha, the cosmic man, you know? According to the Purusha, the head is the priest (Brahmin), his arms the soldier (Kshatriya), his thighs the commoner (Vaishya) and his feet the slave (Sudra). Mayer's sketch for the assembly, though modern, looked like the Buddhist stupa in Sanchi. All the government buildings were to be constructed in native limestone which was creamy pink to deep red. Nowicki's designs blended with the Indian way of life. The bazaars contained all the Indian features: shops where one could sit on the floor, a separate area for hawkers. Houses had screens instead of windows and terraces since people slept in the open. He had also captured the richness of the craftsmen's ornamentation.'

Our food came and we were busy for the next few minutes. Inevitably, after some general conversation, he picked up the thread of his argument again. 'But Corbusier didn't like it,' he said. 'He found Nowicki's designs rather romantic and too Indian. He did not like the way Mayer had located the capitol buildings at the end of the approach road. Corbusier had a different dream for a city. He felt the present cities were not dense. He dreamed of a city of towers where the buildings would be raised on piles of concrete. The streets would also be on piles at a height of sixty-five feet linking the towers. These piles would leave a lot of space on the ground for services like gas, water mains, sewers. Instead of foundations and excavations and digging up roads to bury pipes and cables in them, the ground would carry them. Cafes and restaurants would not be on pavements, they would be on these elevated streets, as would all other commercial activity. This was Corbusier's dream city, clean, orderly and machine-made.

'But Fry found him authoritarian in style. He felt that Corbusier's idea for the city of tomorrow was only fit for a race of robots. Corbusier had been deeply influenced by the technological revolution. He travelled a lot and everywhere he saw technology replacing the work of artisans. Corbusier wanted to search for new architectural forms, machine art which would be used in an industrial age. He found his new language in the cubist aesthetics, in the geometric forms—cubes, spheres, cylinders, cones and so on. He became an anti-naturalist. He believed that the city was a man's grip on nature—a human operation directed against nature. To him this was creation.

'Art nouveau was popular then. But he did not like the way its followers integrated architecture and nature. He felt a building should be a clear, sophisticated statement and should stand in contrast to nature rather than appear as an outgrowth of some natural form. Architecture and nature should enhance by their differences, creating a harmony by contrast and not by looking similar. Just as the art nouveau designers had argued that nature is honest, and therefore forms taken from nature must also be honest, Corbusier argued that machines were efficient and forms borrowed from machines were efficient too.

'So he had committed himself to a new world of form which the cubists had begun to paint. Secondly, he was committed to reinforced concrete, preferring it over steel. He was committed to the tradition of the Mediterranean, its vigour, strength and the grandeur of Greece, Rome, and the Renaissance.'

Over dessert of lime-green kulfi Sharma wrapped up his elucidation of Corbusier's architectural philosophy. 'Corbusier was particular about standardisation. He went back to the traditional Renaissance rule of measure and proportion and produced the modular system, a basic principle of building with the idea of the Greek golden section. The modular system, with its proportionate scale, makes it possible for an infinite number of variations within a unit system of construction, and it can be used to break the monotony which happens in mass production systems. He also felt that cultural progress was connected to urban density. His preference for raw concrete, timber, unfaced brick and rough stone showed his shift to brutalism. It seems he rediscovered this from his interest in natural orders, primitive societies and sexual relations with women who did not have conventional etiquette or sophistication. So you see there was a duality about him. His renewed interest in women led him to use the curve and this can be seen in the slightly lateral streets in Chandigarh.' I was to remember this remark later when I read in a magazine that the curved street was influenced by Corbusier's unsuccessful efforts at seducing a European journalist, Taya Zinkin!

We drove back to the Piccadily Hotel in silence. I think we were all tired from talking, listening and eating too much. It was dark and Chandigarh appeared like a number of giant matchboxes arranged in a row. Square pockets of light shone through the windows. The skyline was even and perfect, the streets were perfect, the trees also planted in a row were perfect. Yet there was something missing. It was not complacent and joyful like the other typically Indian cities, nor was it hectic and fast-paced as Western

340

cities. I realised that Chandigarh may have been right in its time but then somehow tradition had outlived it. Tradition had survived modernity. Nehru had wanted a modern city and without ties to the past. Corbusier had provided an international city. Perhaps it was wrong for us to look for associations to the past. There weren't any. There weren't supposed to be any. Corbusier was right therefore in not copying tradition but just being inspired by it. So Chandigarh was right at that time. But we had changed, modernism had changed. After all modernism was only a state of mind, it described the changes that took place in the nineteenth century in people's attitude towards their physical world and its artifacts. People in need of a new focus had turned to their roots. Tradition had became popular, and all that was modern became an abomination.

Chandigarh had failed. The modernity of Chandigarh was limited only to its physical attributes. Being different from an organic city which has 'grown' without any centralised planning, a planned city like Chandigarh provided its planner the opportunity to restructure the social and cultural values of people. Perhaps it failed because the planners did not understand the culture and values of its people. It was not necessary to look to tradition to borrow its physical forms, but it was essential that the socio-cultural values of tradition be translated into physical forms. Architecture is not all about beautiful forms and spaces, it is much more. It is about people and how they live together.

Within a few years there were slums on the outskirts of Chandigarh, and within the city there was overcrowding with many families living in dwellings meant for one family. Unauthorised shops and hawkers appeared. As the price of plots included all city services such as schools, museums, clinics, stadiums and so forth, it became too expensive for the working classes. The plots were auctioned to the highest bidder which raised the land value rapidly. The major factor in the growth of unauthorised squatter colonies was the city's poor economic base, because the planners, who were preoccupied with the physical character of the city, paid little attention to urban labour and informal activities.

Corbusier had neatly divided the city into four

functions—living, working, leisure and communications. But in India there are traditional ties between living and working, and single purpose zones meant excluding a large population, which was unsuitable. A total assimilation of all elements of a community was absent. There was no alternate economy besides the formal economic base. Because it broke with the past it was thought to be innovative. However, what was forgotten was that the success of a new town is dependent on not just the planners who create it but on the people who live in it, and the officials who manage it. Chandigarh has been admired for its physical features and open spaces. New designs and construction do not by themselves make the dream of planning and building better urban environments come true.

Chandigarh was a dream. It remained one. With this last thought I waved good-bye to Sharma, Sangeet and his wife and walked away between the columns that held the brise-soleil Corbusier had so fondly designed to keep the shining sun away from the new city.

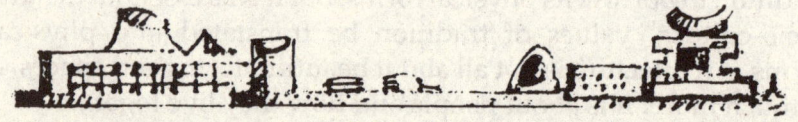

Part IV

Destination

Chapter 21

BANGALORE: MY FATHER DIED FIVE YEARS AGO. ANDAMMA, MY grandmother, died a year after him. As I write this I am in my mother's house in Bangalore. Amma's brother and sister are visiting her for a few days and we all sit together in the evenings in the front veranda (they no longer call it tinnai) and talk about those days in Tanjore we spent together. Tata's house in Selvanagar was sold to a wealthy merchant after his death and Andamma went to live with one of her sons in Mysore. Mama (my mother's brother) tells me about the people who lived in Selvanagar and what happened to them. 'Remember Gita? She lived three houses away from Tata's house. She used to learn Bharatanatyam and you would peep through the gate of their house, see her dance and come home and dance. And Andamma would say to your Amma, you must teach her to dance. She has good rhythm. And Tata would say, no, she will be an engineer. You learned Bharatanatyam and also became an architect.' I remembered everything. I was six years old then and I am forty-four now.

Indiranagar where Amma lives is a new housing colony close to the airport. The houses are built in all kinds of shapes and have a superficial modernity to them. The straight streets are carefully dimensioned and called 100 foot road, 80 foot road, first main, third cross and so forth. There are rain trees, gulmohar and temple flower trees along them. On either side of the street there are mud tracks as there were in Tanjore. The mud, red as it was in Tanjore, becomes moist and slippery in the rain.

The main shopping centre, a huge brick and concrete building on two floors, is thirty minutes away; it is too far to walk to and it is boring. But near Amma's house is the main market street of an existing village which is splitting at the seams trying to cope with the increase in demand. This street is not straight as all the other streets of Indiranagar but curves its way through the shops. There is a temple at its beginning, then a restaurant, a shop selling granite slabs, a jewellery store, a few vegetable shops, a market, a bookshop, a tailor, a video library which is a new addition, a barber's shop. The mud road gets awfully slushy in the rain. Cows and dogs wander around, and there is the smell of wet mud and cowdung, over-ripe fruit and fresh vegetables, and here and there the perfume of white jasmines strung with the orange blossoms of kankambaram.

Amma has not changed much over the years. She wakes up at five in the morning. The watchman, an old Kannada man who lives in the outhouse, washes the paving outside the gate with water. I wake up to the fricative sound of the coconut-stick broom on the wet surface. Then Amma draws kolams in front of the gate and on the doorstep with rice powder. She no longer disinfects the front gate with cowdung water. When I ask her she says, 'Yes, it is a good disinfectant. But where can I get cowdung now? Times have changed. We have to change also.'

She doesn't bathe with cold water as Andamma did. She switches on the electric geyser. Then she makes coffee for us from the milk—delivered now in plastic pouches left over from the previous day. 'The milkman comes late. But the milk stays fresh in the fridge. So I always save some milk for the morning,' she

explains. After a bath she plucks the flowers—jasmine, parijat, temple flowers, shoe flowers—for the puja room. Soon she is doing her prayers, reciting from the Gita, to the accompaniment of chandan incense sticks, burning lamps and the tinkling of the hand bell.

In the evenings I sit back in an old easy chair in the veranda and talk to Amma. I talk to her about the cities I have been to and the book I plan to write. It helps clarify my mind.

What made the cities different was their image. What formed the image? Character and essence. The street's character was formed by its physical-spatial features which were more definite and could be seen in its site, form, architecture and the manner in which their parts were organised. If the site features were different then the street was different. A sloping street was different from a level street. Streets on hills, near the river or the sea, streets with trees, a temple street—they were all different. The form of the street depended in the past on climatic factors. The streets in Udaipur, Jaisalmer were narrow and shaded, and the buildings were huddled together to keep out the sun. Form and architecture were also determined by cultural and historical factors as evident in the ghats of Benaras, the pols of Ahmedabad, the monumental and classical form of the streets in Delhi.

The parts of the street were organised according to function (for example, a commercial street was different from a residential street) and ecology, or natural growth. The natural peculiarities of land, location, climate and culture had become secondary.

Besides the character of the street, its image was also formed by its essence. All these factors—the physical-spatial, their visibility and continuity—formed the image of the street. Its 'essence' was all about traditions, rituals, myths and the way in which people used the street. The essence could not be seen directly. It included attitudes, ideas, philosophies, religious and social sensibilities, and the ways of living. With the passage of time and with activity and ritual, space gained more tangible connotations.

When the traditions and myths disappeared from the street and only the buildings were left, slowly the street's essence also faded. This was the most vulnerable stage, because it was at such a time that change started to occur and then it was so rapid that the street lost its original image completely.

The basic difference in the images of the street, as I had come to realise, depended on whether they were natural or planned. If they were planned they were invariably monumental, because the streets were planned and built for a future and therefore tended to be out of proportion to the immediate needs, as in Chandigarh. On the other hand, the naturally evolved street was a sequence of events which was a result of the interaction between people and several natural forces and changes in them. The planned street was different because it was ordered by economics, climate, material and technology, but not culture.

*

Some streets were 'visible', some not. Some were visible because of distinct natural features and cultural symbols. When streets were close to the sea or a hill, or a temple or market, their pattern was easily visible. Streets that had similarity and contrast became 'visible', but excessive similarity became boring and excessive contrast became confusing. The gridiron pattern of streets, though distinct, looked boring and it lost its character unless there was some hierarchy determined by distinct spaces, edges, corners, intersections and symbols, and they were emphasised by the type and style of buildings and monuments.

Form and continuity made streets visible. A flat, landscape, without any hills or any trees, would be boring. It was the forms of the hills, rivers, trees that gave form to the natural landscape. In the same way it was the pavement, the buildings, the colonnade, the corner, the arcade, the undulations, that lent form to the street.

Short streets, abrupt streets, chaotic streets were not continuous and so not visible because they did not have a perspective quality. There were series of perspective lines on the vertical surface and they moved towards the end of the street; they seemed to vanish so that the edges of the street were not parallel lines but converging lines. This aspect gave continuity to the street and it was important that these perspective lines were not broken. Arcades, pavement, awnings, plinth bands and floor bands, windows, balconies, helped to generate these perspective lines.

A continuous street was not necessarily straight. Often when you asked for directions people said 'go straight' even though the street twisted and turned. The natural street was the most continuous of all streets whereas the gridiron street, though its pattern was legible, lost continuity because of the many intersections. Comparatively, the circular street, although distinct because of its geometric form, was not continuous. It's central focus with radial roads and the strong edge of the buildings encircling it turned it into a node.

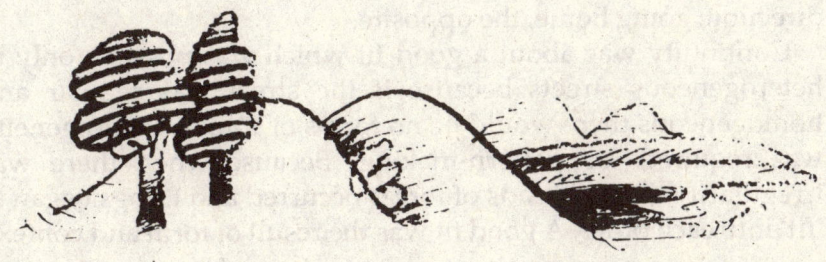

349

When streets were narrow they were continuous and impermeable. Tall buildings, crowds and activity, besides the actual width, reinforced narrowness as also the colour, texture, material and style of the buildings and steps, porches, canopies, shop windows and so forth that connected the buildings to the street. Buildings of the same height enhanced the continuity of the street. So did arcades, colonnades, the alignment of sill and floor levels, colour, texture and material. The concentration of special activities, shops, hawkers, crowds, movement and sounds—all made a street continuous and so visible.

Streets with a definite origin and destination were also clearly visible. For example, a street that ended in a railway station, bus terminus or temple had a strong sense of destination. When one moved from a narrow street to a broad street there was a sense of direction and destination. The origin of some streets became the destination for others and this was dependent on the hierarchy of the street pattern. When a main street ended at a circular node, the node was the destination of the main street and the origin of the subsidiary streets that started from it. If there was a landmark between the origin and destination, the stronger became the destination. The origin and destination was not determined by built forms alone but also by activity, like the market place.

Some streets had a definite direction: they went up or down, they moved towards a focal point, or towards the city centre or a activity. Direction was different from destination and sometimes a street had a direction but no destination.

Destination was a point, a terminal, whereas direction was progression, a number of points in continuity. There was also a positive or negative direction depending on the destination. Going to the city was always a positive direction because the city centre formed a strong destination. Going to work was a positive direction; going home, the opposite.

Continuity was about a good fit which was possible only in heterogeneous streets because if the street was regular and homogeneous there would be no forms or forces. Heterogeneity was required for pattern-making. Because when there was irregularity then all kinds of forces occurred and things began to 'fit' into each other. A good fit was the result of form and context.

It was about what the site was like, whether it was hilly, undulating, flat, full of trees, and whether there was a natural or historical feature which acted like a focus, like a river or an old temple. It was about the plan of the street, whether it was straight, gridiron, circular, curvilinear, the open spaces, the symmetry of the buildings and the street, their asymmetry, the axis, its edges and inside-outside relationship.

Anything new that was added to the street had to fit into the idea of form and context. One of the reasons why natural streets looked so restful and spontaneous was because in them there was a seamless fit between form and context. In modern plans of streets the context was redefined, not entirely, but in a piecemeal way. It was not easy to accommodate variables and even if it was achieved on a smaller scale, it disintegrated on a larger scale. This is because the form can be designed but context is intangible.

So how did it 'fit'? The 'fit' depended on the form-making process or the pattern-making process. Natural forms were gradual, adaptive. The natural street did not begin with a single master-shape, with definite parts that were fitted together. It arranged and rearranged itself, growing part by part like links of a chain. The natural streets had an exaggeration of detail, they had nooks and corners; they had a fluid quality and the pace kept

351

changing. They were ambiguous and therefore dynamic and complex. But in the planned streets the overall pattern decided the shape of the parts; it predetermined the function and position of each part. The planned street focused on the 'whole' image, it ignored the parts.

The problem here was that the context was assumed and the assumptions were frequently wrong or fell short. The natural process was a corrective process, it was unselfconscious and self-organising. Form-making was really a process of subsystems. All the subsystems were interlinked yet free from each other, they were dependent and independent. It worked through cycles of correction and they were restricted to one subsytem at a time. This existed in a natural system but it was never thought of while planning streets or cities.

*

The image of the street was also formed by the space in it. How was space formed? When we looked at the sea, we felt its space because of the shore, the horizon and the sky: they acted as limits to space. Space, like time, was continuous, it had to be contained and defined and it existed only when it had boundaries and when it contained an object. Then there was a relationship between the object and the edges. First it was always right angle relations, front, back, sides, that were visible, and then oblique relations. We saw it in stages: we searched for edges, defined it geometrically, and then established a relationship between the object and the edges. We saw space through the relative size of objects—bigger or smaller, the relations between objects; perspective or convergent or divergent lines; the presence or absence of texture, colour, light and shade variation; steroscopic vision, that is, seeing things in three dimensions; ocular convergence; movement in space and difference between fixed objects and moving objects.

Actually when we saw space, we did so in geometric shapes. We thought of it as a square, rectangle or a circle at the beginning, then we thought of volumes. But it was always geometrical. We created our own axes and points which formed a geometric shape, moving from simple to complex.

There were many factors that made a street and its space visible. Symmetry was one of them, although space by itself was asymmetrical. The hills, trees, architecture were all references for symmetry in space. This was so because we always reacted to a vertical plane before a horizontal plane, just as we reacted to form before a plan. A street with symmetrical buildings was more legible than a street with spaces that were symmetrical, and the verticals, asymmetrical. So the vertical elements structured space. They gave it a sense of location and direction. It was like climbing up the steps of a temple, or going down to the ghats or the river. This verticality had a symbolic meaning. Verticality emphasised hierarchy, isolation, ambition, and competition. On the other hand, the horizontal plane was directed by its axis and because of it there was interaction, movement from place to place, because it was simpler to move horizontally than vertically. The verticality of the houses on high plinths isolated them from the street; and when the plinth was low or almost absent, the street seemed friendly.

Space penetrated into form and form into space. The vertical form of a building penetrated into the ground if its base did not form a horizontal tie to the ground. It was like a capital without a base; it pierced the ground, visually. If the vertical element pierced through the ground then the horizontality of the street was lost. Arcades, dominant plinths, colonnades, prominent bases formed a strong street experience. If entrances were ill defined and too large and if they were without steps, arches, porticos, railings, then space penetrated into the vertical forms and verticality was lost. The buildings on the street had to connect to the ground in the street. The kind of connection could differ: they could be rooted to the ground, raised on stilts, supported by piers, arches, or connected by grand flights of steps.

With a different kind of connection there was a different kind of space. When there was a long dividing line between the building and the ground, the building looked monumental; it did not belong to the ground. A long sprawling building belonged to the ground because it formed a parallel horizontal plane with the ground. The parallel plane did not penetrate, it floated, and appeared rootless, and a number of vertical elements in a horizontal mass helped to connect.

Space at intersections also had to be articulate. A strong focus in the centre of the intersection would have character. A strong centre made the buildings on the corners forceful. When streets crossed and there was no large space, it became a psychological letdown. A square looked good in a street, particularly at an intersection. But if the square was too small then the building facades dominated, the edges became important and the centre lost its potential and the square lost its identity. When it was too large, the line of forces from the building did not reach the centre so there was no mingling of the forces. The boundary of the square became a mere frame.

There had to be a relationship between the vertical and the horizontal plane. Many sociologists and psychologists had studied this aspect; they called it the figure-ground relationship. The figure, the vertical plane, had a definite profile but the ground, the horizontal plane, appeared amorphous, without shape. But in the natural streets there was no defined profile—there was a constant appearing and disappearing, widening and shrinking. In such a case there was a transitory space between the figure and ground that kept running into the figure or ground belonging to both. This inter-space was more an Eastern philosophy than a Western concept, it was more visible in Eastern cities. On the other hand, modern planning was space-blind; it emphasised the vertical plane more and not the horizontal space as natural cities did.

Old towns dealt with space, intimate spaces, more than just vertical forms: they dealt with space on the street, space in front of the house, and space between houses.

The quality of the inter-space gave texture to the street. It was close or loose; there was a continuous expansion or contraction, connection and segregation. The inter-space between the buildings and the sky was activated by the height, mass and profile of the buildings—the architecture diffused softly into the sky rather than marking a dividing line abruptly with flat roofs. That is why the skyline with pitched roofed houses on a hill was very interesting.

This was because of the symbiotic relationship between the part and the whole. We tend to think that the part is incomplete, piecemeal, isolated and meaningless and the whole is something that is complete and to which nothing can be added. Such an absolute whole or part doesn't exist. In the street the whole consisted of a hierarchy of sub-wholes, and each element had the characteristic of being a whole and a part; the parts always carried the idea of the whole. The whole was a sum of parts and the part was a unit of the whole, or a subtraction from it if the idea of the whole existed. You got space by addition or subtraction. For instance, on the vertical plane, in the skyline, subtraction of the form was addition to the sky-space. Additive architecture had the concept of the sub-whole, but subtractive architecture did not because it contained the idea of the whole. So we had to look at parts that were whole, and wholes that were sub-wholes.

There were different kinds of spaces: there was the sociofugal space which kept people apart, and the sociopetal space which brought people together. Old towns had many sociopetal spaces where people met, but the new street spaces were sociofugal. Some streets with arcades, porticos, squares were sociopetal. Crowding did not mean that people were together. In a crowded space like a train or bus or a station, if people were close they were so only physically. There was no interaction between them. Many times people were unfriendly to each other when they were standing close. Proximity was not intimacy. In public spaces the behaviour was formal and constrained but in an intimate space it was informal. There were other kinds of spaces. Streets had both objective and subjective spaces, those that were fixed and permanent and those that kept changing. There was diffused, scattered space also. This often happened in small villages and in the outskirts of cities. Opposing this was the dense space which was compact with smaller distances between objects. The delineated space was bounded and constricted and had an emphatic centre whereas open space had free inward-outward movement.

Whatever the kind of space, it had a certain density. We could feel the difference in the spatial density as we moved from the old parts of the city to the newer parts and then outside the city limits where it became loose and characterless. For a compact and dense street, there had to be a framework for measuring distances, vertical surfaces were also needed and they had to be accentuated, there had to be focus for orientation and landmarks for a sense of place. The street elements had to conform to the acting forces to form good spaces and good perspective lines. If everything was without any relation, there was distortion. Excessive distortion of space destroyed all aesthetic possibilities.

Space was not just physical or visual. It was also social and psychological. For example, there was an aspect of territory and orbit in the street. These were words that sociologists used to study communities. Territory was a space which people felt they belonged to like the shopkeepers on a street, slum-dwellers, residents of colonies, hawkers on a street. The orbit was a wider area having two or more territories. The pols of Ahmedabad, the different galis of Benaras formed territories because the spaces were intimate and communal. Areas like Ballard Estate and Fort in Mumbai and Connaught Circle in Delhi, formed orbits since they were public spaces to which people came but did not belong to a group of any kind; they were mixed. Streets had to provide both territory and orbit, but modern planning encouraged orbits and not territories.

*

Image was not everything to a street; there also had to be order, something many streets did not seem to possess. What caused disorder? One of the reasons I could think of was because people had become commercial and consumeristic; because there were so many ways of thinking and there was no direction and control over the endless possibilities; there was also a lack of cooperation. There was a new individualism, both of people and parts. Because of it and competition, the collective whole based on compatibility and cooperation was destroyed. There was a disparity of parts since all the parts and elements were unrelated. And most of the time it existed because there was no structuring of the whole—no context: historical, geographical or cultural. Most of the streets were ambiguous. If not, it was only because of few focal elements, like a railway station, or a market or a temple or mosque. The station and the market were focal places of utility. The temple or a mosque stood out in a crowded area because of its structure and because it was sacred. But such focal points or places could be truly effective only if the surroundings were cohesive and not ambiguous.

Was ambiguity the cause of disorder then? When a street grew naturally, adjusting, adapting, based on a hidden hierarchy and a set of priorities, there was no disorder, as long as the densities were contained, because it was compatible. There was an inherent ordering force that encouraged the adjustments and adaptations. Ambiguity rising out of ambivalence did not create disorder. Ambiguity only made things slightly unpredictable. It was only when ambiguity led to disorientation that there was disorder, a loss of place and identity. Disorder was the result of fragmentation and erosion. It happened when the street changed drastically, and too soon, and when there was no scope for adjustments. Disorder was also experienced when the relationships between elements were not what was expected or suggested.

What brought about order? In planned streets, it was the physical pattern of the street, its form, its architecture. Order in the natural street was more complex: there was an inherent 'group order'. It was established by the behaviour of the people, the result of a regulating and control mechanism which was built-in. Whether it was a street, neighbourhood, village or town, it contained many groups and each group had a closed domain which was visual, physical and psychological, as in the slum in the city. It had a physical, visual and psychological boundary which characterised and controlled it. It had a threshold which protected and maintained the internal order at the same time formed a communicating link with the outside world. The threshold preserved the group. There were many factors that formed the threshold of the street. In the case of a village or a slum these factors were the focal points of the street, its centre, its boundary, the edges of the building, the consolidation of the building and the entrance to the buildings. The streets that displayed all these aspects had a more legible character, refinement and an organised pattern and a higher degree of independence.

Whereas the threshold defined the borders, the centres, the facades, there was also another factor which preserved and protected the group's order—the interface. It was a common space that interconnected elements and other spaces. The threshold was points of contact and the interface, the connecting tissue.

Some of the order-producing elements were context, harmony, equilibrium, unity, rhythm, symmetry, hierarchy, familiarity, inflection and activity. The streets that appeared orderly had a context, an idea of the whole form and parts, and the parts were compatible to one another and the structure of the whole. So a homogeneity of the whole and a heterogeneity in parts brought about order. Streets were harmonious because of compatibility, like a street winding, climbing up a hill; it was compatible with the terrain. Compatibility was the result of flexibility and conformity. The natural street was far more flexible and compatible than the planned street. It was like a tree that had the capacity to grow as required yet maintain an inner order. Equilibrium in a street had to do with the forces that made it grow. When there were too many external forces then the equilibrium was lost. In a legible street there was a unity of elements of different shapes, sizes, directions, colour, and textures. If this unifying process was absent there was no order. As long as the additions were mere irritants or deviations in an established order, the order was not destroyed. There was a relation of connection and separation, the street worked by it and because of it the street had harmony, equilibrium and unity.

Rhythm in a street also to do with connection and separation. By repetition the parts of the street were visually connected. It gave a feeling of continuity, cohesiveness. But too much repetition also led to monotony. Repetition to be interesting had to be intuitive because intellectual standards and measurements, mindless imitation, piecemeal production, often replaced intuition, and the sense of order disappeared.

As important as rhythm, was symmetry; it created order because one knew what to expect. Hierarchy in the street was established by a sequence of order. This was needed because order was required at all levels—from the smaller elements on the street to the buildings and the relationship between them. The hierarchy was often upset when the older parts of the street changed.

Familiarity was another factor that brought about order. When the surroundings were familiar you had a feeling or order. The abnormalities were less visible. That is why the bazaars looked normal to us. Even the hawkers who crowd the streets were acceptable. There was an additive process by which the street grew in relation to its whole structure and the structure of its parts. As long as this relation was maintained, the street was in order. When this relation was lost the street order was also lost. Eventually, activity as it was most legible and easily identified brought order in the street.

*

The next day a friend visited my mother. He was a swami, a learned man who had given up a good government post to set up an ashram in Pondicherry. He wore a saffron robe and was tall and erect, full of vigour as yogis are. He was well travelled and well read. He stayed with us a few days during which time I talked to him about people, cities, streets and the book I that I wanted to write about them. He listened intently, absorbing everything that I told him. He never said anything but one evening as we sat outside in the veranda he started to speak.

'I have seen many places, buildings, but I did not understand why some of them are special, memorable. I read many books, talked to people to find out. Then I tried to form some idea about metaphysical space. I believe there is a ceremonial order; it is an order that arranges things in a rational way, so that it is honest and beautiful; and establishes a hierarchy, big to small, public to private and so on, giving a functional value to each element and placing it in relation to other elements.'

All this seemed very interesting; I urged him to go on.

'It is my belief,' the swami said, 'that those places or building with ceremonial order have universal principles. There is something intensely real about them and when I experience such a place I feel a sense of wonder and something in me connects me to the whole universe. Actually I am very curious about this place-making process; I was very interested in all that you told me about the streets. I have been thinking.'

He talked about a remarkable study by the Vesica study group, analysing the origin of things and their development. It suggested sixteen archetypal patterns which create ceremonial order. The first one is the idea about the whole. Many traditions believe that the beginning was either nothing or chaos—the void or the bindu, the centre of energy, and from this a wholeness emerged. It is non-spatial, it has no boundary or centre but it is full of sacred power.

The second pattern is the focal point of the ceremonial

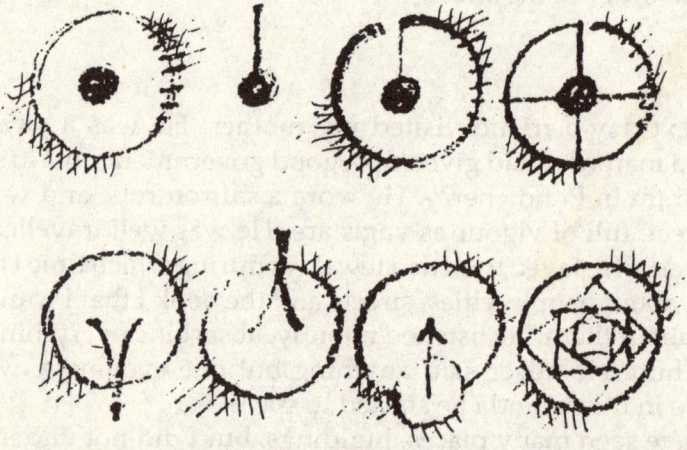

experience. This centre contains the idea of the whole and connects the aspirant and the divine; it is the seed which has the beginning of the essence of form and space and becomes the essence of space. This centre in the physical sense can be a special place, a square, a temple or market, a tree or rock, almost anything. It is a physical focal point and has intense activity and meaning.

The third pattern is the inner gesture. It is an impulse to express. It moves outward from the centre and suggests direction and orientation.

The fourth pattern is the boundary, a surrounding edge in relation to the centre. This relationship is without form. Now there is a centre, boundary and domain. There is unity in the centre where all becomes one, diversity at the edge where different things are distinct and homogeneity within the domain where the parts relate between unity and diversity.

The fifth pattern is direction: there are four basic directions from the centre to the boundary corresponding to the cardinal points. There are also other directions depending on the contours of the site and the view of the sea and other natural features.

Going down into the earth is important as it grounds the energy of the place. This is the descent, the fifth pattern which is related to the deep psyche; there is also a relationship between descent and fertility because a sacred place always has a earth-womb. So the relationship of the vertical walls of the building to earth is very

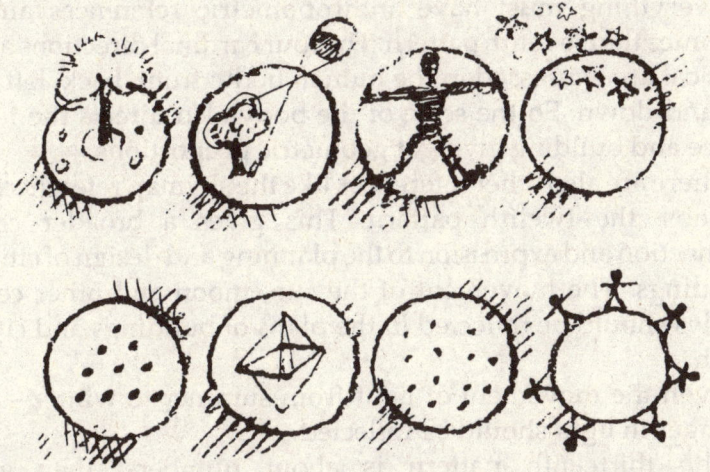

important.

At the same time reaching upward, the sixth pattern is also important. It is verticality—the path from below to above which gives an upward direction to everything that is rooted in the earth. A sacred place or a village, a city or street must have verticality.

The seventh pattern is the passage. When we move from one realm or space to another that is different, there has to be a distinct neutral space, a transition which allows us to travel from one zone to another. There must always be a sense of entering a place and the passage must demarcate the point and the place of actual entry.

The eighth pattern is about making internal order out of chaos. There must be visual symmetry in this order; it must be spatial and can be circular, linear, radial, triangular, orthogonal or spiral, like a mandala, like a lotus. Internal order gives meaning, hierarchy and proportion to the right location of all the main elements in the domain; this order is like a magnetic field and can have many centres or events.

The ninth order is about nature. Nature being vast can also be disorderly, and so it must have order. Chaos can also be reduced by having selected views, and this forms the tenth order. Views should be limited to places of beauty and nature and not allowed to accentuate the mundane landscape. Views of sunrise and sunset are important.

Everything must have anthropometric references and this becomes the eleventh pattern. The four cardinal directions and the vertical are expressed in the human body: front, back, left, right, up and down. So the scale of the body also directs the form of space and building giving it geometric proportions.

There are also other references like the skymap references—the cosmos, the twelfth pattern. This gives a broader context, connection and expression to the planning and design of cities and buildings. The movement of the sun, moon and other celestial bodies should be reflected in the plans of buildings and cities on earth.

Even the movement of light from summer to winter—all the changes in light should be reflected.

The thirteenth pattern is about numbers; they give a quantitative and qualitative character to forms and spaces. The Pythagoreans thought numbers have hidden energies. Even all things about life can be traced back to a number. The number of towers, doors windows, steps are all important. To the Hindus, numbers one to nine are significant and to the Greek one to ten.

As important as numbers, is geometry, the fourteenth pattern; it exists in everything, nature, galaxies, viruses, everything. Geometry is not just an intellectual abstraction but it is based on metaphysics which is then translated visually and physically. Sacred geometry is a key to the relationship between the fixed and the volatile and between proportion and progression. It is a significant relationship between measurable and immeasurable numbers. There are processes by which geometric transformations can occur, like the formative, generative and regenerative.

The fifteenth pattern is about materiality. It is the state or quality of being material; material is a substance that occupies space and therefore has form. So the selection of material is crucial because it seeks to define form and reveal the sacred. Material should always be the reflection of time, level of technology and specific context. The material for ordinary buildings and sacred or special buildings must be different.

The sixteenth pattern is about ceremonial order. There must be rituals to celebrate this order because with ceremony the whole place can be sensed and centre can be felt. Also the vibratory connection between the self and the physical place can be felt. We can feel everything, light, seasons, geometry, gravity, levity; it is a complete experience.

The swami explained the sixtees orders with patience. Concluding, he said, 'Hari Om, Hari Om,' looking at the starlit sky. The swami explained the sixteen orders with patience. Then he went out for a quiet walk before he retired for the night. I thought of all that he had explained to me. Over the years, I had travelled to many cities, walked down many streets, looked into houses of people and their minds—this had taken a long time, but the swami had in a matter of minutes summed up all that I had been trying to understand for some time. I looked up at the starlit sky and a strange sense of fulfilment filled me. I heaved a long sigh and went into the house.

*

I married twenty years ago and have two children. Anshu, my daughter, is sixteen and my son, Ayush, is thirteen. I remember the day when Anshu, then eight, was given an assignment in school. She had to draw a mental map of the way to her school. So she had come to me and asked me how she should draw a road going uphill. I had drawn the plan of the way to her school and she had exclaimed, 'This is not how it is! Where is the road going uphill?' I had explained to her that in a plan one looked at it from above and so everything appeared flat. 'Mark an arrow on the side

and write "up" against it, it will mean a road going up,' I said but she didn't like the idea.

She then had asked me to show her to draw trees. I had drawn several circles with tiny leaves around them just like they had taught us at college and as we did in our design drawings. 'These are not trees, where is the trunk?' she had said. Later she showed me the map she had drawn. It was three-dimensional, axonometric. The road climbed uphill and all the trees had trunks. She had remembered to draw the big flowering trees and in fact she had named them by the colour of the flowers—tree with yellow flowers, tree with orange flowers and so forth. She had remembered to draw every turn of the street and points where other main streets joined it. She had drawn all the bungalows in the street and she had remembered their names. But she had not drawn all the tall buildings except for those in which her friends lived. When I asked her she had said, 'They look all the same and anyway I don't remember all of them.' She had drawn the houses which had dogs. She remembered which house had which dog and had named them accordingly—the house with a bulldog, the house with a Labrador, and so on. She had drawn all the shops on the way. She had coloured the buildings and she had remembered whether they were made of stone or brick, and titled them accordingly. She had drawn birds—crows, parrots and eagles. She had noticed all the details, the singular features—old buildings and new, different activities, animals, turns, shops, trees, terrain.

Often I walk through this street. It appears to have grown naturally; it meanders uphill in turns and bends. At first there were only large bungalows for the rich. Now they have been replaced by tall buildings though a few bungalows still remain. They have tall compound walls and gates, as though they are shy to reveal their extravagance, or at least they attempt to hide it. There are a few clusters of shops along the street and they form points where people gather, focal points. In the evenings the street is full of young boys and girls and parked cars and resounding music. The trees on it are tall and old and their leaves rustle in the salt-drenched sea breeze. There is the smell of the sea. The sea is close by but screened by the hills and all those aging trees.

It is a good street.

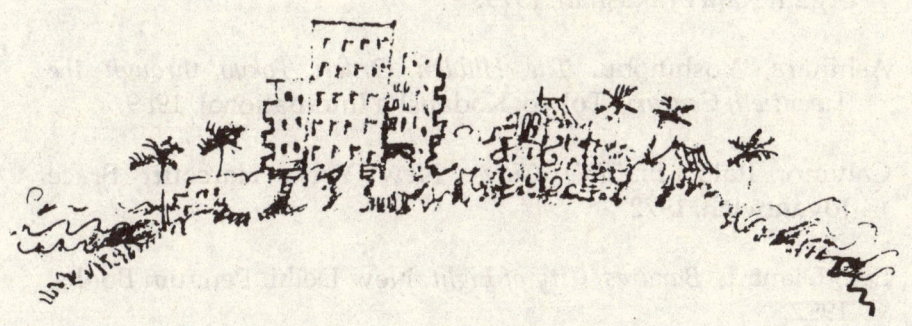

Bibliography

Agarwala, R.N. *History, Art and Architecture of Jaisalmer.* Delhi: Agam Kala Prakashan, 1979.

Ashihara, Yoshinobu. *The Hidden Order: Tokyo through the Twentieth Century.* Tokyo: Kodansha International, 1989.

Calvino, Italo. *Invisible Cities.* New York: Harcourt Brace Jovanovich, 1972.

Eck, Diana L. *Banaras, City of Light.* New Delhi: Penguin Books, 1992.

Evenson, Norma. *The Indian Metropolis.* Delhi: Oxford University Press, 1989.

Fanshawe, H.C. *Delhi Past and Present.* Gurgaon: Vintage Books, 1991.

Hall, Peter. *Cities of Tomorrow.* United Kingdom: Blackwell, 1988.

Jaganathan, Shakuntala. *Hinduism.* Bombay: Vakils, Feffer and Simons, 1989.

Jain, Kulbhushan. *Jodhpur.* Monograph.

Kalia, Ravi. *Chandigarh: The Making of an Indian City.* Delhi: Oxford University Press, 1988.

Khanna, Ashok, and Pramesh Ratnakar. *Banaras: The Sacred City.* New Delhi: Lustre Press Pvt. Ltd., 1988.

Kurokawa, Kisho. *Rediscovering Japanese Space.* New York: Weatherhill, 1988.

Llewellyn-Jones, Rosie. *A Fatal Friendship: The Nawabs, the British and the City of Lucknow.* Madras: Oxford University Press, 1985.

Metcalfe, Thomas R. *An Imperial Vision: Indian Architecture and the British Raj.* New York and London: Faber and Faber, 1989.

Nath, Aman. *Jaipur: The Last Destination.* Bombay: India Book House Pvt. Ltd., 1993.

School of Architecture, Ahmedabad. *Udaipur: The City and its Elements.* Monograph.

Sherring, M. A. *Banaras.* Delhi: Low Price Publications, 1990.

Skelton, Robert. *Rajasthani Temple Hangings of the Krishna Cult.* New York: The American Foundation of Art, 1973.

Sozo Baba (Ed.). *Katsura.* Tokyo: Shinkenchiku-sha, 1983.

Tod, James, and William Crooke. *Annals and Antiquities of Rajasthan*. Motilal Banarsidass, Publishers, 1971.

Varma, Pavan K., and Sondeep Shankar. *Mansions at Dusk: The Havelis of Old Delhi*. New Delhi: Spantech Publishers Pvt. Ltd., 1992.

Wacziarg, Francis, and Aman Nath. *Rajasthan: The Painted Havelis of Shekhavati*. London: Croom Helm, 1982.

*

Illustrations were made from photographs and drawings by:

Prakash Rao (all chapters)
Yatin Pandya (Ahmedabad, Siddpur)
Manish Shah (Ahmedabad)
Nitin Riswadkar (Ahmedabad)
Kulbhushan Jain (Jodhpur)
Sangeet Sharma (Chandigarh)
Murthy Srivatsa (Pondicherry)
Tency Batens (Auroville)
P S N Rao (Delhi)
Rama Natarajan (Madras)